Gift of the Estate of
Robert (1938-2013)
and Gay Zieger (1938-2013)
October 2013

If I Had a Hammer…

IF I HAD
A HAMMER...

The Death of the Old Left
and the
Birth of the New Left

———————

MAURICE ISSERMAN

———————

Basic Books, Inc., Publishers   *New York*

Library of Congress Cataloging-in-Publication Data

Isserman, Maurice.
  If I had a hammer.

  Includes index.
    1. Radicalism—United States.   2. College students—
United States—Political activity.   3. United States—
Politics and government—1945–   . I. Title.
HN90.R3187   1987   378'.1981   87–47510
ISBN   0–465–03197–8

For Marcia

Nothing more was expected by the organizers of this march than that, as usual, one hundred, or five hundred, or a thousand people would turn up, most of them known to one another, and disperse afterwards, while the newspapers commented sourly, if at all, and most of the inhabitants of these islands would know nothing whatsoever about it. Yet by the end of that particular Easter weekend several thousand people had been marching under the black-and-white banners, most of them young, and newspapers and television commented lengthily, and no one could have been more surprised than the organizers.

—Doris Lessing
The Four-Gated City

Contents

Preface: A Renaissance in the 1950s?

The title of this book will appear to many to contain a flagrant contradiction. A renaissance in the twelfth century! Do not the Middle Ages, that epoch of ignorance, stagnation, and gloom, stand in the sharpest contrast to the light and progress and freedom of the Italian Renaissance which followed? . . . The answer is that the continuity of history rejects such sharp and violent contrasts between successive periods and that modern history shows us the Middle Ages less dark and static, the Renaissance less bright and less sudden, than was once supposed.

—CHARLES HOMER HASKINS
The Renaissance of the Twelfth Century, 1927

Once there was a time, 1968 to be exact, when I knew everything that was important to know about the history of the "Old Left." I was a seventeen-year-old college freshman and a proud new member of Students for a Democratic Society (I would say a "card-carrying" member, except things being what they were at the time in Students for a Democratic Society [SDS] national headquarters no one ever bothered to send me a membership card in return for my five dollars annual dues). I knew that the Old Left had existed an immeasurably long time before, back in the 1930s; terrible things had been done to it, and it had done (or at least believed in) some terrible things itself, then had disappeared. Utterly. Without a trace. The only survivors I knew of were a few relatives in my parents' generation, wonderful and well-loved people who kept the most recent copy of *Political Affairs* on a shelf in the bathroom for convenient reading, but who *were* getting on and were, besides—I thought a little guiltily—irrelevant.

About a decade later, a little older myself, and perhaps a little humbler, I took another look at the history of the Old Left, this time in the form of a doctoral dissertation resulting eventually in the publication of my first book, *Which Side Were You On? The American Com-*

munist Party During the Second World War.[1] By the time I entered graduate school SDS was a fading memory, and my investigation of the Communist party's history was inevitably informed by memories of the political disasters I had witnessed in the past decade. I wanted to know how it was possible for a movement seemingly as powerful as the Communist party had been during the Second World War to unravel so completely in the years that followed. Some of the answer, I decided, could be found in the failure of the Party's brief experiment with "Americanization" during the war. In the final chapter of the book I undertook a short survey of the Party's history in the late 1940s and early 1950s, climaxing in the "deStalinization crisis" of 1956 to 1958. I had conceived those years as a time when the Communists were, purely and simply, victims battered senseless by a relentless assault on the part of the FBI and the House Un-American Activities Committee. (If I glance over at my bookshelf to the section where I keep books on the 1950s, I can see such titles as *Scoundrel Time, The Haunted Fifties, The Nightmare Decade, A Journal of the Plague Years, The Time of the Toad, The Great Fear,* and two different books entitled *The American Inquisition.*)[2] Obviously any consideration of the political history of the 1950s has to include the enormous impact of "McCarthyism": the Left *was* victimized. But as I read over the letters to the editor of the *Daily Worker* in 1956, I was struck by some of the daring and sensible proposals to rebuild and redirect the Communist movement that were offered there. The letter writers were expressing notions that I thought of as the invention of the New Left. As it turned out, no matter how fresh their thinking at that moment, the Communists were involved in a doomed enterprise. In the closing pages of *Which Side Were You On?* I tried to suggest the historical irony involved in the fact that such a short interval of time separated the collapse of the Communist movement, the major component of the Old Left, from the appearance of SDS, the most important group in the New Left—nothing like the immense gap I had imagined back in 1968. In the last lines of the book I argued that the valuable political lessons Communists had learned from their own experiences in the years between the 1930s and the 1950s "came too late to be of use to the generation that had learned them, and too early to be of use to the generation that followed."[3]

Once again it turned out I had something to learn about the history of the Old Left. I still assumed there was a gap, albeit a shrinking one, that absolutely separated Old from New. But the more I looked into the history of radical movements in the 1950s, the more it became apparent that I was laboring under a misconception about both the death of the Old Left and the birth of the New Left. I gradually came to understand that the early New Left had emerged from the Old Left in ways that made it difficult to perceive exactly where the one ended and the other began. Not only were "the dark ages" of the 1950s less dark and static than I had supposed, but the "renaissance" of the 1960s (I use the term advisedly) was also "less bright and less sudden" than I previously had assumed. The recent history of American radicalism began to seem less spasmodic, and more a continual process of unfolding. The ideas and the political choices made by earlier generations did affect later generations, though often in ambiguous and ironic fashion.

"Wisdom comes by disillusionment," George Santayana once remarked, and as the Old Left disintegrated organizationally, some of its adherents did the best thinking of their political careers. If we are to understand the 1960s as something more than a brief and bizarre aberration from the fundamental conservatism of post–World War II American political life, we need to examine how this older generation on the Left came to discard the dogmas to which they once subscribed, and in so doing, how they helped give new direction to an emerging generation of younger radicals.

"It's no accident" (as Marxists of a certain vintage are wont to say) that I turned to the history of a defeated movement in the early 1980s. Although the political dynamics shaping the Eisenhower and Reagan presidencies are by no means identical—Eisenhower actually administered the "American Century," whereas Reagan has merely pandered to nostalgia for that bygone era—the marginal position occupied by the Left in both eras is certainly similar. Historians are naturally attracted to periods in which the movements they study are at the peak of their influence (take, for example, my own research into the Communist party's history during the Second World War); but there is as much or more to be learned by studying these movements at their nadir. In defeat, the partisans of a political movement may reveal aspects of their thought, as well as capacities for reflection and change, that would have remained obscured in more propitious times. Political history should not be simply a chronicle of winners and losers: rather, it should seek to understand and portray the response of human beings to political victory and defeat.

It is a truism that history is usually written by the winners. The "winners" of the present era are those for whom the decade of the

1960s presents itself as a time of bizarre and even sinister maladjustment, now thankfully put behind us. It has long been a matter of journalistic convention to take the most violently apocalyptic moments in the history of the New Left and present them as the sum and substance of the movement; *Time* magazine, in a 1977 retrospective essay on the New Left, casually dismissed its history as the "long, wild hallucination of the '60s."[4] Essayists in journals with more ambitious intellectual agendas hold the New Left responsible for what they see as the "Vietnam syndrome" that has paralyzed American foreign policy makers; for the "blame America first" attitude that animates a large portion of the nation's opinion makers; and for a wide variety of other ills plaguing contemporary American government and society.[5]

There are marked similarities between the "politics of revenge" of the 1950s, with its preoccupation with the preceding "twenty years of treason," and the analysis that now scorns the twenty years of "adversary culture" that preceded the Reagan administration. The first book-length treatment of the New Left to embody this analysis is Stanley Rothman and S. Robert Lichter's *Roots of Radicalism: Jews, Christians, and the New Left*, in which the average New Leftist is portrayed as a seething cauldron of narcissism, self-hatred, sexual inadequacy, declining ego strength, irrational power drives, and other unpleasant characteristics.[6] While there is no reason to dismiss such interpretations out of hand, the discrediting of psychological interpretations of the appeal of communism written in the 1950s (all of which, like Rothman and Lichter's study, were supposedly grounded on the most objective clinical techniques available) does suggest that a degree of caution is in order.[7] *Roots of Radicalism* illustrates the problems inherent in devising such interpretations without adequate historical preparation. Rothman and Lichter rely upon existing secondary sources, anthologies of New Left writing, and autobiographies by a few New Leftists to illustrate the generalizations they draw from their questionnaires and Rorschach tests. The danger of such ahistorical theorizing becomes evident in their attempt to read back into the early 1960s the excesses of the New Left's last days. For their argument to work there could never be a moment of innocent idealism in the New Left's history; the movement had to have been born in sin, flawed from the start in ways reflective of its adherents' psychological infirmities:

The New Left was implicitly revolutionary from the beginning, despite an initial reliance on liberal rhetoric. . . . Freedom meant the destruction of a decadent, rotten society, rather than access to its rewards. And "now" meant showing adults that there would be no wait for change, that no delay would be tolerated, that gratification must be immediate.[8]

The evidence they produce to document this assertion is a single "keynote speech" by an unnamed speaker at a 1962 SDS conference on "Race and Politics" held at the University of North Carolina, a speech in which the speaker declared: "We shall succeed through force—through the exertion of such pressure as will force our reluctant allies to accommodate to us, in their own interest." This is a bloodcurdling threat, to be sure, and seems to substantiate the Rothman-Lichter thesis—until one refers to the source cited in the footnotes in *Roots of Radicalism* and discovers that the speaker in this instance is not Tom Hayden, nor Al Haber, nor any other person central to the founding and early development of SDS. It turns out to be Tom Kahn, who although technically an SDS member in 1962 was hardly a typical "New Leftist," as anyone who reads the final chapter in this book will discover. In fact, within a few years of making this speech, Kahn would become as strident a critic of SDS as Rothman and Lichter—and would share roughly the same political perspective. If their psychological portrait does fit Kahn—I have no more basis for deciding whether or not it does than they do—then I suppose one could argue with equal validity that it is lapsed-radicals-turned-neoconservatives who hate their fathers, and envy the sexual potency of blacks, and so on and so forth.[9]

Before we can pretend to understand the psychological or sociological "roots of radicalism" in the 1960s, we would do better to become familiar with the actual historical roots of the movement, and that is the project I have undertaken in this book. What follows will not be a narrowly descriptive narrative; I see no virtue or even possibility of fashioning a historical treatment that offers "just the facts" about the emergence of the New Left. I am offering a political interpretation of the New Left's history that resembles Rothman and Lichter's thesis to the extent that it, too, seeks to establish connections between the character of the early and late New Left. The difference is that my interpretation presupposes the good intentions and psychological soundness of those involved (when I think otherwise, as in a few instances, I indicate as much). One need not have been suffering from any psychological disturbance to have been appalled by the prospect of nuclear war, or the conduct of the Vietnam

War, or the persistence of American racism in the 1960s. The New Left's radicalism consisted not in any inherent propensity for violence, irrationalism, or sympathy with totalitarianism (though all three became far too prevalent among sections of the New Left by the end of the 1960s) but rather in the attempt to understand the interconnection of such diverse issues as the danger of nuclear annihilation, the war in Southeast Asia, and racial injustice. If sane and well-meaning people can create movements that ultimately culminate in something like the Weathermen, the violence-obsessed faction that led Students for a Democratic Society in its final apocalyptic days, then it is all the more important to understand the internal political dynamics of such movements.

Chapters 1 through 4 of this book examine, in sequence, the American Communist party; the various groups led by Max Shachtman; the journal *Dissent*, edited by Irving Howe; and the Committee for Non-Violent Action. The emphasis in each instance is on how those groups influenced—and failed to influence—the "New Left" that emerged at the end of the 1950s. If the adherents of these groups could agree on little else, they at least arrived at a rough consensus in the course of the decade that the New Left, whenever it should appear, should represent something very different from what came before it. When the New Left finally did appear, there existed among its youthful adherents the belief that they *were* different, that their elders had compromised themselves, and that honesty, openness, and moral intensity would prevent them from repeating the mistakes of the past. As it turned out, honesty, openness, and moral intensity were not enough.

This book does not pretend to be an encyclopedia of the Old Left. Not every group's history comes under scrutiny. In choosing which groups to focus upon, I used two criteria. First, I was interested only in those groups that underwent a significant shift in perspective in the course of the 1950s (thereby excluding sects like the Socialist Labor party, whose ideas remained pure, unchanging, and sterile throughout). And second, I was interested only in those groups who either went on to develop a significant influence within the early New Left, or who might have been expected to have such influence (thereby excluding such lively but obscure groupings as the followers of C. L. R. James and Raya Dunayevskaya, who figured into the history of the Detroit Left in the 1960s but who developed little influence elsewhere).[10]

The underlying theme unifying these chapters can be summed up in two words: Politics matters. The civil rights movement, the anti-war movement, and the campus radicalism of the 1960s did not just materialize out of thin air. Nor, obviously, were they simply summoned into existence by small groups of radical conspirators. The upheavals of the 1960s were produced by a complex interaction of demographics, economics, and politics (both mainstream and radical). The political climate would probably have remained much the same as in the previous decade had it not been for the following factors: the baby boom and the resulting postwar expansion of American higher education; the redistribution of the black population from the rural South to the urban South and North and the resulting increase in potential black voting strength; the general prosperity that prevailed in the early 1960s and the resulting willingness on the part of politicians and opinion makers to consider the plight of the "other America"; and finally, a lessening of the immediate prospects for nuclear confrontation, resulting in a greater public willingness to question or at least to tolerate questions about the direction of American foreign policy. Given the new situation created by these factors, it then *did* begin to matter what political choices radicals made. Veterans of the radical movements of the 1950s provided a political language in which those swept up in the new movements of the 1960s could begin to make sense of their own discontents and desires.[11] Although the New Left did not respond with equal enthusiasm to all the advice proffered by the Old, I will argue that the movements of the 1960s were set on a particular trajectory because of that initial interaction of Old Left with New.

The term "Old Left" carries with it (at least for someone of my generation) a connotation of unbending rigidity, but in reality the politics of some of the established radical groups were in the midst of a process of dynamic change in the 1950s. A debate about fundamental beliefs took place within each of the groups examined in these pages. Precisely because the political climate was so unfavorable, radicals were forced to reexamine earlier assumptions. They had to respond to the great social, cultural, and political changes of the postwar years, however much they might have preferred to cling to the verities of the depression era. In the course of the 1950s many radicals came to reject the notion that an American version of the Bolshevik Revolution was inevitable, necessary, or even desirable. The dilution of ethnic working-class cultures brought about by Hollywood, television, and *Life* magazine, the dispersal of ethnic working-class neighborhoods brought about by suburbanization,

VA mortgages, and the interstate highway system, left radicals bereft of the old reliable constituencies and issues and suggested the need for new organizational forms and new political priorities. The growing stockpiles of nuclear weapons in both camps of the Cold War meant that war, rather than serving as the midwife of revolution, could spell an end to all human aspirations, revolutionary and reactionary alike. The debates in radical circles over how to respond to these dramatic changes tell us much about the Left in the 1950s, and they also can tell us something about the United States in that same period. American radicalism has never been blessed with much power, but it has on occasion found itself in possession of some insight. In the course of the 1950s the Left discarded many old illusions and developed new ideas of continuing relevance. If "renaissance" is too grand a word to describe the process, it was at least, as one Communist wrote in July 1956, "a period of discovery . . . giving us freer eyes, ears, and hearts to perceive the world with."[12]

In considering the chapters that follow the reader should bear in mind that what is being described is a very small and somewhat incestuous community. For narrative and analytic reasons I have chosen to treat each of these groups as if it stood apart from the others, but a careful reader will soon note that many of the same names reappear in successive chapters. The debates and changes taking place within one group were related to those taking place in the other groups. Imagine standing at the edge of a small pond and tossing a handful of stones into the still water. Each stone independently sends out its own spreading ring of concentric circles, but very soon the circles will overlap, intermingle, and disrupt the initial simple pattern, until, at the end, only a kind of general disturbance laps up against the shore. The pond is the Left in the 1950s, the stones are the various groups of the Old Left that I have chosen to examine, the shore is the New Left of the 1960s.

Halfway through the writing of this book I had the interesting experience of sitting, literally and figuratively, in the middle of a panel devoted to the history of the American Left in the 1950s, with a former Shachtmanite to one side and a former Communist to the other. The two of them went at each other tooth and nail (hammer and sickle?) throughout the session, neither willing to concede a single criticism that the other had to make of their respective political pasts. I tried to keep my head down. It so happened that I had previously interviewed these two seemingly inflexible dogmatists for

this book—on separate occasions, of course—and listened while
each of them offered self-critical judgments just as damning as any
of the charges that their ancient and unesteemed factional opponent
had to offer on this more public occasion. Interviews with participants many years after the events being described can be of uncertain value as historical evidence, but on the whole it has been my
good fortune to have interviewed people who themselves really care
about history. Far from being self-serving, their reminiscences often
prove to be too self-deprecating—even if they would never give
"that damn Stalinist" or "that damn Trotskyite" the satisfaction of
hearing them say the kinds of things they were willing to tell me. I
could not have written this book were it not for the candid and in-
sightful recollections offered to me by Stanley Aronowitz, Paul
Buhle, Joseph Clark, Lewis Coser, David Dellinger, Betty Denitch,
Bogdan Denitch, Ralph DiGia, Hal Draper, Barbara Epstein, Harry
Fleischman, John Gates, Emanuel Geltman, Todd Gitlin, Albert
Glotzer, Max Gordon, Michael Harrington, Gordon Haskell, Doro-
thy Healey, Richard Healey, Irving Howe, Julius Jacobson, Phyllis
Jacobson, Arthur Lipow, Gail Malmgreen, Steve Max, David
McReynolds, Debbie Meier, David Montgomery, Juanita Nelson,
Steve Nelson, Wally Nelson, Joni Rabinowitz, Ronald Radosh,
George Rawick, Vera Rony, Bernard Rosenberg, Andre Schiffrin,
Michael Thelwell, Freijof Thygeson, Dorothy Tristman, Michael
Walzer, George Watt and Saul Wellman. I also appreciate the helpful
letters I received from Sam Bottone, Sidney Lens, Ralph Shapiro,
and Ernest Erber, and the copies of some of his private correspon-
dence from the 1940s that Erber sent along with his letter.

In addition, I am grateful to Eileen Eagen, who sent me her unpublished paper on postwar student activism; to Jon Bloom, who sent
me his unpublished paper on the Workers Party in World War II; to
Mary McFeely and Elaine Miller of the Smith College library, as well
as to the librarians and archivists at the Tamiment Institute, the
Swarthmore College Peace Collection, and the Columbia University
Oral History Collection; to the National Endowment for the Humanities for providing a summer stipend to aid in my research, and to
the Mellon Fellowship for the Humanities and the Smith College
Committee on Faculty Compensation and Development for further
financial assistance. For the original publication of sections of chapter 1, see *Socialist Review*, No. 61 (January–February 1982), and for
sections of chapter 4 see *Peace and Change Journal*, 11, No. 3/4
(1986): I am grateful to the editors of these journals for permission

to reprint this material. Permission to reprint excerpts from the Max Shachtman oral history has been granted by the Columbia University Oral History Research Office, which is the holder of the copyright to this memoir.

Steve Fraser of Basic Books has been a wonderful editor; not the least of the satisfactions involved in this project has been that of becoming friends with him over the past several years. Friends of longer standing, including Mark Erlich, Michael Kazin, and Peter Mandler, provided their usual indispensable advice and dissent when I discussed early drafts of the book with them. Finally, I am grateful to Marcia Williams, the woman who foolishly agreed to marry me just as I was beginning to jot down my first notes on 3 × 5 cards for this book, who has gracefully suffered the consequences ever since.

1

The Collapse of the Communist Party

The title of Mr. Hoover's book *Masters of Deceit* is . . .
a misnomer. The CP here never mastered the art of
persuading very large numbers of Americans, decep-
tively or otherwise. The only deception at which it
proved adept was self-deception—the basic cause of
its demise as an effective political trend.
                                                    —JOHN GATES
                        The Story of an American Communist, 1958

A thorough housecleaning: a self portrait of
American Communist dissidents, autumn 1956.

BETWEEN 1956 and 1958 the American Communist party (CP) for all intents and purposes collapsed. What has come to be known as the "deStalinization crisis" was a critical development in both the death of the Old Left and the birth of the New Left. The unprecedented scope and duration of the crisis, and the importance of the issues being debated, marked a point of no return for the Communists as well as for other American radicals. A generation of political activists who in better years had built and led powerful movements now abandoned the Party to which they had devoted themselves since their youth. The Communist party's collapse significantly altered the setting in which the coming generation of young radicals tried to make sense of the world. In the aftermath of 1956, for the first time in the twentieth century, the United States was left without any significant nationally organized party espousing socialism.

For all the confusion and pain that was so evident in the ranks of the Communist party in 1956, the year was not simply a moment of defeat. Despite the years of repression endured by the Communists, and despite a series of crippling political mistakes imposed upon them by their leaders, as many as 20,000 Americans were still members of the CP at the start of the year, more members than the Party had managed to assemble during the first four years of the "Red Decade" of the 1930s. The Party had been, by and large, a movement of young people in the 1930s: although it was an aging group by 1956, most of its veteran members were still only in their forties at the time of the deStalinization crisis, still in the prime of their lives. In the course of the 1930s and 1940s the Communists developed invaluable political skills—although those skills were not matched by a commensurate measure of political wisdom. For American Communists, 1956 was both a time of accounting for the mistakes of the past and a time—or so it seemed for a few months—of rebuilding for the future. No longer sustained by the comfortable orthodoxies of the past, some among them hoped that they were at last about to embark upon a truly "American road to socialism." If it seemed unlikely that the CP itself would ever again play as commanding a role in radical politics as it had in the 1930s, at least the experience the Communists had gained and the lessons they had learned so painfully could be put at the service of a new Left, whatever organizational form that new Left might finally assume.

Background to Crisis

The decade leading up to 1956 had not been a good one for American Communists. The rapid deterioration of the Soviet-American "Grand Alliance" after the Second World War brought Cold War abroad and Red Scare at home. Congressional investigating committees, newspapers, and Hollywood portrayed Communists as a subversive and sometimes as a virtually demonic force. Communists had to endure persecutions that ran the gamut from the draconian to the ridiculous. Over a hundred Communist party leaders were convicted under the Smith Act, a law making conspiracy to advocate the teaching of the desirability of overthrowing the government a federal crime; others were indicted under state sedition laws; some endured conviction for the same "crime" in both state and federal courts. Steve Nelson, a veteran CP leader in western Pennsylvania, received a twenty-year sentence in 1952 for violating the Pennsylvania sedition statutes; the following year he was sentenced to an additional five years in prison under the Smith Act. Communists were denied passports, found their social security and military disability payments cut off, and if they were unfortunate enough to have been born overseas, risked deportation. Thousands of those accused of Communist affiliation or sympathies were fired from jobs in government, the universities, public schools, and private industry. New York State made its own contribution to national security by denying Communists the privilege of purchasing fishing licenses.[1]

The Communist party, which had played a major role in organizing the new Congress of Industrial Organizations (CIO) unions and had been a significant political force in New York, California, and several other states since the mid-1930s, found itself powerless and isolated by the start of the 1950s. The decisive blows fell from 1948 to 1949 when Henry Wallace's Communist-backed Progressive party campaign failed to mobilize the shrinking battalions of New

Deal liberalism around an anti–Cold War banner, and when the CIO expelled eleven Communist-led or -influenced unions.

The Communists added to their troubles by disregarding many of the lessons they had learned in the 1930s and early 1940s about American political realities. The man most responsible for their post-1945 course, Party chairman William Z. Foster, had been an important figure in the CP's internal factional struggles since the 1920s. During most of the New Deal era and World War II he had been kept on the sidelines by his one-time lieutenant Earl Browder, the Communist party's general secretary from 1934 through 1945. Browder became a staunch advocate of "Americanizing" the Party's public face (though he left its authoritarian internal structure largely unchanged). For years Foster fumed impotently at the "right opportunism" he saw revealed in Browder's policies. The CP's steady gain in members and influence (interrupted only by the setbacks they had to endure during the Nazi-Soviet pact) disarmed Foster. In a report to the Party's top leaders in 1944, Browder sneered at Foster's continued criticisms: the aging Foster had become "terribly confused, tragically confused; I think he has lost his way."[2]

Browder overstepped himself that year. Carried away by the wartime rhetoric of national unity and international collective security, he decided to dissolve the Communist party and replace it with a "Communist Political Association." He argued that it made no sense for the Communists to pretend to be a party contesting for power in their own right when the chief form of their electoral activity consisted of supporting candidates from other more significant parties. Communists had moved into the mainstream of American political life in the course of the 1930s and early 1940s, through their involvement in the union movement and their support of the New Deal, and needed to discard the organizational relics of their earlier marginal existence as a self-styled revolutionary opposition. Browder coupled this change in organizational perspective with predictions of postwar Soviet-American cooperation and domestic labor-management harmony. The lion was to lie down with the lamb: capitalism would coexist with socialism, and employer would reach out a friendly hand to worker in Browder's militantly benign view of the postwar world. Except for Foster and one or two others, American Communist leaders went along with Browder. But Soviet leaders evidently decided that he was straying too far from the fold, and in the spring of 1945, French Communist leader Jacques Duclos published an article accusing him of a "notorious revision" of Marxism. Browder's colleagues interpreted Duclos's article as a directive from Moscow to change both direction and leader, and in short order Browder was expelled from the reconstituted Communist party as an "enemy of the people."[3]

Foster, who had been privately humiliated by Browder and publicly demoted to the rank of "vice-president" in the Communist Political Association, was once again made chairman of the CP. Exercising real power in the Communist movement for the first time since the early 1930s, Foster made up for lost time. Over the objections of more cautious CP leaders (including Browder's successor as general secretary, Eugene Dennis, who never was able to exercise the kind of authority that Browder had brought to the post), Foster pushed Communists to embrace policies that even he would later admit were "left-sectarian" in character. War between the Soviet Union and the United States, he argued, was all but inevitable (this became known within the Party as the "five minutes to midnight line"—the phrase was coined by Dennis, but the impetus behind its adoption came from Foster). The coming economic collapse, Foster believed, made Wall Street eager for war; and with war would come fascism. Under such conditions, normal politics were impossible. The Communist party's primary responsibility in the harsh times to come was to maintain its ideological integrity, whatever short-term political losses that entailed. The example set by the Communist-led resistance movements in Nazi-occupied Europe was much on Foster's mind in the late 1940s and early 1950s. After the impending catastrophe had run its course, the CP would emerge from the ruins, fighting spirit intact and political honor unsullied.[4]

If the Communist party had been an isolated sect, like most of its competitors on the Left, it might have survived this change in direction with few losses. But given the power and influence that the Communists had built up so painstakingly since the early 1930s, in the union movement and in sections of the Democratic party, Foster's insistence that it was "five minutes to midnight" entailed real sacrifices that the Communists could ill afford. The decision to form an independent third party in 1948, rather than following a more cautious strategy such as supporting a challenge to Truman's candidacy in the Democratic primaries, cost the Communists valuable political allies, particularly in California, where they had been well entrenched in the left-wing of the Democratic party. The Communists suffered irreplaceable losses when they forced their trade union "influentials" to support the Wallace candidacy and oppose the Marshall Plan—positions that were anathema to top CIO leaders, providing them with a readymade case to justify the expulsion of such Communist-influenced unions as Harry Bridge's International Longshoremen's and Warehousemen's Union (ILWU). The severe demands the Party placed on its union supporters extended even to bread-and-butter issues. The Party's insistence that its members within New York City's Transport Workers Union (TWU) oppose any increase in subway fare (an issue linked to the prospects for wage increases for transport workers) led to the disaffection of TWU president Mike Quill, despite the fact that his staunch support of the CP over many years grew out of genuine radical conviction. More opportunistic union leaders (like Joe Curran of the National Maritime Union) who had joined hands with the Communists only because of the practical support the Party was able to deliver in return, required even less provocation to turn vehemently against their former allies now that they were in trouble.[5]

The gravest threat the Communists faced in these years was the legal attack mounted by the federal government, through the Justice Department, the Federal Bureau of Investigation, and various congressional committees. The Communists had weathered the "little Red Scare" of the Nazi-Soviet pact years, in part because the Roosevelt administration was not wholeheartedly committed to the attack, and in part because many non-Communists were, if not sympathetic to the Communists, at least fearful of unleashing another period of reaction like that of the early 1920s. Most of that liberal goodwill had been squandered by the Party's "flip-flops" in 1939 and 1945, and the Communists were doomed to hard times in the postwar years regardless of what political path they chose to follow. But Foster made it even harder for them to find defenders outside their own ranks by insisting that defendants in the first Smith Act trial, in 1949, engage in a protracted defense of Communist political theory, rather than rely on constitutional and civil libertarian arguments as some of the defendants and their lawyers would have preferred (defendants in later trials of "second string" party leaders in New York, California, Washington, and elsewhere battled Foster for the right to abandon the earlier, disastrous trial strategy). As the Communists by necessity grew preoccupied with courtroom battles, their political organizing suffered accordingly. With Communist headquarters and meetings the target of vigilante and mob violence, it became all but impossible to show the "public face" of the Party. Once again at Foster's insistence the Communists made a difficult situation worse,

7

contributing to their own isolation by sending hundreds of their most experienced cadre into hiding, while purging thousands of members regarded as potentially "unreliable." The Communists developed an elaborate system of underground leadership that was enormously expensive and cumbersome to maintain and proved easily penetrable by the FBI. The shift to an underground existence at first only reinforced the Party's apocalyptic outlook. Those who dissented from the five-minutes-to-midnight perspective were whipped back into line with charges of "Browderism," the most damning epithet in postwar CP polemics.[6]

Despite external and internal pressures for ideological conformity, some Communists grew dissatisfied with Foster's habitual ultra-leftism. Those very Communists who endured the enforced inactivity of prison or the underground were among the first to raise disturbing questions within the Party. The signing of the armistice ending the Korean War in 1953, followed by the first postwar summit meetings between Soviet and American leaders, suggested that war was not as inevitable as Foster assumed. The Senate's censure (in December 1954) of its most prominent Red-hunter, Joe McCarthy, and the Supreme Court's decision a year later to hear appeals from Steve Nelson and other Communists convicted under the Smith Act, suggested that fears of fascism had been greatly exaggerated. In 1955 the Communists began to come up from underground; as the *Daily Worker* spoke tentatively of "the revival of the democratic spirit" in the United States, fugitives from the Smith Act turned themselves in to federal authorities. Many of those assigned to the Party underground apparatus had been forced to sever links with family and friends for years, living bleak lives in strange cities, dodging the FBI, and now they bitterly questioned the justification for their self-imposed exile.[7]

The excesses to which Foster's policies had led were not the only source of dissatisfaction. Events in the Soviet Union and Eastern Europe since Stalin's death, in 1953—including the arrest and execution of Lavrenti Beria (head of the Soviet secret police), the rehabilitation of the defendants accused of conspiring to murder Stalin in the so-called "Doctor's Plot," and Khrushchev's visit to Yugoslavia and apology to Tito, in 1955—all fed a growing sense of unease within the American Communist party. When Tito defied Stalin in 1948, American Communists had repeated obediently the Soviet charges that the Yugoslav leader was an American hireling, just as ten years earlier they had taken it as an article of faith that Trotsky was an agent of the Gestapo. Now that Stalin's case against Tito had exploded, what were Communists to make of the charges against such "Titoists" as Laszlo Rajk in Hungary, Rudolf Slansky in Czechoslovakia, Traicho Kostov in Bulgaria, and other Eastern European Communist leaders who had been tried and executed in the postwar purge trials? If those trials were frame-ups, what did that suggest about the prewar Moscow trials? And finally, if the Soviets could now acknowledge the right of Yugoslav Communists to find their own independent road to socialism, might they have been similarly mistaken when they engineered the removal of Earl Browder, scorned by his once-devoted followers as the American Tito?

Joseph Starobin, former foreign editor of the *Daily Worker*, published a book in 1955 called *Paris to Peking*, that in cautious fashion raised questions about past Soviet and American Communist policies; the book won a substantial readership among Communists despite official disapproval. Joseph Clark, Starobin's successor as the *Daily Worker*'s foreign editor, raised similar questions in private memoranda in late 1954 and in public CP forums in the summer of 1955. After serving their Smith Act prison sentences, John Gates and Eugene Dennis returned to active roles in the Party leadership at the end of 1955, with Gates as editor of the *Daily Worker* and Dennis as general secretary. Both Gates and Dennis suggested to a Party audience in January 1956 that it was time for Communists to take a "new look" at the causes of past failures. Few if any American Communists had made the connections between their dissatisfaction with domestic Party policies and their uneasiness about events in Eastern Europe, but once the first forbidden questions were asked, they suggested a hundred others. Starobin would later describe the mood in Communist circles both in America and abroad as "a vast intellectual black market in which many of us traded, half in a daze, unable to voice everything on our minds."[8]

Impact of the Twentieth Congress

Whatever doubts the Communists may have harbored about the past, they still regarded the Soviet Union as the homeland of socialism, and the Soviet Communist party as the indisputable first among equals in the international Communist movement. When the Soviet

CP met in Moscow in February 1956 for its Twentieth Congress, American Communists paid close attention to published reports of its deliberations. In the public sessions of the congress, the Soviet CP's new leader, Nikita Khrushchev, pledged to pursue policies of peaceful coexistence with the West. Khrushchev and other speakers attacked repeatedly the now safely buried "Beria gang," as well as an abstract entity referred to only as the "cult of personality," for past abuses of power in the USSR. Not all the congress's sessions were open to the press and foreign observers, and it soon became known in the West that Khrushchev, in an unpublished speech, had made much more extensive criticisms of the "cult of personality," generally understood to be a euphemism for Stalin. The *Daily Worker* carried detailed reports on the public sessions of the congress and promised a full discussion of the significance of the secret sessions as soon as "the texts and materials discussed become available."[9]

The *Daily Worker*'s first editorial response to the Twentieth Congress was resolutely cheerful; mistakes had been made in the Soviet Union and were now being acknowledged by its leaders; such mistakes were already or soon would be corrected. For several weeks after the end of the congress the newspaper had little more to say on the subject. But the placid tone of this first reaction was misleading. The *Daily Worker*'s staff was, in fact, already shaken by the "violations of socialist law" revealed in such oblique fashion in published reports of the congress's sessions. By late February a revolution began to brew in the paper's New York editorial offices.

The most minute details of the *Daily Worker*'s editorial policies had always been controlled by national Party leaders, and its reporters and columnists were expected to toe the line on all significant questions of Party theory and policy. Even the letters column had been kept free of dissenting views, except for a short period around the time of the appearance of the "Duclos letter" in 1945. In the spring of 1956, the *Daily Worker*'s staff realized that they shared some common political concerns that put them at odds with the official Party line. *Daily Worker* editor John Gates; Alan Max, the managing editor; Joseph Clark, the foreign editor; Lester Rodney, the sports editor; Abner Berry, a black columnist; Max Gordon, who covered New York State politics; and others on the staff were part of the generation of Communists who joined the CP or the Young Communist League (YCL) in the early days of the Great Depression. Despite the Party's official repudiation of Browder's "revisionism," the *Daily Worker* staffers, like many other Communists of their generation, looked back to the years of Browder's leadership during the Popular Front and World War II as a golden era in which the Party's political success had grown out of the loosening of the rigid ideological bonds of earlier years.

Browder and the Popular Front

Browder's strength as a leader lay in his skill as a political tactician, shaped by a driving personal ambition. Many veterans of the earliest years of the Communist movement, especially those who were foreign-born, were almost indifferent to the Party's actual political influence within the United States. They derived a sense of destiny from belonging to a world movement that already held power in the Soviet Union ("one sixth of the world," as Communist publications habitually noted) and that seemed to be on the verge of a serious contest for power throughout Europe and Asia. Browder himself, a native-born radical of midwestern Populist parents, joined the Communist movement in 1920. In the early part of the 1920s he served as Foster's aide in the Party-organized Trade Union Educational League; in the latter half of the decade he spent much time in Moscow and went to China as a representative of the Profintern, the Soviet-controlled international trade-union organization. In the early 1930s he found himself catapulted into the leadership of the Communist party, over the head of his former mentor, Foster, who had long coveted the position. Browder must have made a good impression on Soviet leaders in his years in Russia and China, but his absence from the United States during the worst of the American CP's internal factional struggles of the 1920s was among his most important qualifications for leadership.

Despite the image he cultivated during the Popular Front, Browder was not at heart a Jeffersonian democrat. With years of training in the hard school of international communism, he knew better than to oppose Soviet-imposed policies, however inappropriate they might seem to American conditions. But he was also an ambitious man, and he wanted to be the leader of a national movement with power and influence of its own, like Maurice Thorez in France or Mao Zedong in China. His sense of self-preservation and his personal ambition would be at war with one another at several critical moments in his career.

Since political innovation paid off in the United States, Browder became an innovator; once given the green light by the Communist International's adoption of the Popular Front policy in 1935 (which made antifascist unity rather than proletarian revolution the Communists' main concern), he hastened to clear out the deadwood, ideological and individual, that cluttered up the Party's policy making. Party membership increased dramatically from around 25,000 in 1934 to triple that level five years later. And, though harder to measure, the Communists' indirect influence extended far beyond their own ranks. Communists no longer sought to stand aloof from and in hostile opposition to all other organized movements. They learned to work in coalition for common goals with people as diverse as Father Divine and John L. Lewis. Browder proved a shrewd tactical leader who knew how to extract maximum gains for the Party without damaging the goodwill of the Party's new allies. He also knew a good slogan when he heard one (witness the contrast between his "Communism is 20th century Americanism" and the party's earlier slogan "Towards a Soviet America"; Foster's book of that title would be a recurrent source of embarrassment to the Communists in the later 1930s as they attempted to allay the suspicions of mainstream church, union, and political leaders). Perhaps the most important step Browder took in terms of the long-term evolution of American communism was to open up secondary leadership positions throughout the Party and its auxiliaries to politically talented young people, like Gates, Gordon, and Clark, who entered the movement in the early 1930s through the Young Communist League and various Party-organized student groups.[10]

Thousands of these young people, many of them the native-born children of Jewish and other Southern and Eastern European immigrants, joined the Party in the course of the 1930s. Hundreds went on to become full-time Party cadre. As paradoxical as it may seem, even as they were swept up by the internationalist vision of the Russian Revolution, they also felt that becoming Communists was a step toward "Americanization," breaking down the distance between the insular immigrant communities they grew up in and the American working class. The new generation of Communists replaced most of the Party's older foreign-born functionaries by the mid-1930s, and became the most enthusiastic adherents within the movement of the Popular Front line. By the late 1930s, graduates of New Utrecht High

School and City College in New York could be found organizing Slavic steelworkers in Youngstown, black packinghouse workers in Chicago, or the polyglot collection of workers on the San Francisco docks.

The Communist movement was born in the wave of revolutionary enthusiasm that swept outward from the Soviet Union after the Bolshevik triumph. It took many years of painful learning before Communists in the West were able to distinguish between enthusiasm and imitation; longer still until some of them learned that part of their responsibility as revolutionaries would be to understand the limitations of the first revolution successfully undertaken in the name of socialism. Popular Front communism, whatever its limitations and whatever the intentions of its Soviet sponsors, turned out to be a step in that learning process.

American Communists from 1936 to 1939 entertained a strange hybrid of democratic and antidemocratic ideas. Socialism had its origins in the nineteenth century as a critique of the limitations of democracy under capitalism, not as the repudiation of the principles and institutions of "bourgeois democracy." Large sections of the Left had lost track of this distinction in the years since the "dictatorship of the proletariat" had been transformed from an unfortunate choice of words by Marx to the harsh reality of the Soviet system. The Popular Front, with its emphasis on the defense of existing democratic rights against fascism, restored a measure of democratic content to Communist ideology even as Communists continued to celebrate the supposed virtues of the "higher form of democracy" that the Soviet people enjoyed under Stalin. This contradiction led some political opponents to label them "Red Fascists" who hypocritically mouthed democratic slogans they did not believe in. But fascist ideology began from frankly stated antidemocratic premises, glorifying national or racial supremacies, sexual inequality, military conquest, and dictatorship. Communism began from other premises. The basic texts of their movement instructed Communists that men and women of all races and nations were equal, that war was a ghastly pursuit, that ordinary people had the potential to control their own destinies, and that any cook should be able to aspire to govern the state. This did not prevent the Communists from glorifying the very aspects of the Stalinist dictatorship that some among their ranks would later find repellent: the "monolithic unity" of the Party, Stalin's "irreplaceable leadership" and his "iron hand" in dealing with enemies of the Soviet Union. Still, there remained a potential for tension within the American Communist movement around questions of democracy, a potential that did not exist in any fascist movement. This tension led to a constant stream of individual defections from the Party in the 1930s and 1940s and provided a background necessary to understand the crisis that overtook the Communists in 1956. The Popular Front permitted Communists, for a time, to take their own arguments about the value of democracy seriously, and Browder's ambitions made it possible for younger Communists to begin to experiment with new forms of political activity. By World War II a few members of the new generation of Communist leaders were asking questions that went far beyond a purely tactical or temporary concern over how to reshape the Party's image for political gain. As one Communist recently returned from military service asked Browder in 1943:

Isn't the Leninist Party designed for an immediate, sharp and final struggle? Is it possible to build a mass Marxist party to meet the challenge that lies in front of us today on such a basis?[11]

Browder's downfall in the spring of 1945 cut off such questioning. The fact that his predictions of postwar international and domestic harmony had proven empty discredited the other innovations that had been undertaken under his leadership. Government repression during the Cold War made internal Party unity a necessity. But with the first thaw in that repression, doubts and questions began to shoot up from a long period of underground dormancy.

The Crisis Goes Public

Until the Twentieth Congress, Communist leaders of both reform and orthodox persuasion had carefully kept all signs of internal dissent hidden from the Party rank and file. In the months after the Twentieth Congress discretion was thrown to the winds, and the deep divisions within the Party became obvious.

Daily Worker writers had carried the heavy burden, year in and year out, of reassuring their readers that any criticism of the Soviet Union, regardless of its source or evidence, was capitalist slander. If Stalin and Hitler signed a nonaggression pact it was a "brilliant stroke for world peace," even if the Second World War broke out a week later. If Communist leaders were shot in Eastern Europe, they were "imperialist agents," even if they were personally known to American Communists as veterans of the International Brigades, the European resistance, and Nazi concentration camps. If Jewish writers and artists disappeared in the Soviet Union, they were on vacation or had decided to move to some inaccessible corner of the country, even if no one was ever able to contact them again. Joseph Clark was the *Daily Worker*'s correspondent in Moscow for three years before taking over as its foreign editor. In a series of articles reprinted as a pamphlet in 1954, Clark set out to refute the unflattering picture of Soviet society that Harrison Salisbury was drawing for *New York Times* readers. In the "real Russia," Clark insisted, there was no anti-Semitism, no political terror, no harsh treatment of the few Soviet citizens sentenced to prison: "The Soviet penal system is based on labor rehabilitation," Clark insisted. "Prisoners are paid for the labor they perform."[12]

But it was Clark, until that moment among the most skilled apologists the Party possessed, who broke the *Daily Worker*'s silence on the significance of the Twentieth Congress. In a column appearing 12 March 1956, Clark noted that East German CP leader Walter Ulbricht had criticized Stalin by name for fostering "the cult of the individual" during his years in power in the Soviet Union. Stalin, Clark suggested, was not the only one bearing responsibility for this mistake: "Ulbricht would have been a lot more candid if he had only admitted that he himself had contributed to sponsoring the 'cult of the individual.' "[13]

Mild as Clark's comments may seem, they shocked his readers to the realization that a new and unprecedented crisis was upon them: in the past Communists had *never* criticized the leaders of other Communist parties in public, unless that criticism had the sanction of Moscow (as in the case of the Duclos article attacking Browder, in 1945). Clark's column did leave a larger question unanswered: if East German Communists were now to be criticized for contributing to the shortcomings of the Stalin years, what did the *Daily Worker* have to say about its own responsibility? The answer was to come the next day in a column by managing editor Alan Max entitled "US Marxists and Soviet Self-Criticism." Max declared: "Any Marxist who says he has not been jolted is either not being honest with himself . . . or minimizes the extent of the developments now in progress in the Soviet Union." He admitted that American Communists had "glossed over" problems in the USSR, particularly the suppression of civil liberties, but he pledged that would never happen again. Max concluded with yet another unprecedented gesture, asking *Daily Worker* readers to write down responses to the Twentieth Congress and send them in for publication.[14]

With the appearance of the Clark and Max columns the deluge began. Over the next twelve months hundreds of Communists, ranging from top leaders to the humblest rank-and-file members, used the pages of the *Daily Worker* and other Party publications to raise and debate fundamental questions about the nature of Soviet society, the American Communist party's past history, and its future prospects. It was an angry debate, never free of bitterness and recriminations, and toward the end grew increasingly despairing in tone. But in its first six months, from mid-March until the suppression of the Hungarian revolution in November 1956, the debate also conveyed a sense of emancipation from old dogmas, of self-discovery, and of renewed hope.

The first issue that had to be debated was whether there should be any debate at all. Foster tried his best to squelch it before it could get started. Three days after Max's column appeared, Foster acknowledged in the *Daily Worker* that Stalin had committed "serious errors." But, he insisted, "our task is neither to rush indignantly to the defense of Stalin nor to tear him to political shreds, as some in our ranks seem inclined to do." The necessary reevaluation of the Stalin years "can be done most authoritatively by those leaders who have worked closely with him in the Soviet Union." A week and a half later Foster returned to the attack, warning that "capitalist apologists" would use criticisms of Stalin by American Communists to discredit the socialist cause. The capitalists hoped to "turn rank and file Communists in the various countries against their leaders over the Stalin issue." Collective leadership, the ideal enunciated by Soviet leaders at the Twentieth Congress, "does not mean no-leadership and the abolition of party discipline."[15]

Foster had brought out the heavy guns—loyalty to the Soviet Union, the tradition of Bolshevik discipline, and the fear of lending ammunition to hostile forces. In previous Party crises these had never failed to batter down dissenters. But this time the old weapons did not prevail. "N. J." wrote in to criticize Foster's position (except for well-known Party spokesmen, most of those who wrote to the *Daily Worker* used their initials or adopted pseudonyms as a measure of protection against anti-Communist harassment): "At the time

[the] Duclos letter on Browderism was published in France, Foster did not feel that critical evaluation of another party concerning American affairs was ruled out." Why then did Foster believe the Soviet CP should be spared similar treatment from fraternal parties?[16] "A Reader" challenged Foster's assertion that frank criticism of the Soviet Union aided capitalism:

Some people fear that to be critical of injustice under socialism plays into the hands of those who hate socialism. To the contrary, to remain silent plays into their hands.[17]

"Hank" brought the issues raised by Foster's attempted suppression of debate closer to home in a letter published 29 March 1956.

We demand of the bourgeoisie that they permit free discussion of socialist ideas, quoting at them the dictum that truth has nothing to fear from free discussion. Too often we have failed to apply it within our own ranks. It seems to me that a certain contempt for the rank and file is implied in the constant fear that "destructive" criticism has to be stifled.[18]

Events abroad, interpreted with increasing candor and independence by the *Daily Worker*, fueled the debate. Between the end of March and the middle of April the newspaper carried reports from Eastern Europe on the posthumous "rehabilitation" of Rajk, Slansky, Kostov, and other victims of the postwar purge trials. On 11 April the *Daily Worker* cited a report from a Warsaw newspaper on the suppression of Yiddish culture in the Soviet Union in the last years of Stalin's life, including the execution of a score of prominent Jewish writers and artists.[19] The *Daily Worker* admitted that it had until now accepted all too slavishly the official lies about "why Jewish culture had disappeared in the Soviet Union in the late 1940s. Had we not done so, we would have served the cause of Socialism better."[20]

The Reevaluation of the Past

The impact of the events of 1956 on the Communists was compared to a religious crisis by outside observers. "In the eyes of a Communist," Irving Howe and Lewis Coser wrote in their critical history of the Party, published in 1957, "it was as if St. Paul, suddenly and without warning, had bitterly charged Christ with depravity and deceit. . . . Faith had been shattered at its very source."[21]

The religious analogy was not without merit. Moscow had been both Rome and Jerusalem for the Communists, both the seat of doctrinal authority and the Promised Land. Once that authority was tarnished, the whole Communist system of beliefs was thrown into jeopardy.[22] But the analogy should not obscure the *political* response that disillusioned Communists made that year: continuing Howe and Coser's analogy, it was as if those early Christians—shaken as they were by St. Paul's revelations—had then reread the Sermon on the Mount, decided it required a humbler and less dogmatic interpretation than they had previously given it, appended a paragraph warning against messianic abuses of power, and vowed to do a better job in spreading the remaining and abiding gospel truths.

Many letter-writers in the *Daily Worker* now complained of the ritualistic, pseudoscientific style of writing and speaking that over the years had allowed the Communists to shut out uncomfortable realities. They had used language as a shield against emotion and uncertainty: if something could be named, then it could be safely pigeonholed and forgotten. Top Communist party leaders came under repeated attack for seeking to explain away the recent revelations from the Soviet Union and Eastern Europe with the catch phrases used by Khrushchev at the Twentieth Congress. Foster was a frequent target: he was clearly unmoved by the fate of Stalin's victims and repeated listlessly the now obligatory condemnation of the "cult of personality."[23] The Party's general secretary, Eugene Dennis, also came under attack. Dennis at first seemed genuinely disturbed by the post–Twentieth Congress revelations but proved unable or unwilling to abandon his habitually cautious, stilted approach to controversial issues.[24] A reader named Alex Leslie wrote to the *Daily Worker* to praise the paper's new outspokenness. He took issue with those readers who were upset at "incorrect formulations" in some of the newspaper's editorials.

I would rather read one of those "incorrect" editorials with their vivid communication of personal outrage, than a dozen wordy and passionless "correct formulations" by Dennis . . . *et al.*, whose emotions, if they have any, are buried in "cult of the individual," "Soviet achievements," "violations of legality," and all the rest of the conventional clichés.

Leslie offered a personal challenge to Dennis:

After the mistakes you have admitted, a few sloppy formulations won't make much difference. Tell us how you feel—about the lies you swallowed, about the years wasted in propagating those lies, about the innocent men and women destroyed.

Dennis never responded. Leslie was not calling for breast-beating for its own sake; rather, he had come to believe that if the Communists ever hoped to make headway in the United States, they needed to relearn some lessons understood by an earlier generation of American radicals. Eugene Debs, leader of the Socialist Party in its great years before the First World War, had not been addicted to the "correct formulation." Debs built a powerful movement for socialism because, Leslie argued, he

understood what too many Communist leaders seem to have forgotten: that socialism is a moral movement, a movement against the cut-throat, belly-crawling world of capitalism, a movement to exalt not this or that "great leader" but all humanity.[25]

The Communists had never before considered the possibility that earlier radical movements might have possessed virtues that their own movement lacked. But that was a mild heresy compared with those that could be found in other letters published that spring in the *Daily Worker*. By the end of April some readers were no longer simply criticizing Stalin for betraying the original purity of Leninism: they found in Leninism itself a primary cause of the American Communist party's failures. The Leninist party had proved itself prone to become a self-absorbed world unto itself, providing its members with an illusory sense of purpose and accomplishment. Why, "A. W." asked in a letter printed at the start of May, did the Communists refer to their own leaders as

"leaders of the American working class," "leaders of the Negro people," "Great women leaders," etc. If these self-proclaimed titles were true, our troubles would be over. The truth of the matter is that CP leaders and functionaries have been for most of their lives inner party functionaries, isolated from the people, and have no organizational ties with the mass organizations of the people.[26]

Even "mass work" was no guarantee against self-deception, according to "E. S.," a Bronx Communist whose letter appeared in the *Daily Worker* on the Fourth of July:

When an issue arose, we got together, planned a protest meeting, chose one another as speakers, sold tickets to one another, and finally went to the meeting where we had a wonderful time saying hello to this or that comrade whom we hadn't seen in years. . . . After everything had been planned down to the last detail . . . including what was to "come out" of the meeting . . . we cordially invited the people in the community to step right up and be sponsors.[27]

Words could be great deceivers, and some Communists turned to parody to demystify the ritual language of Leninism. Jessica Mitford's inspired guide to left-wing usage, "Lifeitselfmanship," is one of the few documents generated by the deStalinization crisis to have escaped total obscurity, reprinted as an appendix to her autobiography, *A Fine Old Conflict*. A typical passage went: *"Question*: What does one do with cadres? *Answer*: One develops them, trains them and boldly promotes them, poor things."[28]

One reader offered a "glossary of sectarianism" in his letter to the *Daily Worker*, mocking Leninist pieties with such definitions as "vanguard role—first roll out of the oven."[29] This was a rueful form of humor: there was nothing funny about what American Communists had done to one another in acting out their illusions. "A. B.," a Brooklyn housewife, wrote in at the end of May, recounting the dozen years she spent in the YCL and the CP. She had always been willing to do the work assigned to her by her local Party branch, but

it was never enough, and I never felt that anyone in the leadership of my neighborhood had any respect for the efforts of women like myself. Pride in the work of the housewife was never appreciated or understood. Even women leaders seemed a little contemptuous of the desire of man and wife to spend quiet times at home with just each other and their children. This was "bourgeois."

Her own feelings of inadequacy and the harsh demands continually placed on her for ever-greater sacrifices of time and effort finally forced her to quit the Communist party. Communists, she concluded, had to recognize "that people can be chased away more easily than they can be recruited."[30]

Now that old ideological barriers were falling, the Communists began to look critically at many aspects of their own history. Letters came in criticizing the Party's policies during the Nazi-Soviet Pact, the failure to defend Trotskyist leaders indicted under the Smith Act in 1941, the decision to launch the Progressive party in 1948, the internal Party purges of the late 1940s, and the creation of the underground in the early 1950s.[31] A number of Communists began to reappraise Browder's leadership, a daring step considering the anathema in which his name had been held over the past decade. The most enthusiastic defense of Browder came from Chick Mason, a New York Communist with a quarter-century of involvement in the CP. Mason wrote a 20,000-word article entitled "Sources of Our Dilemma," which he circulated in a mimeographed edition and eventually published in abridged form in *Party Voice*, the monthly internal bulletin of the New York State CP, controlled by anti-Foster forces. Mason argued that under Browder the Party "began to speak a language that could be understood, at least by us [and] that could almost be understood by millions of Americans."[32]

The great strength of the Communist party under Browder, Mason went on, was that it had been deeply involved in day-to-day political activities, giving Communists the kind of grasp on reality that seemed to elude them after 1945. Under Foster the Communists had retreated to a catastrophic determinism, believing in a

fantasy of socialists huddled in a corner, predicting depression and wars, awaiting the call from suffering humanity for help. Then Socialism would emerge from its hiding place on a white charger, shouting "To the Rescue."[33]

Other taboos were discarded by Communists that summer. American Communists had looked to the Soviet Union for cultural as well as political guidance, and since the early 1930s they had echoed the Soviet cultural establishment's condemnation of artistic modernism. They now discovered, or in some cases rediscovered, modern painting and writing. "Allegro" wrote to the *Daily Worker* in July:

I used to be an avid reader of our contemporary poets, but I pretty much gave it up about ten years ago when I joined the Communist Party. . . . The elaborate preparations many of us made to exclude all ideas in the arts but those we mistakenly believed conformed with "socialist realism," have done us and American culture great harm.

Like others who wrote in to the *Daily Worker* in defense of modern painting, of previously disparaged novelists, and of the value of Freudian psychology, "Allegro" felt that the months following the

Twentieth Congress had been "a period of discovery and liberation, in a very personal sense, of ourselves as human beings, giving us freer eyes, ears, and hearts to perceive the world with."[34]

The Struggle for Control

The forces of orthodoxy within the Communist party were clearly on the defensive in the spring and summer of 1956. The *Daily Worker* did print letters from some leaders and rank-and-file Communists disapproving of its new course. "F. M.," a Party member since the 1920s, wrote in March: "I was for Stalin, I'm for Stalin, and I will be for Stalin."[35]

But the old guard's position was shaky. After all, Soviet leaders had initiated the reexamination of the Stalinist era at the Twentieth Congress. Communist leaders in Eastern Europe were taking steps to liberalize their own regimes without suffering public rebuke from Moscow. It remained unclear how far Khrushchev intended to go in discarding Stalin's legacy in the Soviet Union, and the last thing the American CP's old guard wanted was to find itself out of step with Moscow. When Khrushchev's "secret speech" was finally made public in June 1956 it seemed to sweep away the more orthodox Communists' last hope of stifling the reform movement in the American Communist party.

Through one or another covert means, the U.S. State Department obtained a copy of Khrushchev's speech and released it to the press on 4 June 1956. The *Daily Worker* printed a condensed version of the 26,000-word text the next day, and the full text appeared in the Sunday *Worker*.[36] The Party's leaders had already received a private preview of its contents at the end of April when a copy of the speech (passed on to them by the Soviet embassy) was read aloud at a meeting in New York. The élite of the Party, 120 people who had known each other and worked together for decades, many of them defendants in Smith Act trials or veterans of the underground, gathered in the auditorium of the Party-run Jefferson school. They were ordered not to take notes on what they were about to hear. Steve Nelson called the meeting to order, and Leon Wofsy, Dennis's personal secretary, read Khrushchev's speech to the dumbfounded gathering. The speech gave substance to the sparse euphemisms employed in public at the Twentieth Congress. Stalin stood revealed to these hard-bitten Communist veterans as the vain, bloodthirsty tyrant he was, the man who had unleashed a reign of terror against his own Party. "Honest Communists," Khrushchev declared, "were slandered, accusations against them were fabricated, and revolutionary legality was gravely undermined."[37] He cited the fate of the 139 members of the Soviet Communist party's central committee in 1934, nearly three-quarters of whom would be arrested as counter-revolutionaries by the end of the decade. The same fate swallowed up over half of the 1,966 delegates to the Soviet Party congress that year. Dorothy Healey, one of the representatives at the meeting from California, remembered the several hours it took to listen to the speech as the most devastating experience of her life. Like many of the other people in the room, she wept as she heard

this voice going on, piling up facts upon facts, horrible facts about what had happened there. . . . We had marched for so many years with the purity of the Soviet Union as our banner. It was not just a public thing, you felt it, believed it. You had no difficulty in dismissing the stories that were told about the Soviet Union as lies, nonsense. And here you were being told that not only were those stories true but that they went beyond anything you ever heard from enemies of the Soviet Union.[38]

At the end of the meeting, Nelson, a veteran of more than thirty years in the Communist movement, could only comment "This was not why I joined the Party." Ben Davis, the former Communist councilman from Harlem, who on most occasions was one of Foster's closest allies, seemed genuinely shocked. He told the national committee the following day that the most devastating effect of hearing the Khrushchev speech for him was the realization that if American Communists had been in power, they would have been capable of committing the same crimes against one another. Or, as Dorothy Healey put it many years later, "I was a little Stalin. I'm not talking about anybody else."[39]

The weeks just before and after the publication of the Khrushchev speech were the high tide of "reexaminationist" sentiment in the American Communist party. The dissident forces were in position to cement their control of the Party, if they chose to do so. At the April meeting of the national committee, Dennis, as general secretary, submitted a report scathingly critical of the CP's "left-sectarian" bent over the past decade, and proposed that Communists work with other American radicals to establish a new "united mass party of socialism."[40] Of forty or so voting delegates at the meeting, Foster alone voted against Dennis's position. Reform-minded forces controlled the Party's state organizations in New York (where half of the total Party membership was concentrated), New England, New Jersey, western Pennsylvania, and California. They controlled or strongly influenced the editorial policy of almost every important Party publication, including the *Daily Worker*; the *People's World*, in San Francisco; the *Freiheit*, the CP's Yiddish daily; the magazine *Jewish Life*; and the *Party Voice*. The dissidents had a sense of *élan*, believing themselves to be the wave of the future, not just in the American Communist movement but in the international movement. Clark kept *Daily Worker* readers abreast of the latest developments in Poland, where Wladyslaw Gomulka returned in triumph to the leadership of the Polish Communist party after years of imprisonment and faced down a Russian challenge to the liberalization of the Polish regime; and in Italy, where Palmiro Togliatti, leader of the Italian Communist party, called for a "polycentric" Communist movement and challenged Khrushchev to explain how and why other Soviet Communist leaders had allowed Stalin to acquire his despotic powers. A cartoon on the cover of the September issue of *Party Voice* showed a group of American Communists vigorously sweeping out and polishing up the house of socialism, and captured the optimistic spirit of reform-minded Communists that summer.[41]

Foster, although thrown on the defensive, was not without resources of his own. He retained a small but significant base of support within the CP. Communists in the Midwest and Northwest, isolated and fiercely persecuted during the McCarthy years, tended to regard the activities of their more freewheeling comrades in New York City and Los Angeles with suspicion. Even in those centers of the dissenters' strength, Foster retained a significant base of supporters. Among his backers were many of the older Yiddish-speaking workers from the needle trades, for whom the Party had become a comfortable retirement home; many of the Communist party's remaining maritime workers, syndicalist by tradition and unsympathetic to political experimentation; and some, though not all, black Communists, to whom the claims of "bourgeois democracy" rang especially hollow.[42] Foster was the best-known American Communist and, at least within the Party, a charismatic figure. As the principal organizer of the 1919 steel strike, and the sole important CP leader to have opposed Browder's "revisionism" during World War II, he seemed to his followers to personify the spirit and tradition of class struggle in the United States. (Foster liked to depict his own forces as the real workers in the Party; interestingly enough, however, he could also count on the support of many Communist doctors, dentists, and lawyers who looked upon him as their proletarian conscience.) Foster also retained the advantage of being well connected in Moscow, maintaining private liaison through John Williamson, a Scottish-born Communist leader who had been deported to Britain after serving his Smith Act sentence.[43]

Foster had a shrewd grasp of his opponents' vulnerabilities. The *New York Times* and other outside observers in 1956 described the "Gates faction" as though it were a tight-knit group with commonly agreed upon goals and established leadership: Foster and his allies found it useful to attack the "Gates-Starobin-Clark line" as a comprehensive plan for the "liquidation" of the Communist movement.[44] In fact, Gates did little to organize a faction to consolidate his sympathizers' potential power within the Party, nor did the dissenters share a common program for the future. This seems surprising, because those who opposed Foster included the most articulate, experienced, and talented political organizers in the Communist party. They were not naive about the means by which power is gained and exercised. Yet by early 1957 they lost the initiative to Foster, and by the end of the year were decisively defeated.

What Went Wrong

The initial strength of the dissenters bred a fatal complacency among them. Foster was so isolated in the spring and summer of 1956 that it seemed vindictive and pointless to take decisive steps against the old man and his few followers. Many of the reformers were now openly critical of the way the Party had treated Browder in 1945, and the idea of giving Foster the same treatment by expulsion and vilification seemed hypocritical as well as unnecessary. "We were attempting to reverse the party's deep-seated sectarian isolation," Max Gordon recalled, "and what could be more sectarian at the time than a factional struggle within the party?"[45]

In this last and most decisive battle of his life, Foster drew upon his long training in intrigue. Having vanquished two former general secretaries of the Communist party, Jay Lovestone in the 1920s and Earl Browder in the 1940s, Foster was not about to surrender to John

Gates in the 1950s. By the start of the Depression, when Gates and Gordon and most of the other prominent dissenters joined the Communist party, the power struggle had subsided and "factionalism" became a dirty word. (The intense clashes between Foster and Browder at the top were kept well hidden from the lower ranks.) Because they joined the Communist party at a moment when its political opportunities in the outside world were rapidly expanding, the 1930s generation of Communists turned their organizing energies outward. They were by no means political *naifs*, but they lacked Foster's skill at, and perhaps even his enjoyment of, "inner party" warfare.

Gates and other dissenters failed to strike decisively at Foster in the summer of 1956. Gates himself lacked the political support necessary to oust Foster and succeed him as Party leader. Many people who agreed with Gates on the issues facing the Party refused to accept his leadership. Short, pugnacious, and hard-driving, a veteran of two wars and four years in a federal penitentiary, Gates won respect but not many friends. As Alvah Bessie, who had served under Gates in the Abraham Lincoln Battalion in Spain, once wrote of him: "Gates was liked only by those who knew him well, and his job was such that it was almost impossible for the men to know him."[46]

No other plausible candidates for Party leader stepped forward. There was, of course, Eugene Dennis, who had never been particularly effective in the post of general secretary, but he was well regarded within the Party. For a long and fatal period the dissenters hoped that they would be able to win Dennis over to an unequivocal "reexaminationist" position. Since delivering his relatively bold report to the April national committee meeting, Dennis had backtracked from any statements that might have been taken the wrong way in Moscow. If he could have been persuaded to display the courage of his April convictions, he would have been the ideal candidate to unite the Party around a new and independent political course. But Dennis, a tall, shy, aloof man, was unsure of himself and the direction the Party should take. While Dennis wavered, Gates and others in his camp moderated some of their own outspokenness in the hopes of keeping him from slipping irretrievably into the camp of orthodoxy. The longer Gates temporized by waiting on Dennis, the more his own potential support within the Party eroded. Communists who had adopted a wait-and-see attitude in the spring and early summer of 1956 were voting with their feet in large numbers by the fall. In early November David Solomon wrote to the *Daily*

Worker, declaring that its independent editorial stance represented "the sentiments of most of what is left of the rank and file." But he warned:

A schism is developing between the Old Guard bureaucrats and those who feel that the party will disintegrate unless it breaks sharply with its undemocratic past. The issue is simple: those members of the party who cannot give up the self-comfort of dogmatism . . . will succeed in wrecking the party if their attitudes and policies prevail.[47]

Foster had inertia and tradition on his side: as defender of ideological orthodoxy, he understood that all he had to do to win was sit tight. The dissenters had to come up with alternatives to past policies, a far more difficult task even at a moment when so many felt that the old policies were hopelessly discredited. The "Gates faction" could agree on the large abstract issues: they sought a genuinely independent and democratically organized movement, free to set its own policies and to criticize the shortcomings of the Communist regimes; they believed that the American road to socialism would be democratic and peaceful, that when socialism was finally established in the United States it would guarantee full civil liberties (including the right to advocate a restoration of capitalism); and they no longer considered their own Party to be the sole repository of political wisdom, and hoped to unite or at least cooperate with other, non-Communist radicals. As they attempted to move from such abstractions to practical matters of policy, they found less and less they could agree upon. "We had no difficulty," Dorothy Healey recalled of a meeting with Gates in 1957, "in finding unity on what we didn't want."[48]

Gates argued in the fall of 1956 that the Communist party should be transformed into a "political association" rather than continuing to maintain its marginal existence as a Party. The change in organizational form, he argued, would be "more in line with the modest role we actually play in the country, facilitate the improvement of our relations with the labor movement [and] help to legalize our status."[49] The change would be fraught with obvious symbolic significance, dispelling once and for all any lingering notion in Communist ranks that socialism in America would come via a Bolshevik-style revolution. But Gates was vague in describing what just such an "association" would actually do, and the Browderist sound of the name made it easy for Foster to attribute to Gates all kinds of beliefs he

27

did not hold. Rumors of Gates's heresies were so widespread by the end of 1956 that his wife, Lillian, felt compelled to recite the Communist catechism in an article in the *Party Voice*: "Can anyone really believe that we have lost our understanding . . . of the existence of the class struggle, of the profound meaning of historical and dialectical materialism, of the theory of the national and colonial question, or that we question the existence of American imperialism?"[50]

Apparently many Communists did fear something like that to be the case, because the political association proposal failed to win significant support outside of New York. Any proposal to revamp the Party would need the support of the other major center of dissent in the Communist party, the California state organization, which was the second largest in the country after New York. In California the Party had weathered the worst of McCarthyism with proportionately fewer losses than elsewhere in the country: the Los Angeles County CP still had more than 3,000 members in 1956, down from 5,000 in 1949; elsewhere losses ran up to two-thirds of total membership. Having retained enough members to keep the Party a going concern, California Communists tended to regard Gates's proposal as unnecessarily drastic, panicky, and "liquidationist."[51] Another proposal discussed that year favored retaining the Party's current status for the time being, but left open the possibility of eventual merger with other socialist groups. But the "united party of socialism" proposal, voiced at different times by Dennis and Steve Nelson, made as little headway as Gates's political association. It was all very well to talk about unity, but in the political climate of the mid-1950s, just who were the Communists going to be able to unite with that would make any real difference in their potential strength? The lack of persuasive alternative strategies made it easier for Foster to argue that Communists should continue "to build the Communist Party and not some futile, opportunistic substitute for it."[52]

Above all else, dissenting Communists needed time to come up with real political alternatives to the sterile sectarianism of the past decade. A breathing space of a few years would have given the Communists time to sort through and attempt to put into practice some of the many ideas that were only sketched out in the months after the Twentieth Congress. They were not so fortunate. The de-Stalinization campaign had consequences in Eastern Europe that Khrushchev had not anticipated. In June 1956, rioting broke out in the Polish industrial city of Poznan, with workers attacking secret police and Communist party headquarters. The democratic demands of the workers that set the stage for Gomulka's return to power made Khrushchev very nervous. He warned Polish leaders that future outbreaks could lead to Soviet military intervention. Gomulka temporarily was able to satisfy both his own people and Khrushchev with a measure of mild reform and a reassertion of Party control. In Hungary, popular discontent led to clashes with Soviet troops and the installation of Imre Nagy, a liberal Communist leader, as prime minister in October 1956. A Polish-style solution seemed in the works and Soviet troops were withdrawn from Budapest. But unlike Gomulka, Nagy was unable to restore order. Nagy then made a brave but suicidal gesture when he announced that Hungary would withdraw from the Warsaw Pact. Soviet tanks rolled into Hungarian cities on 4 November 1956, overturned the Nagy government, and after a few days of bitter fighting, put down popular resistance.[53]

American Communists followed the events in Hungary with growing apprehension. Before full-scale fighting between the Red Army and civilian insurgents broke out, the American CP national committee had adopted a resolution declaring that any Soviet military intervention in Hungary would violate "the essence of the Leninist concept of national self-determination."[54] Foster did not attend the meeting at which the resolution was approved, and Dennis abstained on the vote. A week later, with fighting raging in Budapest, Dennis made it unmistakably clear that he was parting company with Gates. He argued in the *Daily Worker* that the Soviet army had the right to intervene in Hungary to prevent the establishment of "an imperialist salient threatening the vital security of all the people's democracies and the USSR."[55]

The CP's old guard now rallied around the familiar battle cry "Defend the Soviet Union." When the national committee met again on 18 November 1956, it found itself hopelessly deadlocked on the question of Hungary. According to the rough notes that survive from the meeting, Gates warned the other CP leaders that "membership [of the American Communist party] is questioning very basis of socialism. Filled with shame at actions of leadership of CPSU [Communist Party of the Soviet Union]. . . . Socialism a bigger thing than any country. . . . Split here—one view must prevail." Dennis, in flat contradiction of his publicly expressed views, agreed that the Soviet decision to use troops was a "gigantic error," but he would not go along with those who wanted a public condemnation of Soviet actions: "Why rush? What Washin[gton] may do? danger of interven-

29

tion." Other reform leaders, like Steve Nelson and Dorothy Healey, who would have sided with Gates on most issues, decided that the situation in Hungary offered too great a possibility of a "White Guard" or fascist restoration to justify an open challenge to Soviet intervention. Given this internal division, the best the committee could come up with was a resolution stating that American Communists neither condemned nor supported Soviet intervention.[56] It was not enough to hold the Party together. Rank-and-file Communists split over the issue. Meetings of Party clubs were scenes of angry debate. "B.N.," a Brooklyn Communist, wrote to the *Daily Worker* to condemn its critical treatment of Soviet actions in Hungary: "The Soviet troops there are like a mother watching her young ones."[57] "T. M.," a New York Communist, wrote in mid-November:

I have been a member of the Communist Party for 19 years and of the YCL for five years before that. When the "Stalin revelations" broke last spring, many members felt this would be the end of the CP. I felt there was still hope, that if we really analyzed and corrected our mistakes we could still become the party to lead the American people to socialism. But now I do not want to belong to an organization whose members feel socialism should be imposed on the ends of bayonets. This is not the socialism I worked for and dreamed of.[58]

Earlier in the year the dissenters had benefited from the uncertainty over Soviet intentions. In July it was still possible to believe that Khrushchev was prepared to tolerate a significant measure of ideological diversity within the international Communist movement. The events of early November dispelled such notions.

The Dissidents in Retreat

Though it took Gates and his allies some time to realize it, the suppression of the Hungarian revolution marked the end of their chances for winning control of the American Communist party. The Party national convention, which met in New York City in February 1957, adopted resolutions reflecting many of the dissenters' ideas. Foster voted for those resolutions, but he clearly understood that passing resolutions and putting them into practice were two very different matters. Dissident Communists were dismayed by Soviet actions in Hungary and also by their leaders' continued compromises (Gates agreed not to bring up his political association proposal at the convention, and Hungary was scarcely mentioned). At the convention's final session, William Mandel, a New York delegate, offered a gloomy assessment of the results: "This convention, having patched up unity between two irreconcilable viewpoints, has failed in what appears to be its very success." He predicted that Gates's supporters around the country would not bother to attend the state Party conventions scheduled to follow the national convention, and that within a short time the "Foster-Dennis forces will be in full command."[59]

Mandel proved a good prophet. While dissenters retained a slim majority on the Party's national committee for the rest of the year, they no longer had any real claim to speak for the remaining membership in most districts. In the two years after the Twentieth Congress, the Communist party lost roughly three-quarters of its remaining membership. As had been the case at the height of McCarthyism, California survived with proportionately fewer losses, but many of its most prominent leaders and more than half of the rank and file quit. Dorothy Healey, who remained in the Party leadership in Los Angeles, watched while county membership dwindled to less than 1,500 members at the end of 1957.

My generation was leaving, the generation that had grown up in the Young Communist League, that had a great deal of experience in both mass work and in party leadership, the people who had done the writing. . . . It was a far more significant blow than we'd recognized at the time, just in terms of competency, just to be able to do . . . the ordinary things that preoccupied you 90 percent of your time as a revolutionary.[60]

By May enough of the dissenters had resigned in New York to allow Foster to regain control of the state organization, a shift in power that was symbolized when Ben Davis, a long-time Foster ally, took over as its leader. Foster was not greatly concerned with the membership losses: as he told Healey at the end of the February convention, "It's better to have fifty true members than 50,000 people who are not genuine Communists."[61] Foster began to describe the convention as a "rejection of revisionism" and a mandate for his own version of orthodoxy. Soviet leaders, relatively restrained until that point in their dealings with the American CP, now made clear their preference for Foster over his opponents. Soviet publications repeatedly attacked Gates and Clark as revisionists. When Clark finally resigned in September 1957, Gates wrote a column wishing him well, adding, "I have not lost hope, as has Clark, that the opponents of our new policies will be decisively defeated."[62] Gates's optimism sounded strained, and his own days in the Party were numbered. The dissenters' remaining stronghold, Gates's editorship of the *Daily Worker*, was under siege. Foster's allies controlled the Party's funds, and systematically choked off support for the chronically financially ailing newspaper. In October the paper cut back from eight to four pages, and from six to four issues a week. Three months later it was forced to shut down. Gates handed in his resignation from the Communist party, declaring that it had "ceased to be an effective force for democracy, peace and socialism in the United States." Nelson, Rodney, Gordon, and most of the other leading dissenters who had remained in the Party soon followed his example.[63]

Two years after the Twentieth Congress the Party had shrunk to under 5,000 members. Perhaps as many as 15,000 former Communists newly set adrift were added to the tens of thousands who had left the Party over the previous decade. If all the ex-Communists living in the United States in the mid-1950s had been gathered together in one radical organization, they would have constituted the largest movement on the Left in American history, with a membership running into the hundreds of thousands. At the height of the dissenters' strength, in the summer of 1956, a Buffalo Communist who signed his letter as "Steelworker" wrote to the *Daily Worker* and called on Communists to take immediate steps to organize a "new party of socialism." The Communist party, he had reluctantly concluded, was past resuscitation. And he warned of the consequences of inaction: "Dissolution without the existence of a new organization would only lead to thousands of good fighters scattered and splintered, with a resulting body blow to the cause of socialism."[64]

Gates, Clark, and other leading dissenters did meet for a few years after 1957 in informal discussion circles, but they made no effort to retain contact with the thousands of rank-and-file Communists who had left the Party with them. They started no newspapers or journals to spread their ideas. They were exhausted from the struggle with Foster and remembered, perhaps too well, the futile sectarian existence led by other opposition movements that had been set up by former Communists, like the Lovestoneites and the Trotskyists. Many were distracted by the more immediate question of how to support themselves and their families: credentials as Communist party functionaries or *Daily Worker* columnists would not get them through many prospective employers' front doors. In the heat of their battle with Foster, they had not had time to create a meaningful alternative political program or vision: phrases like "political association" and "mass united party of socialism" had little meaning once divorced from the struggle to retain control of the Party machinery. No longer bound together in common opposition to the old guard, they soon found themselves drifting apart politically and personally.[65]

Some former Communists eventually did find a way to become politically active again. In the mid-1960s Irving Howe provided an unfriendly but astute analysis of their new role. The Party itself may have been reduced to an ineffective remnant, Howe wrote, but many of those who had been in or near its orbit before 1956

continued to keep in touch with one another, forming a kind of reserve apparatus based on common opinions, feelings, memories. As soon as some ferment began a few years ago in the Civil Rights movement and the peace groups, these people were present, ready and eager; they needed no directives from the CP to which, in any case, they no longer (or may never have) belonged; they were quite capable of working on their own *as if they were working together.*[66]

In the course of the next decade, J. Edgar Hoover and various congressional investigating committees had no difficulty in turning up ex-Communists at work in the civil rights and anti-Vietnam War movements, proving to their own satisfaction that the political upheaval of the 1960s, like that of preceding decades, was the product of the international Communist conspiracy. Former Communists, or people who had been close to the Communist party, were indeed effective in the role they found to play within those movements. As Howe put it, these were "people who could offer political advice, raise money, write leaflets, sit patiently at meetings, put up in a pleasant New York apartment visitors from a distant state."[67] It probably would not be going too far to say that the most influential adult radical group in the 1960s was this "party" of ex-Communists. It was a party that could do *almost everything* that a more formally organized radical group could do in the same situation: everything, that is, except recruit new members.[68]

The upheaval in the Communist party that followed the Khrushchev revelations had dramatic consequences for others on the American Left. The Communists' misfortunes provided rival radical groups with a unique opportunity. Since the Communist party would be unable to play any direct role in assisting at the birth of a "New Left," if there was to be any organizational continuity linking Old Left and New, someone else would have to step in to provide it.

2

Max Shachtman,

A Sectarian's Progress

> The tradition of all the dead generations weighs like
> a nightmare on the brain of the living. And just when
> they seem engaged in revolutionising themselves
> and things, in creating something entirely new, pre-
> cisely in such epochs of revolutionary crisis they
> anxiously conjure up the spirits of the past to their
> service and borrow from them names, battle slogans
> and costumes in order to present the new scene of
> world history in this time-honoured disguise and
> this borrowed language.
>
> —KARL MARX
> *The Eighteenth Brumaire of Louis Bonaparte*

THE NEW INTERNATIONAL
A MONTHLY ORGAN OF REVOLUTIONARY MARXISM

VOLUME VI   APRIL 1940   NUMBER 3

For the Third Camp!

The Shactmanites set forth: the large dreams of a small sect,
spring 1940 (Reprinted 1969 by Greenwood Press, Westport, Conn.)

N O ONE in the 1950s attempted with such single-minded fervor as Max Shachtman to act as the midwife at the birth of a new American Left. At first glance, his qualifications for playing that role were less than impressive: his own political career consisted in large measure of an endless stream of sectarian squabbles and splits. Since 1940 he had been the leader of a tiny sect—known initially as the Workers party (WP) and by the 1950s as the Independent Socialist League (ISL)—that had never managed to gather more than 500 adherents at any one time. But Shachtman was not an ordinary sectarian. The groups he led had from the beginning displayed an unusual commitment to preserving the right of internal dissent and an unusual tendency to question their own political assumptions. Shachtman himself had challenged no less an authority than Leon Trotsky in developing a new theory of the nature of Soviet society, and by the 1950s had discarded much of the Leninist baggage with which he began his political pilgrimage. Throughout his career he had displayed a singular talent for attracting and training younger protégés, of the caliber of Irving Howe and Michael Harrington. Any new Left was bound to be in large measure a young Left, and by the 1950s Shachtman had had three decades experience as a "youth leader." So Shachtman's candidacy as a potential shaper of a new Left was not as farfetched a proposition as it might initially appear.

Unlike the bourgeois revolutionaries whom Marx had mocked in *The Eighteenth Brumaire of Louis Bonaparte*, Shachtman, by the 1950s, was willing to discard the "time-honoured disguise" and the "borrowed language" of earlier revolutions, both so dear to his fellow-sectarians, if that would help him attain his political ends. But in the end Shachtman faltered. He could put aside the external dress of the sectarian, but he could not truly "revolutionize" himself. At a moment of apparent triumph, the habits of sectarianism reasserted themselves, and he squandered his long-sought opportunity to remake the American Left.

Max Shachtman and the Trotskyist Movement

One of the few things that surviving veterans of the Workers Party and the Independent Socialist League still agree upon is that those groups would never have existed without Max Shachtman. Shachtman was born in Warsaw in 1904 and was brought by his Jewish immigrant parents to New York City as an infant. Shachtman's father was a tailor, whose socialist sympathies did not prevent him from trying to rise out of the working class. Though a failure as a small businessman, he was able to move his family from the Lower East Side to more comfortable quarters in upper Manhattan, and eventually to the Bronx. He was determined that his son would never have to labor with his hands. In 1920, as a precocious sixteen-year-old graduate of Dewitt Clinton High School, Max Shachtman entered City College in New York. His father hoped he would pursue professional training as a doctor or engineer. But a bout of ill health, and then more pressing political interests, intervened. After two false starts Shachtman dropped out of college for good in 1921.[1]

Shachtman came of age politically in the confusion and excitement of the post–World War I Red Scare. In 1919 the Socialist party splintered: its Left wing, infatuated with Lenin's success in Russia, went on to found two rival Communist parties. By the time Shachtman enrolled in City College, both groups had gone underground in response to official persecution and in emulation of the Bolsheviks under the Czar. While still a student, Shachtman listened eagerly to street corner speeches by Communist agitators, and made sympathetic remarks from the edge of the crowd in the hope of being approached as a likely recruit. But such was the temper of the Communist movement of the time that Shachtman's facility with English made him a suspect character, and no invitations from Party recruiters were forthcoming. Only at the end of 1922, with the formation of a unified and aboveground Communist organization was Shachtman able to become a Communist.[2]

In the 1920s the Communist movement was a place where a talented and ambitious young man could make his mark in a hurry. Despite his lack of formal higher education, Shachtman was widely read, fluent in French, German, and Yiddish, and, at least in his youth, a prolific writer. His talents were recognized by Martin Abern, national secretary of the newly organized Communist youth

group, the Young Workers League (YWL). Abern persuaded Shachtman, who since his arrival in the United States had never left New
York City, to move to Chicago and assume the editorship of the
YWL's newspaper, the *Young Worker*. Shachtman seemed to thrive
on the drudgery of the movement: associates from those days remember him writing an entire four-page edition of the *Young Worker*
overnight. Shachtman would later fondly recall the heroic asceticism
of his new life: living on a ten-dollar-a-week stipend from the Party
(when it came), sleeping on a cot, and cooking his meals on a hot
plate in the back of the YWL office.[3]

The history of American communism in the 1920s, like that of
American Trotskyism in the following decade, is largely a story of
internal factional squabbling. Abern and Shachtman enlisted as lieutenants in the camp of James Cannon, then one of the top contenders
for Party leadership. As an up-and-coming young Communist
leader, Shachtman got to visit Moscow twice on official missions in
the 1920s (on the first occasion he was given the task of smuggling
back money to subsidize the Young Workers League's activities). He
did not attend the Sixth World Congress of the Communist International, held in Moscow in 1928, where a beleaguered Leon Trotsky
was staging a last-ditch defense of his waning power in the Soviet
leadership. But Shachtman's mentor James Cannon did go. Cannon
was so impressed by Trotsky's analysis of the reasons for the stagnation of the Communist movement that he smuggled a copy of
Trotsky's criticisms of the Comintern's draft program out of the Soviet Union. Shachtman and Abern were among the first to see it in
the United States, and both were immediately converted. Trotsky's
challenge to the Comintern program helped his new American disciples to see their own political disappointments as part of a larger
pattern of defeats that Communists had experienced in Europe and
Asia in the 1920s, the responsibility for which Trotsky laid at Stalin's
door. When news of the Cannon group's apostasy reached other
Communist leaders, they were promptly expelled. They then
formed the Communist League of America (Opposition), which under various names served as the nucleus of the Trotskyist movement
for the next decade.[4]

Shachtman, Cannon's lieutenant in the 1920s, became his partner
and eventually his rival in the course of the 1930s. They made an
odd couple. Cannon was fair, handsome, and, according to his associates, "American" in appearance. Like his one-time comrade Earl

Browder, he delivered his revolutionary message with a Kansas twang. Shachtman, in contrast, had a swarthy complexion and a calculating demeanor. He sported a thin mustache and favored professorial tweeds. He spoke with a New York accent and, according to Irving Howe, had "a face you'd expect to find in a bazaar or a diamond center."[5]

Within the Trotskyist movement Cannon and Shachtman divided responsibilities and constituencies. Cannon was the movement's public figure. He represented the heroic tradition of native American radicalism and had a colorful past as one of the Industrial Workers of the World's (IWW) hobo organizers. He was an effective if bombastic orator, out of the Debs tradition. Shachtman was much more of an inner party intellectual, theorist, and link with the Russian revolutionary tradition. He served as editor of the movement's newspaper, the *Militant*, as well as its theoretical journal, *New International*, met with Trotsky on numerous occasions, and helped marshal evidence to discredit the Moscow trials.[6]

The working class was supposed to provide the bone and sinew of the revolutionary movement. But Shachtman, who had minimal experience in organizing workers, proved better able than Cannon to influence the kinds of recruits who actually joined the Trotskyist movement in the 1930s. Apart from some limited gains from the 1934 Minneapolis Teamsters' strike, in which the Trotskyists played a leading role, they recruited few union members during the 1930s. They were far more successful in appealing to intellectuals disillusioned with Stalinism, particularly in New York City's highly politicized academic and literary world. This was not Cannon's milieu. He was suspicious of intellectuals, whom he regarded as "tourists in the proletarian movement." Cannon was much more comfortable with the older trade unionists, and they, in turn, were his most loyal supporters within the movement. Shachtman, by contrast, had always been a "youth leader." Though he had once served a spell as a YWL organizer in the Illinois coal fields, he was at his most effective in working with college students, particularly the young Jews who provided the bulk of the movement's recruits in New York. From the early 1930s Shachtman and Cannon squabbled over the proper role for these young Trotskyists: Cannon regarded them as a threat to the "proletarian" character of the Party, whereas Shachtman sought to sponsor their rise into its leadership. The 1930s marked an important transition in the history of American radicalism. Radical youth groups were beginning to rival the adult groups that sponsored them in their importance to the movement. Although neither Cannon nor Shachtman realized it at the time, by thus dividing responsibilities between the unions and the youth movement, it was Shachtman who had been entrusted with the Left's future.[7]

Shachtman inspired his young followers with the sense of being part of the elect, the designated heirs to the international revolutionary tradition. He became renowned for his bravado performances as a public speaker. Phyllis Jacobson, a young Trotskyist recruit, recalled that Shachtman's speeches "were always full of irony; they had very mordant wit. He knew words; he knew how to fire your imagination; he was a great mimic." Like George Whitefield, the itinerant revivalist of the eighteenth century's Great Awakening, who could reduce his audience to tears by pronouncing the word "Mesopotamia," Shachtman was able to reduce his audience to a fit of scornful hilarity simply by his pronunciation of the words "Viacheslav Molotov." Irving Howe, who became known as one of "Max's boys" while still a high-school student in the Bronx, commented in his memoirs: "If Shachtman, during one of his marathon speeches, made a joke about Karl Radek or threw out a fleeting mention of 'the August bloc,' those of us in the know felt as gleeful as a philosophy graduate student pouncing on a subtle point in a Wittgenstein blue book." Julius Jacobson, like Howe a product of the Bronx socialist youth movement, remembered Shachtman as "a young man's person. It was part of his personality. He was a kibbitzer; he was fun to be with; you could make jokes with him; he was bawdy; he'd hug you; he'd pinch your cheek."[8]

There was also a darker side to Shachtman's personality. He ridiculed his own followers behind their backs. He was manipulative: he encouraged and flattered his protégés but never let them forget who was supposed to have the last word. He enjoyed debate, but only up to a point: if one of his followers obstinately continued to fail to accept his viewpoint, he grew petulant. He would withdraw his attention and refuse to speak to or even acknowledge the presence of the offender, an effective sanction in a group where leaders and followers were in constant close contact. For all his cheek-pinching, he remained a reclusive figure, confiding fully in no one. He had associates and protégés, but with the exception of one or two people whom he knew from his Chicago Young Workers League days, he sought no close personal friends among his movement comrades. Despite formidable talents, he had limits as a leader, which became more apparent to his followers over the years. Gordon Haskell, who joined the Trotskyists while a student at Berkeley in the late 1930s, remembered Shachtman as a "great *inside* speaker," but someone who was of little use as public spokesman.

The people who already agreed with you loved to have him come and speak. He could always draw a big crowd because there were always enough of a periphery who had heard about him, and knew they were going to have a good time at the expense of the Stalinists or whoever his target was. He was absolutely devastating as a polemicist, but we didn't attract new people with that.[9]

Shachtman could entertain and instruct the faithful; he could not attract outsiders to the cause. That made him the perfect sect leader, but there would come a time when neither he nor his followers would be satisfied with having him continue to play that role. There was a constant degree of tension in Shachtman's relationship with his young disciples: an enormously charismatic figure, he also left his followers nettled and dissatisfied. His leadership was of the kind that inspired emulation and—in time—rebellion.

Trotskyism in the 1930s

Though American Trotskyists had little impact on the broader politics of the 1930s, they were by no means idle. By mid–decade the exiled Trotsky began to despair of ever returning to the Soviet Union. He undertook a series of increasingly erratic political maneuvers, marching and countermarching his European and American followers into and then out of the Socialist movement and finally into their own independent "Fourth International." In the United States the Trotskyists negotiated an informal merger with Norman Thomas's Socialist party in 1936. In the beginning, it was not clear whether they were to regard the Socialist party (SP) as a temporary or a permanent home. Whatever the initial purpose, the effect of their brief sojourn was disastrous for the Socialists. As Cannon later boasted, in a classic expression of the sectarian mind:

Partly as a result of our experience in the Socialist Party and our fight in there, the Socialist Party was put on the side lines. This was a great achievement, because it was an obstacle in the path of building a revolutionary party. The problem is not merely one of building a revolutionary party, but of clearing obstacles from its path. Every other party is a rival. Every other party is an obstacle.[10]

Even before the appearance of the Trotskyists, the SP's youth affiliate, the Young People's Socialist League (YPSL) had swung far to the left of the adult party. The adult Socialist party was increasingly detached from any real political activity, with its most active members drifting off into New Deal politics or CIO organizing. The Communists could discard revolutionary rhetoric, portray themselves as loyal followers of Franklin Roosevelt and John L. Lewis, and still retain their revolutionary *élan*. The Socialists could not. Revolutionary gestures like adopting manifestos on the "seizure of power" became increasingly important to young Socialists in forging a political identity. The Trotskyists and the YPSL (the latter usually referred to as "yipsels") were natural allies in the SP's inner battles. The Trotskyists proved to the young Socialists that one need not become one of "Stalin's minions" in order to lay claim to the reflected glory and authority of the Bolshevik Revolution. By the end of 1936 the Trotskyists had gained effective control of the YPSL and were making inroads into other sections of the SP.[11]

Despite the success his followers were enjoying in the Socialist party, in 1937 Trotsky decided that it was time for them to reassemble under their own banners. Some Trotskyists had misgivings, feeling that they would do better within a larger sheltering movement than on their own. But Trotsky's prestige, as always, proved difficult to resist. The issue became moot when Socialist leaders, fearing that they were losing control of the party, began expelling Trotskyist leaders. The Trotskyists pulled their followers out of the SP, and in 1938 organized the Socialist Workers party. Most of the yipsels went with them. Ernest Erber, YPSL national chairman, had been a Trotskyist sympathizer since the mid-1930s. He recalled that when he first heard of the plan to split the SP he was "mildly shocked," but quickly overcame his hesitations, determined to prove to his new allies that he "was now a hardened Bolshevik who had shed his SP illusions."[12]

The Origins of the Workers Party

The onset of the Second World War brought a long simmering crisis within the Trotskyist movement to a boil. In the course of the 1930s a number of Trotskyists wondered how they could condemn everything Stalin said or did and still regard the country that he led as the Socialist homeland, a "degenerated workers state," as Trotsky described it. The events of the late summer and fall of 1939—the Nazi-Soviet Pact, the Soviet occupation of Eastern Poland, and finally the Soviet invasion of Finland—made it impossible to ignore the question any longer.

Trotsky insisted that his followers keep the "defense of the Soviet Union" as one of their main political priorities. When two capitalist nations fought one another, it was axiomatic that revolutionary socialists refused to back either side. In the First World War, the Bolsheviks had been "revolutionary defeatists," pursuing the class struggle at home without regard to its effect upon Russia's war with Germany. But in a war between capitalist and socialist nations, revolutionaries did not enjoy the luxury of adopting a "plague on both your houses" attitude. No one knew better than Trotsky the sins of the then present Soviet leaders, and for over a decade he had called for an anti-Stalinist revolution in the Soviet Union. Nevertheless, he insisted, true revolutionaries would rally to the Soviet Union's defense when it was in danger, because in the Soviet Union the basic step of expropriating the bourgeoisie and nationalizing the means of production, (prerequisites for any genuine social advance) had already been accomplished. The state owned the nation's productive resources: its industries, mines, and farms. In capitalist nations, a *social* revolution would be necessary to enable the working class to come to power and build socialism. All that was required in the Soviet Union was a *political* revolution, a change of leadership, to return to a healthy socialism.

Shachtman and James Burnham, coeditors of the *New International*, disagreed with Trotsky's analysis. In the debate that followed they won most of the younger members of the Socialist Workers party—the former yipsels—to their position. The USSR, they argued, was in no sense of the word socialist, "degenerated" or otherwise. The Stalinist bureaucracy was not something simply fastened onto an otherwise healthy socialist society: rather, it represented a new kind of ruling class that collectively controlled the means of production through its control of the state. The Soviet Union was thus an entirely new kind of society, neither capitalist nor socialist, which Shachtman called "bureaucratic collectivist." State ownership of the means of production in itself was not socialism; indeed it could be the basis for fastening upon the working class a subordinate status more absolute and degrading than that which prevailed under capitalism. What was required in the USSR was not simply a *political* revolution, as Trotsky assumed, but a full *social* revolution.

Burnham soon gave the bureaucratic collectivist argument a twist that both Shachtman and Trotsky would find abhorrent: he abandoned his own revolutionary convictions and wrote a book extolling the virtues of the "managerial revolution" that was sweeping aside all other powers in capitalist and collectivist nations alike. Shachtman stuck to his revolutionary guns. He insisted that Stalinism, like capitalism, carried within itself the seeds of its own destruction. One did not have to choose between the two systems. There was a third choice, a "third camp," the camp of genuine socialism, which stood equally opposed to capitalism and Stalinism. Regrettably this third camp had no country (and in most places did not even have a party) to call its own. But in the upheaval that surely would follow the war, both capitalism and Stalinism would be fatally weakened, and the workers of the world could resume their march down the path Lenin and Trotsky had blazed in 1917. The "bureaucratic collectivism" thesis would go on to become very influential on the anti-Stalinist Left, anticipating the influence enjoyed by Hannah Arendt's analysis of totalitarianism in the postwar era. The Soviet Union had been an embarrassing ideological problem for anti-Stalinist socialists. Conservatives argued that the Soviet Union proved that socialism equaled tyranny. In the early 1930s even Norman Thomas felt compelled to distinguish between the good and bad aspects of the Soviet experiment. Shachtman's "third camp" analysis dispensed with all that: bad, good, or indifferent, there was no need to apologize for any aspect of the Stalinist system, because what went on in the Soviet Union was no more representative of genuine socialism than Hitler's "national socialism."[13]

The immediate prospects for this third camp, at least as measured by the size of the Workers party, seemed anything but promising. Before the split with the Socialist Workers party, at a time when the Communist party counted its members in the tens of thousands, the entire Trotskyist movement had no more than 2,000 members, by a generous estimate. Perhaps 800 of these followed Shachtman out of the SWP. By the fall of 1940 the Workers party could count a mere 323 members in good standing within its ranks.[14]

War and Fulfillment

American involvement in the Second World War breathed new life into the group. Within a few months of its founding the Workers party embarked upon a strategy of "colonizing" its members in industrial jobs in cities across the nation. Gordon Haskell, who became WP organizer in the Bay Area during the war, was struck by the contrast with the movement's prewar fortunes: "When the war started most of us had been unemployed for a long time. We'd learned to live with no money at all. Now we all had industrial jobs and we felt as rich as Croesus. We had guys giving a week's pay out of a month without feeling it." Flush with the "income tax" it levied on its members' paychecks, the Workers party invested in two linotype machines, paid off its back debts to the printer, and by 1943 had increased the press run of its weekly newspaper *Labor Action* to 40,000 copies per issue.[15]

By 1943 *Labor Action* was filled with firsthand accounts of the wildcat strikes that were breaking out across the country in open defiance of the "no-strike pledge" that top union leaders had taken after Pearl Harbor. WP members, who had moved from New York to take jobs in Buffalo, Detroit, San Pedro, and other centers of war industry, were often in the thick of the action. Through a selfless devotion to organizing, and with skills honed in inner-party factional battles, many of them were able to win election as shop stewards, chairmen of grievance committees, and even as the presidents of some union locals. For the first time anti-Stalinist radicals were able to mount an effective challenge to Communist influence in some CIO unions. While the Communists championed "all out production" to aid the Soviet defense against the Nazis, the Shachtmanites, as "revolutionary defeatists," professed indifference to the outcome of the war and encouraged strikes. Though few American workers shared the Workers party's international perspective, many could respond sympathetically to its call for militancy in the workplace after a decade of economic hard times. The "class struggle" was no longer simply a term to be thrown around in debates in the City College cafeteria; Workers party members felt that the moment of historical reckoning was at hand.[16]

Or was it? The former YPSL leader Ernest Erber had become WP organizer in Philadelphia during the war. In 1943 he sent a memorandum to the WP's national leaders, arguing that the group's wartime gains might prove illusory. *Labor Action's* circulation of 40,000 was "80 times as many as we have party members"—which meant that in its fourth year the WP still had only 500 members. Erber felt there was a good reason why so few of *Labor Action's* readers joined the Workers party:

We live a life apart from our surroundings. We develop our own sense of values, our own moral concepts, our own habits, and even our own jargon. . . . Our training is in the tradition of the Jesuits. Money, position in life, family, personal inclinations as to kind of work, place of work, place of residence, must all yield when necessary to the requirements of the party.

Erber argued that if the Workers party ever were to grow beyond its present size and social composition, it would have to abandon the model of the party of professional revolutionaries it had carried over from the Communist and Trotskyist movements and make less stringent demands upon the time and financial resources of its members.[17]

Not so, responded Chalmers K. Stewart, the WP's organizer in Akron, Ohio. "Our failure to recruit broadly is due to the political retardation of the working class," he argued, rather than to any mistakes on the part of the Workers party. Stewart opposed any tampering with the party's internal organization or political outlook: "Our party constitutes a revolutionary staff, bold, resourceful, self-sacrificing, educated. Let us not be impatient with history." Shachtman was equally unsympathetic to Erber's plea.[18]

Even at the moment when its members had their greatest contact with and influence upon the real world during the struggle against the "no-strike pledge" in the Second World War, the Workers party displayed many of the classic characteristics of left-wing political sectarianism, including what Daniel Bell later described as "the illusions of settling the fate of history, the mimetic combat on the plains of destiny, and the vicarious sense of power in demolishing opponents."[19] The Shachtmanites struck a habitual public pose of tough self-assurance, when an objective assessment of their strength and prospects might have suggested that a humbler mien was more appropriate. Stewart's defense of orthodoxy against Erber certainly had the flavor of Bell's "mimetic combat on the plains of destiny." He appealed to "history" as the deus ex machina that would deliver the Workers party from insignificance. The purity of the party's devotion to a set of unalterable principles, rather than any short-term gain in members or influence, was its guarantee of eventual triumph.

The WP's ingrained capacity for self-deception was also evident in the fetish its members made of the written word, mistaking the passage of resolutions and the publication of editorials for meaningful political activity. For a small group scattered across many cities, *Labor Action* and the *New International* fostered a sense of community and purpose—which could become a form of myopic self-satisfaction. A WP member in Akron might grow discouraged over the group's apparent lack of political success. Even Stewart, in his dispute with Erber, commented in passing that of ten new members the Akron Local of the Workers party had managed to recruit since 1942, only two were "bona fide proletarians." But once a week the bundles of *Labor Action* would arrive, crammed full of accounts of the success the party was apparently enjoying elsewhere around the country. If a thousand workers in a Philadelphia shipyard walked out on strike, wasn't it just possible that they—or at least a few key activists in their ranks—had been set in motion by reading an editorial in *Labor Action*? Those tens of thousands of copies of *Labor Action* they distributed every week were seen by WPers as so many seeds sown for a revolutionary harvest.[20]

The Bolshevik Revolution was the model the Workers party dreamed of replicating. When the WP was formed, the revolution was an event of the still recent past. Some of the revolution's principal organizers were still alive (at that time those who had died, as a rule, did so at the hands of Stalin's secret police rather than of old age). Trotsky's life was proof that individuals and small groups could change the course of history. Reasoning by historical analogy, readers of *Labor Action* and the *New International* could imagine themselves as the cutting edge of an international vanguard. How many socialists in Europe had stood with Lenin in 1914 in opposing the war? Probably not many more than were now enrolled in the Workers party in America. If the Second World War was in essence a repetition of the First World War, then it stood to reason that in time the working classes of the respective belligerent nations would become as war-weary and rebellious as they had by 1917. "Fascism Falls—Revolution in Italy Has Begun!" banner headlines in *Labor Action* declared after Mussolini's overthrow in 1943: "Masses Want Peace, Bread and Freedom." Never mind that the Italian Communist party—the Stalinist enemy—was leading the Italian resistance movement: "In the midst of turbulent events, a new revolutionary leadership—an internationalist, Marxian party—can be swiftly formed and tempered."[21]

Revolution was not imminent in America, to be sure. But the events from 1917 to 1919 in Europe had shaken up the traditional Left and inspired the creation of a Communist movement out of the wreckage of the old Socialist party; similar events in the aftermath of the Second World War could be expected to brush aside the wreckage of the CP, the SP, and the SWP, which would leave the WP as the largest and most dynamic party on the American Left.

In the fetish it made of the written word, in its habit of draping itself in the mantle of the Bolshevik Revolution, in its highly selective reliance on historical analogy, and in its willful misreading of the temper of the American working class, the Workers party seemed no different from the myriad of tiny radical sects that preceded or followed it into oblivion. But the WP was not simply another collection of revolutionary flagellants confidently awaiting the millennium in blissful discomfort. From the beginning there was something that distinguished it from its competitors on the ultra-Left. The political language favored by the Workers party was one of stern confidence: "history," "the masses," the "tasks of the moment," and so forth. But there was a growing tension between the conceptual limitations imposed by this language and the dynamics of the political culture that had begun to develop within the group. This was a party founded on doubt rather than on certainty. In a 1944 article reviewing the origins of the Workers party, Shachtman remembered:

> I had developed some doubts . . . on the correctness of our traditional position, without being able to say to myself, and therefore to others, that this position was fundamentally false and that an alternative position had to replace it. . . . Doubts are bridges you cannot stand on for long. Either you go back to the old views or move on to new ones.[22]

Shachtman wrote as if all doubts had been resolved. But for some of his followers, one question led to another. If Trotsky was wrong in his assessment of the nature of the Russian state, why should it be assumed he remained the ultimate authority on other questions of revolutionary strategy, organization, and goals? Eventually the Shachtmanites would have to confront the possibility that the Bolshevik Revolution was of little relevance to American socialists, save as an example of what to avoid. They would spend the next decade crossing the bridge from old certainties to new and more problematic beliefs.

Postwar Troubles

The aftermath of the Second World War made it difficult for even the most orthodox members of the WP to remain content with the party's founding assumptions. One by one, the premises that underlay the organization's optimism in the war unraveled. Nineteen forty-six did not prove a repeat of 1919. No wave of revolutionary fervor swept Europe. To the extent that there was any turn toward the Left among the European working classes after the war, it worked largely to the benefit of the Communists, hardly what the Shachtmanites had in mind. The creation of new "people's democracies" in Eastern Europe brought them no joy: Stalinism, rather than being destroyed by the war, emerged stronger than ever.

After the Communist coup in Prague in 1948 destroyed the remaining vestiges of pluralist democracy in Eastern Europe, Irving Howe wrote a revealing article in *Labor Action*. He was, he said, "sick with sorrow and apprehension" after hearing the news from Prague.

It was time to abandon "myopic and opiatic forms of 'official optimism' " because "the world is today in a far worse state than it was ten years ago." "Honest pessimism" required Howe to admit that the Communists enjoyed the support of the Czech working class. The workers' sense of what socialism was "has been debased and corrupted as a result of the . . . barbaric experiences of recent history." Socialists of Howe's persuasion had hitherto regarded the working class as the motor force of social change, but the triumph of totalitarian systems like Stalinism and fascism was evidence of "a general, total decline of modern class society." The only question left for true socialists was "Would you stand with the cops or their victims, with the hunters or the hunted?"[23]

The revolutionary optimism that had sustained anti-Stalinist radicals in the late 1930s was in the process of chilling into a mood of apocalyptic gloom. In 1939, in the midst of his battle with Shachtman and Burnham, Trotsky had argued that *if* Stalinism should prove more than an accidental and transitory phenomenon, then the whole socialist project would be revealed as a fantastic chimera. For Howe, in 1948, the qualifying *if* had fallen away. Mass society spelled an end to class struggle. Socialism was no longer the road to power. It was now reduced to a simple moral choice: to be a "cop" or a "victim."

Howe was approaching the outward bounds of what was considered acceptable discourse in the Workers party. Shachtman was in Europe when Howe's article appeared on 8 March 1948. E. R. McKinney, the WP's labor secretary, took up the cudgels in Shachtman's absence. Two days after the publication of Howe's article, McKinney wrote to Shachtman to denounce it as a "disgraceful . . . frightened, piss in the pants, looking down from my Princeton Parnassus, petty-bourgeois bundle of Howe verbiage." He was only slightly more restrained in his public response in *Labor Action*.

I am not much impressed or moved by Comrade Howe's "sorrow," his "oppression," or his "feeling of discouragement." I don't believe that sorrow, oppression and discouragement are very helpful qualities in the struggle against Stalinism or capitalism. . . . Socialists, that is revolutionary socialists, REAL communists must be made of sterner stuff.[24]

"Official optimism," of the variety that McKinney had to offer, might have weathered a season of dismal events overseas, if only the Workers party had managed to find a little sunshine closer to home. The postwar strike wave momentarily raised the Shachtman-ites' hopes, but the conservative mood of the postwar labor leader-ship and their close ties with the Democratic party left the Workers party little political space in which to maneuver. At the same time, the WP found itself with a dwindling number of cadre in the labor movement. Lacking seniority, many of the group who had found industrial jobs during the war lost them during the first wave of post-war layoffs. In places where WPers held on in the labor movement, they did so increasingly from the security of union office or staff positions rather than as rank and filers.[25]

The romance had gone out of the industrial colonization strategy for Shachtman's followers. With the end of the Depression, many Workers party members found new professional outlets opening up for those verbal and writing skills they had honed in inner-party debate in the 1930s. Gordon Haskell sent a bleak report to WP head-quarters in 1948 on the state of the Bay Area branch, which had not grown at all in the previous year. Of twenty-three active members, only ten held industrial jobs. The remainder stubbornly resisted sug-gestions to do the same.

A comrade who is asked to leave a relatively interesting professional job for industry quite naturally says: Yes, I understand why this is important. But we have ten members in industry right now. Yet not one of these seems to be able to bring a single fellow-worker to our forums or socials, leave alone to recruit them to the party. . . . Isn't it a little foolish for me to leave my present good or interesting job for a hard and unpleasant one just on the basis of a theory which looks good, but which so far doesn't seem to produce any practical results?[26]

According to an internal party report, national membership dropped almost 100 from 1946 to 1947, down to 389, little more than the Workers party had begun existence with in 1940. Their eth-nic, geographical, and social composition remained virtually un-changed in the same period: 199 members lived in New York (40 members of other branches were originally from New York); 202 members were of Jewish background; and the average member's age was thirty-two years old. After seven years of frenetic activity in-volving immense personal and financial sacrifice, the Shachtmanites found themselves back where they started.[27]

Questions

In the midst of a crisis, or in response to some dramatic and disillusioning event, new ideas sometimes arrive with the force of revelation. But if the crisis takes another form, such as the long series of disappointments the Workers party experienced in the aftermath of the Second World War, new ideas are likely to emerge by a gradual process of accretion rather than through any sudden revelation. What could begin as a moment's hesitation in repeating an old slogan that had begun to sound a little trite, a slight embarrassment in rereading a yellowing copy of *Labor Action* and discovering how shrill some editorial sounded, or a desire to find a more persuasive way of phrasing some standard argument in the WP's repertoire, could lead to unexpected results.[28]

Shachtman was willing to tolerate dissent within the Workers party, as he proved when Howe, Erber, and others raised questions about the party's current policies and outlook. But tolerance for dissenting views was not the same thing as genuine freedom of discussion. When Erber finally resigned from the organization in 1948, he conceded in a letter to a friend who remained in the group that "the Workers Party has done more in the years of its existence to establish conscientiously the rights of members in discussions, the party bulletins, etc. than any party I know of."[29] But he then went on to distinguish between the "formal democratic rights" that were observed so scrupulously and "real democracy."

Real democracy requires the proper party atmosphere. This is possible only if there is respect for another's opinions. Despite everything we have done to create a democratic machinery in the WP, such respect for opinions is still singularly lacking.

Even with the best of intentions, a movement modeling itself on the Bolshevik Revolution developed habits of thought that undermined internal democracy. Erber proposed early in 1948 that the Workers party endorse the Marshall Plan as a means of staving off the spread of Stalinism in Western Europe. The Political Committee voted in favor of the proposal, despite Shachtman's opposition. When the proposal went before the National Committee, which consisted of delegates from WP branches around the country, Shachtman succeeded in getting it voted down by denouncing Erber as a "social patriot." As in so many debates within the party, historical analogy proved to be the most potent argument. Lenin had denounced the prowar socialists in the First World War as "social patriots" who had placed the interest of their respective bourgeois governments over the interest of the international proletariat. "The movement," Erber complained, "is asked to vote for or against social patriotism when everyone has been taught for years that [it] constitutes one of the worst crimes against Socialism and the 'social patriot' is a loathsome person." Formal democratic rights had been duly observed; Shachtman had personally assured Erber that he would not be expelled for his "social patriotism." But the substance of free and open debate had been fatally undermined.

How can an atmosphere conducive of intelligent discussion be possible when "Menshevik" and "social patriotism" are attached to one position and spoken of . . . in the manner of a Catholic theologian discussing fornication and blasphemy?

In ordinary times, as in times of heated internal debate, the rigid, formalistic structure of "democratic centralism" worked against free inquiry. To act responsibly within the Workers party, particularly for those who were leaders, meant raising only those questions that were compatible with the party line, as defined at the last convention. Since 1943 Erber had chafed at the restrictions of the Leninist model, and at a meeting of the Political Committee in 1948 he had "thought out loud."

I questioned the need for a Bolshevik type of organization and stated that I thought a wide educational group that would include Marxists from varied backgrounds, including non-Trotskyists and anti-Trotskyists was the direction in which we should move. . . . [Other WP members attacked] me for "vagueness," "confusion," failure to present definite propositions, etc.

In order to stay within the rules, Erber either had to accept the WP's fundamental outlook, or be prepared to present an entire new program for consideration at the next party convention. Erber complained:

Shachtman now charges that I worked out my position in seclusion and sprang it upon the PC. . . . To the extent [that] is true, I found it unavoidable. *The movement affords no opportunity to think out loud, above all, when one is thinking what are considered "dangerous thoughts."*

Leninism, he concluded, "places a straightjacket on the ideological life of the leadership." In the CP, or the SWP, or in most of the horde of tiny left-wing sects, Erber would have been expelled, or would have checked his own unorthodox inclinations, long before he arrived at such an insight. In the WP he had been given enough freedom to reach a point where he could no longer tolerate the remaining boundaries on free thought and free expression imposed within the group.

The polemical fury that Shachtman could bring to bear on those departing from the WP (inflicting 120 pages on Erber alone) led most members who quit to do so quietly: the leader of the Buffalo branch simply disappeared one day, and none of his party comrades ever saw him again. Irving Howe and his close friend and ally Stanley Plastrik made their own departure in 1952 in a more public fashion. In a joint letter of resignation they argued that the Workers party

has always been characterized by a political split personality; between its ties with the heritage of Trotskyism and its healthy fumblings toward a new view of American socialism, between its needs for "orthodoxy" and its need for reassessment. It has repeatedly struck out toward new ideas and then retreated to familiar formulas.

Events outside the control of its members had restricted the Workers party to the size and influence of a political sect. That was bad enough, but what finally made life in the WP intolerable for Howe and Plastrik was the fact that "the shell of isolation has begun to seem almost comfortable, and what was once felt to be the tragedy of sect life has now covertly become glorified in the psychology of the 'saving remnant.' "[30]

In fact, Shachtman was not at all comfortable with the role of leader of the "saving remnant." Though he took every resignation from his movement as a personal betrayal, he too had been slowly changing his own ideas since the war years. His natural secretiveness, and what he considered to be the best interests of the Workers party, led him to do his best to disguise such doubts for as long as he could. In their letter of resignation in 1952, Howe and Plastrik complained of the "dreary pattern" of recent years in which Shachtman "advances a necessary modification [of theory] . . . the 'diehards,' primed by their intellectual frustration to seek factional struggles, pounce on this latest 'deviation,' and the ISL [Independent

Socialist League] chairman, to keep peace in his house, retreats behind a smoke-screen of diplomacy and maneuver." Without bringing anyone into his confidence, Shachtman was beginning to rethink his ideas about foreign policy, about independent labor politics, and about the Leninist heritage. His entire political career had seen him moving from relatively large groups to ever more isolated sects: from the Communist party to the Trotskyist opposition, from the Socialist party to the Socialist Workers party, from the Socialist Workers party to his own Workers party. Having worked his way so far out into isolation, he was now beginning to search for a way to return to some larger sheltering movement.[31]

One of the less controversial changes Shachtman proposed to his followers was the adoption of a new name for the Workers party, which became the Independent Socialist League (ISL) in the spring of 1949. It was a gesture toward recognizing political realities. *Labor Action* explained that "while it has been the custom for small socialist propaganda groups to assign themselves the name of a party, the WP has decided to break with this custom and to call itself what in actuality it is and has been—a socialist propaganda group." In proposing this change, Shachtman carefully maintained the appearance of political continuity. His resolution for dissolution of the Workers party contained no criticisms of the Leninist model of party organization or theory of revolution, and Shachtman continued to insist, on ceremonial occasions like May Day and the anniversary of the October Revolution, on the relevance of the Bolshevik example for his followers.[32]

The dissolution of the Workers party coincided with Shachtman's growing interest in the British Labor government, and implicit in the shift in name was a new conception of the proper role for American socialists. Shachtman argued that the British Labor government had "demonstrated the *possibility* of expropriating the bourgeoisie by parliamentary means." This new position was a long way from Lenin's suggestion that British Communists should support a Labor government the way a rope supports a hanged man. The Labor government was not to be a Kerensky-style prelude to the real revolution: Socialists in Britain could support the government in good conscience, while encouraging it to take much bolder steps toward the establishment of a truly socialist society.[33]

So, whether they chose to admit it to themselves at the time or not, the Shachtmanites had crossed an important ideological divide.

They were putting aside the revolutionary beliefs of their youth; they might remain Bolsheviks in temperament and training, but they no longer expected to see a repetition of the Bolshevik Revolution in America. With the formation of ISL, Shachtmanites were turning toward a new role: that of acting as what British socialists called a "ginger group," the socialist conscience within a broader movement for social change. The trouble was, there was no such movement in the early 1950s. In practice, the ISL remained as marginal as the WP had ever been.

By the early 1950s the Independent Socialist League's prospects could hardly have been bleaker. The movement had stagnated since 1946, it was losing many of its best and most devoted members, and Shachtman was withdrawing into semiretirement. The only really active ISLers were the national staff, who somehow managed to get out a newspaper every week that made the organization sound like a large and important movement. Except for occasional gala events, such as the famous Shachtman-Browder debate in 1951 (when Shachtman had brought down the house by pointing to an ashen-faced Browder and intoning, "There but for an accident of geography sits a corpse"), the movement had almost no public life.[34] *Labor Action* was strapped for material because local members weren't doing anything they could write in about. When the first issue of Irving Howe's new journal, *Dissent*, appeared in 1954, *Labor Action* editor Hal Draper ridiculed it as "a temporary halfway-house for backsliders from the struggle." Howe responded: "Except for a handful of ISL trade-unionists, who command my respect, what struggle is the ISL conducting? What struggle does Draper have except the very real one to fill the pages of *Labor Action* every week?"[35]

Postwar Campus Radicalism

As *Labor Action*'s coverage of the labor movement declined, its columns began to be filled with reports of political activities on college campuses. The Workers party established a youth affiliate, the Socialist Youth League (SYL), shortly after the end of the war. By the late 1940s *Labor Action* was carrying as many stories about the meetings and demonstrations staged by SYLers at Brooklyn College and at the University of Chicago as it had once devoted to wildcat strikes in Buffalo and San Pedro.[36]

For a brief moment, the late 1940s promised to be a hospitable time for campus radicalism. American colleges and universities were beginning the period of vast expansion that would culminate in the 1960s. After a decade of depression and a half-decade of war, a flood of older students (many of them paying their tuition through the GI Bill) enrolled in college. This was not yet a "silent generation": the 1930s were still part of recent memory; the phrase "Cold War" had just been coined; Roosevelt was only recently buried; and Joe McCarthy was a newly elected and still obscure junior senator from Wisconsin. The Nazi-Soviet Pact had killed off the American Student Union, the major left-wing group on campus in the later 1930s, but several new radical and liberal student groups got off to promising starts in the aftermath of the war. The Student League for Industrial Democracy (SLID), a group with a mildly social democratic perspective, was one of the smaller groups. It was organized in 1946 and claimed 700 members by 1948. Americans for Democratic Action (ADA) had been organized by anti-Communist "vital center" liberals in 1947; its campus affiliate, Students for Democratic Action (SDA), had 3,500 members in 1948. The largest campus radical group, controlled by the Communists, was the Young Progressives of America (YPA), the student affiliate of the Progressive party. Henry Wallace stirred a wave of enthusiasm on campuses that had not been demonstrated for a radical presidential candidate since Norman Thomas's 1932 campaign. In 1947 thousands of students turned out to hear Wallace give a speech from a sidewalk adjoining the Berkeley campus of the University of California when the university authorities refused him permission to speak on campus. During the campaign the YPA grew to some 10,000 members nationwide. The Communists recruited heavily during the Wallace campaign, and in 1949 organized the Labor Youth League (LYL) as a replacement for the Young Communist League, which Browder had dissolved during the war. The LYL soon claimed 6,000 members. Finally, chapters of the American Veterans Committee (AVC), a liberal alternative to the existing veterans organizations, flourished on campuses immediately after the war.[37]

But as the fortunes of the adult left-wing groups declined, so did those of their campus counterparts. The YPA expired with the end of the Wallace campaign. The LYL was virtually forced underground by the early 1950s, retaining a single open chapter at the University of Wisconsin. Cold War hysteria did not spare the anti-Stalinist Left on campuses. By 1953 SLID had declined to a few dozen active members, with no functioning campus chapters. When Andre Schiffrin helped organize a SLID chapter at Yale, shortly after his arrival as a freshman in 1953, he discovered that even the few people who came to meetings were not willing to put their names on mailing lists: as for its five active members, "everybody had prepared the speech he was going to deliver to the House Un-American Activities Committee." The SDA suffered a similar fate. And the AVC was torn apart in internecine battles between Communists and their liberal and anti-Stalinist opponents.[38]

While the more significant groups lost ground, the Socialist Youth League (the Shachtmanite youth affiliate) and its successor, the Young Socialist League, held their own, and became the most visible if not necessarily the most admired radical group on campuses. In part, this was because they were so small to begin with that they had little to lose. The Communists went through the demoralizing process of being reduced to a hard core; the Shachtmanites began with the hard core and could only build up from there. But there was another reason why the Shachtmanites survived and, by the dismal standards of the time, flourished. For a small group of students, they offered a sense of community and identity, representing a fusion of cultural and political radicalism that could not be found elsewhere.

In the 1930s the Trotskyists had derided both the political and the cultural content of the Communists' Popular Front "Americanism": the differences between the Communists' decidedly middle-brow cultural sensibility and the Trotskyists' interests in élite culture carried over into the youth movements they sponsored after the war. By the later 1940s folk songs had long been a staple of Communist gatherings: the Weavers were at the height of their popularity, and People's Songs and its successor organization, People's Artists, were experimenting with the "hootenanny." All of which combined to make folk songs anathema to the anti-Stalinist Left: as the joke told in and around the Workers party had it, two CP organizers got together and divided up responsibilities for the next meeting: "You bring the Negro, I'll bring the folksinger."[39]

The Socialist Youth League also displayed a very different cultural style. Vestiges of the Trotskyist appeal to intellectuals in the late

1930s survived into the late 1940s in the link between the Shacht-manites and a group of left-leaning writers and critics in New York and Chicago. Sunday forums sponsored by *Labor Action* in New York could draw on writers and intellectuals in the WP like Irving Howe, and also on a wider group who were sympathetic to the anti-Stalinist Left even if they were probably skeptical of the WP or the ISL's political prospects. Clement Greenberg, Norman Mailer, and Alfred Kazin were among the speakers who agreed to appear under the auspices of the Socialist Youth League. Michael Harrington re-membered the Shachtmanites drawing their supporters in the late 1940s and throughout the 1950s from a "radical Bohemian milieu," in New York, Chicago, and San Francisco. They found themselves rubbing elbows with the progenitors of Beat culture. Folklore in Shachtmanite circles had it that the Beat poets Lawrence Ferlinghetti and Allen Ginsberg used to come to SYL meetings (Ginsberg seems to have found the proceedings a little staid: a line in *Howl* commem-orates a more lively than ordinary occasion when Shachtman, in the midst of delivering a lecture on Dadaism, was the target of a bowl of potato salad hurled by a direct action-minded Dadaist in the audience).[40]

There were few rebels, cultural or political, on college campuses in the 1950s. Looking back at his college years from the perspective of the mid-1960s, radical journalist Jack Newfield described the 1950s as a time of abject conformity and passivity. His fellow-stu-dents at Hunter College were "bereft of passions, of dreams, of gods. . . . If any single characteristic bound them together it was withdrawal. Not the experimental, alienated withdrawal of the Beats, but a timid, unfeeling withdrawal."[41]

But at a few schools, students came out of the 1950s with different memories. Betty Denitch, a student at Antioch College in the mid-1950s, recalled that her fellow students were

attracted to a style we associated with the Left Bank in the 1920s. We read Hemingway. We were wearing clothing that became part of the uniform of the sixties, jeans, long hair, sandals, berets. We believed in sex. We knew the Beat poets. We were interested in some other way of life, some other values, some other symbols besides those we had grown up with. There was a sense that something was really wrong, something inhuman about the way of life that people were encouraged to live in our society.[42]

As a freshman at Antioch Denitch joined a socialist discussion group where she encountered and was impressed by the Shachtmanites because they seemed part of this underground cultural milieu.

The 1950s generation of young Shachtmanites had grown up in the last years of the Depression and during the Second World War. They had a sense of having missed out on the great events that had formed the world they grew up in, but rather than admit to powerlessness, they came to think of themselves as a saving remnant destined to play an important role at some unspecified future date when political conditions were again propitious. They were mostly Jewish, some the children of 1930s Socialists, a few foreign-born.

Michael Harrington, who came out of a middle-class, midwestern, Catholic background was *sui generis*. Although atypical sociologically, Harrington fit the mold culturally, and it was not by chance that he emerged as the most influential of Shachtman's young recruits in the 1950s. He had been a graduate student in English literature at the University of Chicago, was a contributor to *Partisan Review*, and a regular at the White Horse bar, a bohemian haunt in Greenwich Village where alcoholic poets traded complaints with frustrated radicals. Harrington came to socialism via the pacifist Catholic Worker movement. He joined the Young People's Socialist League at a time when it and its parent organization were at a low ebb of membership and morale, and broke with it almost immediately over the issue of the Socialist party's support of the Korean War. Harrington had considerable reserves of charm and ambition to draw upon, as well as a fresh-faced "American" visage—"a good person," as one former Shachtmanite recalled cynically, "to present our ideas to the unwashed masses." Bogdan Denitch, a young YPSL organizer, recruited Harrington shortly after meeting him at a picket line in New York supporting exiled Spanish Republicans. As Denitch recalled their meeting: "I immediately noticed this smart guy who didn't look as flaky as the rest of the Catholic Workers, or as nutty as the anarchists." Harrington and Denitch became a team within YPSL, and later within the YSL. Denitch would describe their relationship as "good cop" and "bad cop," with Harrington the public spokesman and Denitch in charge of behind-the-scenes maneuvers. Harrington thrived on the life of an itinerant organizer, maintaining a penurious existence through a succession of ill-paying movement jobs, regularly hitch-hiking across the country as a kind of Bolshevik version of Jack Kerouac's "Dean Moriarty." In the course of the decade he became an effective writer and a charismatic speaker, echoing Shachtman in style and inflection. He prided himself on being a man of letters as well as a radical organizer, as interested in "literary decadence" as in Marx's theory of immiseration. When he made his annual visit to Antioch College in the 1950s he usually gave two lectures, one on politics and one on literature. And like Irving Howe and others before him, he found Shachtman an appealing mentor.[43]

Harrington, Denitch, and the small group of yipsels who followed them into the Shachtmanite camp represented a prize catch for the Independent Socialist League. But the Shachtmanites met little success in their attempts to influence other youth groups: at one time or another both SLID and SDA enacted bans on advocates of "totalitarianism" to keep out the Shachtmanites. SLID went through a major internal upheaval when Denitch, still in the YPSL but closely aligned with the Shachtmanites ("we thought the Russian Revolution started going sour with Kronstadt, for them it was when Trotsky got bounced out") organized a "Red Caucus" in SLID and gained control of the evening session campus chapter at CCNY. After a two-year battle, the Red Caucus members resigned in the face of an ultimatum to do so or be kicked out. In 1955 the Shachtmanites, with Harrington and Denitch in the lead, captured the New York regional office of SDA, and came close to gaining control of the national organization. They were defeated only when the leaders of Americans for Democratic Action threatened to cut off the student group's financial stipend. In both episodes the Shachtmanites gained a few recruits, and a lasting reputation for factional unscrupulousness. As one SLID officer complained in the 1950s, the young Shachtmanites' "predilections for intra-organizational warfare verge on the pathological."[44]

The Young People's Socialist League and the Socialist Youth League merged in 1954 to form the Young Socialist League (YSL), which proclaimed itself "the major socialist youth organization in the United States." In reality, as Harrington admitted in his memoir, *Fragments of a Century*, that didn't mean very much: the union of YPSL and SYL in 1954 produced an organization with a grand total of eighty-three members. Still, it was the first occasion in recent radical memory when two groups had actually joined together rather than splitting apart. Tiny as the YSL was, it represented a major asset to the Shachtmanites in the 1950s, and it is doubtful they would have survived without it.[45]

Although radical movements had always recruited heavily among

the young, the emergence of the "youth group" was a relatively recent innovation. The Young People's Socialist League was the first
radical youth organization in the United States. Organized in 1913,
it grew to about 10,000 members by the end of the First World War
but played a relatively minor role in the large Socialist party of the
pre-war era. In the 1930s, youth groups emerged as a far more important factor in the fortunes of the various radical parties. The
Young Communist League provided the Communist party with the
bulk of its English-speaking secondary leaders: many former YCLers
went on to positions of prominence in the Party or in the CIO. The
Young People's Socialist League was equally important, in turn, to
the Socialists, the Trotskyists, and the Shachtmanites. Traditionally
the adult movement was supposed to guide the youth movement,
but as the fortunes of the adult parties waned, the balance of influence between the two began to shift the other way. Saul Mendelson,
an ISL member who had been a leader of the Shachtmanite group
at the University of Chicago, made a half-serious proposal in
the mid-1950s that the ISL dissolve into the YSL, on the grounds
that the youth organization was real and the adult organization
was not.[46]

As YSLers must have understood in more reflective moments, being the "major socialist youth organization" in the United States was
not much of a distinction in the 1950s. But there were occasional
stirrings on campus that gave them hope of being lifted by a rising
wave of student radicalism. The *Young Socialist Challenge*, which appeared as a regular supplement to *Labor Action*, offered extensive
coverage to the short-lived "green feather movement" of 1954.
When *Robin Hood* was banned from Indiana's public school libraries
as a subversive text (who but a Communist, local authorities reasoned, could applaud that tale of armed insurrection and revolutionary expropriation?), students at Indiana University began selling
pins displaying a green feather, mocking the excesses of McCarthyism. The movement spread to Wisconsin, Michigan, University of Chicago, and a number of other campuses. At UCLA an
unlikely coalition of campus Communists and Shachtmanites organized a green feather march across campus, in defiance of the
administration's ban on such activities, and attracted some 500
participants.[47]

The Shachtmanites might applaud an act of impudent audacity
like the green feather movement, but it is unlikely they would have

come up with the idea themselves. Their fixation on radical movements of the past and their cumbersome political style worked to their disadvantage. Even among the few students who already thought of themselves as radicals, the Shachtmanites had a hard time overcoming a reputation for deviousness. Dave McReynolds, leader of the YPSL chapter in Los Angeles, worked with the Shachtmanites on various common enterprises in the 1950s but never shed the distrust left by his initial encounter.

I went to a garden party they were having, because I wanted to know more about them. They had everything set up in the backyard, pitch pennies and darts and other games. There were about twenty people there. So I went out in the backyard and pitched pennies and threw darts at balloons for about ten minutes, and then someone said, "Well, why don't we go inside and talk?" I soon discovered I was the only person there who wasn't in their group. We had a drawing for the door prize. Who do you think won? The whole party was going on for my benefit. What would have happened if I hadn't come along, I don't know.[48]

Ideologically, the YSL seemed to be plowing the same barren ground as its parent organization. Its mimeographed internal bulletin, the *Young Socialist Review*, was filled with articles describing "the death agony of capitalism and the crisis of the proletarian movement." In his memoirs Harrington self-mockingly described a debate on Indochina at the first "plenum" of YSL in September 1954.

What, precisely, should we say to the workers in Saigon and Hanoi? Should we advise them to create a new movement which would fight both the French colonialists and the Stalinists within the Viet Minh? Or should they enter into the Viet Minh and contest with Ho Chi Minh for leadership?

Appropriate quotations from the Bolshevik classics were brandished by both sides and in the end, late at night, the YSL resolved that "the Indochinese proletariat should organize independently."[49]

Despite its deeply inbred sectarianism, the YSL began to grow—slowly, to be sure—but that it grew at all made it stand out on the campus Left in the 1950s. New college chapters were started at Columbia, Oberlin, Antioch, Boston University, the University of Washington, and elsewhere: fifteen in all by 1958, with about 250 members nationally. Harrington developed a network of contacts on other campuses, like the University of Wisconsin and University of

Michigan, where he visited on his annual campus tours. The YSL grew because few alternatives were available to radically minded young people in the 1950s but also because it possessed certain virtues of its own. It antagonized many on the campus Left, but it did not mindlessly inherit the enemies of its parent organization. When *Dissent* appeared in 1954, Shachtman forbade ISLers from writing for it. But the YSL, much to his annoyance, adopted a resolution a few months later welcoming *Dissent*'s appearance as "a new forum for socialist views," and Harrington became a frequent contributor. Narrow and self-centered as many of its debates were, the YSL did offer its members an education in both radical theory and current events. They knew the history of the Indochinese conflict at a time when most American students would not have been able to find Vietnam on the map. They could tell one faction from another in the Algerian independence movement. They were, at least initially, enthusiastic backers of Castro's July 26 movement. They mastered an exotic but ultimately useful jargon: they learned the meaning of words like "imperialism" and "national liberation," which would come to have much wider circulation a decade later. And at a time when the "myth of the happy worker" (as former Shachtmanite Harvey Swados labeled it in mid-decade) held virtually undisputed sway in the American mass media and the academic world, the YSL retained contact with the remnants of an earlier radical tradition within the labor movement. For left-wing students in the 1950s it was of no little import that a UAW shop steward would be willing to come and give a talk or offer a class under YSL auspices.[50]

The Socialist Youth League and the Young Socialist League were tiny groups: probably no more than 500 people were members of either at one time or another in the course of the 1950s. The YSL's "Marxist sophistication," Harrington would later write, "stood in inverse ratio to any possibility of changing the world." But to focus only on the absurdities of such debates, he added, would "obscure the real, and rather astounding, truth: that theories of considerable importance were being conserved and even deepened in apparently silly little debates; and that the ideas generated there would influence the mass movements of the 1960s."[51]

New Opportunities

For a decade, Shachtman had been looking for a way out of the dead end in which his movement had found itself. The formation of the ISL had not done it, but the deStalinization crisis in the Communist party revived his hopes for a breakthrough. Thanks largely to the YSL, the Shachtmanites had something to offer when the political climate began to change in the later 1950s. Battered and shrunken as it was by the mid-1950s, the Communist party was still a formidable force in the eyes of the Shachtmanites, its 20,000 or so remaining members "more people than we had ever seen," as Harrington recalled. At first, the Shachtmanites greeted reports of the denunciation of Stalin coming out of the Soviet Communist party's Twentieth Congress with practiced skepticism. What difference did it make if Stalin was in good or bad odor in the Soviet Union? "Bureaucratic collectivism" was not the product of Stalin's personal flaws and ambitions: it was a new social system, whose ruling class was made up of the very people who were now criticizing the "cult of personality." All that Khrushchev had to offer, *Labor Action* avowed in March 1956, was "Stalinism without Stalin." As for the American CP, the Shachtmanites had seen it weather many crises before, and at most they expected "defections of ones or twos."[52]

But when the magnitude of the CP's crisis became apparent to Shachtman, he suddenly came to life, after years of lethargy. In mid-April he gave a talk on the meaning of the Soviet Twentieth Congress and presented the usual analysis of bureaucratic collectivism. What was unusual about the evening, as *Labor Action* reported, was that about a dozen members of the Labor Youth League had come to hear him in response to leaflets that YSLers had handed out at the CP's Jefferson School. For the first time *Labor Action* chose to address Communists as fellow socialists, sincere, if misguided, in their beliefs.

We want to discuss our ideas with you, and we do so as independent socialists, not as apologists for capitalism who merely use anti-Communism as a justification for the status quo.[53]

Thus began an intricate courtship process that ultimately would involve most of the organized Left in America. Shachtman's initial goal was probably limited to picking up a few dozen new recruits from the CP and LYL, as the WP and ISL had over the years scooped up an occasional individual or small group from the YPSL or the SWP. But that spring another development caught Shachtman's eye and led him to decide that much more was potentially at stake.

Dave McReynolds had had his differences with the Shachtman-ites over the years. He stuck with the Young People's Socialist League when Harrington and Denitch led the split that resulted in the founding of the YSL. But like those who departed, he remained opposed to the Socialist party's support of the Korean War and what he felt to be a general rightward drift in its political orientation. In 1954 he organized a caucus within the SP called the "Committee for a Socialist Program," which counted a few dozen adherents scattered among the SP's thousand or so remaining members. In 1956 the Socialist party began to consider the possibility of a merger with the Social Democratic Federation (SDF), a small group of "Old Guard" Jewish needle-trade unionists who had left the party in 1936 to support Roosevelt. They now wanted to come back—as McReynolds later realized—"to die in the Socialist Party." McReynolds initially opposed the SDF merger, feeling it would only strengthen the SP's inclination to function as an old people's home rather than as an activist group. But then he realized he could use the merger as an argument for bringing in other groups who would strengthen the Socialist party's activist wing. As he wrote in May 1956 in *Hammer and Tongs*, the SP's internal bulletin:

There are . . . very few groups with which we could seriously consider merger. Perhaps the SDF, perhaps the Jewish Labor Bund, perhaps the ISL. . . . The real objective would be to create a new climate in which the Socialist party would again be the dominant, moving force on the scene— to create the kind of environment and atmosphere in which it would be natural for radicals to come into the Party individually.

McReynolds had his eye on bigger game. When he lived in Los Angeles he had met with and come to respect the local and somewhat unorthodox Communist leader, Dorothy Healey. What would happen to people like Healey and the thousands of other Communists who were responding to the Khrushchev revelations with horror and disillusionment? He deliberately did not mention the Communist party by name in his article in *Hammer and Tongs*, not wanting to alarm right-wing SPers with the specter of thousands of "Stalinists" flooding into their organization. But the hidden message came across clearly to those—like Shachtman—who knew how to read it: "While few groups could actually merge with the Party, almost every group contains good, hard-working Democratic Socialists who belong in the Party and who would come as individuals if they felt they were wanted and if the Party showed some sign of life."[54]

McReynolds hoped that by bringing in the Shachtmanites the Socialist party would shake off some of its lethargy, and thus become more appealing to individual Communists as they left their own Party. The Communist party had been built in 1919 on the ruins of the Debsian Socialist party; in essence, what McReynolds now hoped to do was to rebuild the Socialist party on the ruins of the Communist party. McReynolds did not get very far with his proposal at the SP's national convention in June 1956. Norman Thomas rejected the idea out of hand: "I know this group," he said, referring to the SP, "and the Shachtmanites would take this bunch over in about a year." For most SP leaders, memories of the last merger with Trotskyists were a powerful argument against any repeat performance, a lesson only recently reinforced by the Shachtmanites' role in the splitting of YPSL. McReynolds' proposal was voted down by an overwhelming margin.[55]

Until this point McReynolds had acted on his own, without a consultation with Shachtman. But Shachtman now adopted McReynolds's strategy as his own. He sold it to his own initially skeptical followers with the argument that it was the only way by which they could hope to gather in the thousands of people who were quitting the Communist party. The Socialist party as presently constituted was important only as a means to this more ambitious goal. As he wrote to one of his followers in 1958: "Unity with the SP does not mean a real success except if it is understood *exclusively* from the standpoint of a new *possibility* for a movement. . . . We can help tremendously, once we are in the SP, to realize many of the terribly neglected opportunities of the day."[56] Shachtman's arguments eventually won over most of his followers. They knew that ex-Communists, no matter how shaken they had been by the Khrushchev revelations, would be very unlikely to consider joining an organization with a Trotskyist heritage. Old prejudices died hard. And why should anyone leave an organization of 20,000 to join a sect of a few hundred? But the SP, though it had scarcely over a thousand members, could be dressed up in a way that might appeal to the Communists: draped in the mantle of Eugene Debs and the "all-inclusive" socialist movement, it could serve as the center of a general regroupment on the Left.

Having decided at last on a strategy, Shachtman now moved with vigor and deliberation. He hadn't spent thirty-five years in factional maneuvers for nothing. If he could sell the SP on the idea of a merger with the ISL/YSL, given the nearly twenty years of bad blood between the two movements, it would be his political masterpiece, the triumph of his career. ISLer Herman Benson, in close consultation with Shachtman, wrote a long article entitled "The Communist Party at the Crossroads" in the fall 1956 issue of *New International*, which was reprinted and distributed as a pamphlet. It continued the conciliatory tone that *Labor Action* had adopted in April: "Whole sections of the Communist Party honestly have already taken the first steps towards the only authentic socialism, that is: democratic socialism. New hope stirs for American socialism." Benson pointed to the end of McCarthyism, the unification of the AFL and CIO, and the rise of the civil rights movement as evidence of great days coming. "Now is the time for socialism to rebuild. . . . The rebirth of socialism calls for new forms, new methods, a new appeal." The article included favorable references to dissident CP leaders like John Gates and Steve Nelson. Benson urged the Communists to avoid the twin evils of dogmatism and despair.

Thousands of Communists have devoted their full mature life to the fight for a world of socialism, as they saw it, risking personal well-being, gaining experience in the class struggle. Are they now to be scattered to the winds and squandered; are they to waste away in a hopelessly Stalinist sect, justly scorned by the working class?

The place for ex-Communists was with their brother socialists in a broad, democratic socialist movement: "What we are describing is nothing less than the Socialist Party of Eugene Debs."[57]

Local members of the Independent Socialist League began contacting their Communist counterparts. In Pittsburgh, Hugh Cleland met with Steve Nelson and reported back to Shachtman, with apparently genuine surprise, that he found Nelson "a nice guy."

The feeling I had about our conversation and about Nelson was—he used to be miles from us—now he is only a quarter of a mile from us. . . . Incidentally, his explanation for the rise of Stalinism sounds almost like ours![58]

Shachtman personally met with John Gates. As he wrote to Barney Cohen, a member of the Bay Area ISL, in February 1958:

A couple of weeks before he quit the CP [in December 1957], John Gates told Ben [Herman Benson] and me at a confidential meeting that he agreed completely with our orientation and perspective (he doesn't like our "anti-Soviet bias," however!) and that he himself would decidedly like to join the SP but believes that they would have no part of him.[59]

Once ISLers got into the SP, Shachtman concluded, they could make it a place where people like Gates were welcomed.

Shachtman's new strategy met with some die-hard opposition within the Independent Socialist League. Hal Draper argued in *Labor Action* that Shachtman's justification for the merger, the opening to former Communists, was based on faulty reasoning. Socialist party leaders were interested only in opening to their right, not to their left: "If the SP opened itself up as a 'home' to attract . . . a swarm of ex-CPers who want a new left movement, then—such is the slimness of the SP's own cadres—it would literally be swamped." SP leaders, he argued, were not about to commit "political suicide." But Draper and his allies couldn't come up with any alternative to Shachtman's proposal except to muddle along as before, and so they eventually capitulated. Within the YSL the battle was more protracted. About a quarter of the members split away from the group as a result of the proposed merger (in time they found their way into the SWP, where they became the basis of that group's new youth affiliate, the Young Socialist Alliance).[60]

Shachtman's Triumph

For two years Shachtman devoted his persuasive powers to wooing the Socialist party. McReynolds's initial resolution calling for a merger with the ISL had been overwhelmingly defeated at the 1956 SP convention, and Shachtman and McReynolds worked unceasingly to guarantee that the next time the issue came up they would have the votes they needed. One by one they made their converts, including important SP leaders like national secretary Irwin Suall. Norman Thomas was the biggest obstacle they faced, but by the fall of 1957 he had begun to waver. "You know," he wrote to Shachtman in September, "that I would like unity on a proper basis." But he was not prepared to accept the ISL if all it meant was a repetition of the Trotskyist episode of the mid-1930s: "Would the ISL explicitly and honestly abandon existence as an organized caucus, open or secret, in the Party? Where do you stand on Leninism?"[61]

Shachtman responded with a solemn pledge, "We are prepared to lean over backward to prove in deeds that any concept of a 'raid' on the Party or the 'capture' of the Party is utterly alien to our views and intent." As for the question of "Leninism," he still believed that the Bolshevik Revolution had at its inception a democratic potential that was betrayed by the Stalinist bureaucratic revolution, but he promised that his followers would not force their own interpretation "on a subject that is primarily of historical importance" on other members of the Socialist party. Given the importance that Shachtman and his followers had always attached to the "Russian Question," this seemed to be a substantial concession on his part.[62]

Thomas also raised specific objections to some members of the Young Socialist League, like Bogdan Denitch, with the implication that if the merger were to take place, Denitch would not be welcome. Shachtman admitted in his reply that the YSL was not "composed of angels." But on the whole, he insisted, YSL members "would be a pillar and a credit to any movement they supported. I am especially aware that a socialist movement that does not make its greatest headway among the new generation will never succeed in really breaking out of the isolation that afflicts us all." The last was a powerful argument. The SP had revived the YPSL after the 1953 split, but it still had fewer than 100 members. The YSL was two or three times larger, and considerably more active. In the debate in the SP's internal bulletin *Hammer and Tongs*, prounity SPers cited the YSL as the Shachtmanites' chief attraction. Thomas, in any case, was finally persuaded. He knew that the SP, as presently constituted, was a fossil, and had to change if it was to survive. So he gambled on Shachtman's sincerity, using his letter as means of convincing others of the necessity of the merger. (Denitch, meanwhile, was sent from

New York to Berkeley, so he would not be an unpleasant reminder of the Shachtmanites' earlier clashes with the SP.)[63]

The opposition to the merger centered in New York, where the SP had its greatest strength, and its most politically sophisticated members. Robin Myers, former national secretary of the SP, was among the most outspoken opponents of the proposal. She had bitter memories of the battles with the Communists in the American Student Union, and with the Trotskyists in the YPSL in the 1930s. In a letter to other SPers she shrewdly appraised Shachtman's motives:

It was after the Khrushchev revelations and the split in the CP that the ISL policy towards the SP began to take shape. The ISL believed, for their own reasons, that the time was ripe for a regroupment on the left, a rebuilt American socialist movement. The key to making this a successful, American movement was the leadership of the SP. Otherwise, one of two things would happen; it would be a unity (if achieved) of sectarians into a slightly larger sect; or it would be a unity discredited by the communist background of its participants. Hence the first drive of the ISL, now almost successful, was to involve the Socialist Party.

Myers opposed Shachtman for two reasons. First, because she did not want the SP filled with former Communists, which she feared would lessen its appeal to other potential recruits. And second, because she did not trust Shachtman's pledges of goodwill:

Do not think that we would be just taking in 200-odd members to do Jimmy Higgins work. Here are trained functionaries with a well-planned idea of the movement they are trying to build, flush with the accomplishment of their first step—unity with the SP-SDF. We would be carrying out the ISL's program, not ours.[64]

Despite the determined opposition mounted by Myers and others, in June 1958 the SP-SDF national convention voted by a three to one margin in favor of the proposal. In a last-ditch effort to block unity, opponents of the proposal invoked a constitutional requirement to force the party to hold a membership referendum on the question, a process that took most of the summer of 1958.

Midway through the balloting a curious and telling incident took place. McReynolds received a message from Shachtman asking to meet on a matter of importance. Shachtman met with McReynolds, Maurice Spector, and some other pro-unity SPers at Spector's New

York apartment. Spector was a veteran Canadian Trotskyist, and he and Shachtman went back together a long way. He had been in Moscow with Cannon in 1928 and had been converted at the same time. He had left the Canadian Trotskyist movement some years earlier and moved to the United States, where he eventually joined the Socialist party. He was one of McReynolds's most reliable allies in the effort to get the merger with the ISL approved. According to McReynolds:

Maurice wanted Max in the SP, not because he cared about Max but because he wanted to open the party; he wanted to open it to the Gates faction . . . and so on. At the meeting at Maurice's apartment Max said, "Look, I didn't plan to have a division. The whole intent was that we should have a merger. My comrades and I have been thinking this over, and we recognized that, after all, what does it matter what year we come in? If we come in and drive others out what have we achieved? Nothing. So, we have thought that it perhaps would be good if we withdrew the application. Let it rest. Let the comrades see that we're not intent on raiding them. We'll come make an application a year from now."

McReynolds was appalled. He told Shachtman that the ballots from the referendum were even at that time being returned to the SP's national office, and the vote would be counted in any case: a withdrawal now would mean that the merger would never go through. He adamantly opposed Shachtman's withdrawal and finally persuaded him to drop the plan. Spector had remained "strangely silent" during the entire discussion. After Shachtman had left, McReynolds recalled, Spector asked him to stay on a moment.

Maurice said to me, "Wait, I want to talk to you." So I stayed and Maurice said, "I want to tell you something, because we've worked closely together. I'm leaving the party. When Max gets in he's going to go so far to the right that you won't believe it." I said, "No, he's just upset." But Maurice replied, "I'm an old Trotskyist. I know the signs. I can't go on with Max in the party." He was never active again politically. He had seen one great chance, gambled everything on it, and then realized suddenly that night that he had miscalculated about Max.[65]

What Spector realized that evening was that Shachtman was already planning his break with the SP's left-wing (people like himself and McReynolds), and would do anything—even delay his group's merger with the SP—to curry favor with the Party's right-wing. In

73

any case, when the votes were counted in the referendum, unity with the Independent Socialist League carried by a small majority. The ISL stopped publishing *Labor Action* and the *New International* and turned over its assets to the SP. The YSL and the YPSL merged, while individual ISLers, according to a prearranged formula, joined the SP-SDF over the next few months.[66]

Robin Myers had been right about one thing, and wrong about another. When Shachtman and his followers got into the Socialist party, they were able to quickly gain control of the party machinery just as she feared. Myers was mistaken, however, in her concern that Shachtman would open up the party to a flood of ex-Communists. Once safely ensconced in the SP Shachtman showed virtually no interest in what supposedly had been the main purpose for the merger, appealing to those thousands of former Communists adrift since the deStalinization crisis. Some of Shachtman's closest associates came to believe that he never had any intention of following up his promised "opening to the Left." The whole proposal, Hal Draper and Julius Jacobson later decided, had been a fraud from the beginning, designed only to sell Shachtman's proposal to his followers in the ISL. It is also possible that Shachtman was initially sincere in his proposal but developed second thoughts once the merger actually had gone through. Shachtman was an important figure in the tiny Socialist party he joined in 1958, but if it were to grow substantially, and actually draw in experienced radical leaders of the caliber of John Gates and Steve Nelson, the relative weight Shachtman carried in the party could only diminish. The habits of a lifelong sectarianism reasserted themselves, as Shachtman decided it was better to control a narrow group than to risk losing control of a broader movement. Debbie Meier, a veteran of the Chicago ISL and SP, recalled:

One thing that annoyed me when we joined the Socialist Party was that Shachtman wanted to keep it as it was. Especially in New York, which was the center of the national organization, the Socialist Party leadership stayed pretty much the same. It still had the quality of a sect. In Chicago we quadrupled the membership: all kinds of people came in from the pacifist and civil rights organizations. We thought we were about to take off . . . Shachtman's argument was "We can't do it in New York because it would frighten the Old Guard." Afterwards some people argued that wasn't his real reason; the real reason was that he didn't want to change the Socialist Party in the kind of direction that Chicago was moving in.[67]

Shachtman not only moved to close the recruitment door once his own group was in the Socialist party; he was also moving steadily to the right politically, as Maurice Spector had divined. Within a few years some of the very people who had opposed unity with the Shachtmanites because they feared Shachtman would drag the party to the left found themselves instead opposing Shachtman as he dragged the party in the opposite direction.

Shachtman willingly shed the garments and language of revolutionary Trotskyism, and adopted those of democratic socialism. His stated beliefs changed dramatically, but his mode of operation remained that of a staunch sectarian. Within the SP the Shachtmanites continued to function as a small, disciplined cadre, operating in secrecy, persuaded that they alone possessed the truth, at once harsh and unscrupulous and selfrighteous in their attitudes, oriented solely toward the struggle for power and the manipulation of power once gained. It would be of no small consequence for the early New Left that when it encountered "democratic socialism" for the first time, it came to it in the peculiar form offered by the Shachtmanites.

3

Dissent, Journal of
Tired Heroism

There are ironies here. Some who maintained a radical identity during the political desert of the Eisenhower years gave much thought to the "human values" that were lost sight of in the organized radical life of the thirties. Others talked of "ideology" and traditional radical beliefs as if they were a plague from which we had been mercifully delivered. Is it stretching a point to suggest that the students' contempt for "ideology," their stress on the need for "human relationship," and the breaking of the barriers of "impersonality," have been influenced by the reflections of the adherents of the "old Left"?

—Murray Hausknecht
Dissent, 1968

Irving Howe among his classmates at City College: "a pillar of ideological rectitude." (Courtesy of CCNY Archives)

F OR the first thirty years of his life Irving Howe followed closely in Max Shachtman's footprints. Born in New York in 1920, the year that Shachtman spent fruitlessly trying to join the Communist party, Howe, like his mentor, went on to attend DeWitt Clinton High School and City College. Like Shachtman before him, he found left-wing politics infinitely more interesting than his formal college studies—although, unlike Shachtman, he did manage to complete four years at City College and began (though never completed) a graduate program in English literature at Brooklyn College. Howe followed Shachtman from the Young People's Socialist League into the Trotskyist movement, and from there into the Workers party and the Independent Socialist League. And Howe, like Shachtman, would devote much of his energies in the 1950s to the attempt to summon up a new American Left. But when it came to choosing a vehicle to reach that goal, Howe and Shachtman at last parted company. Shachtman was dissatisfied with the limits of sectarian politics, but he thought he could use the instrument of the sect to create a new political role for himself and his followers. For Howe political medium and message were inseparable: in order to create a new, nonsectarian politics he abandoned the sect and sought new ways of binding together a political community. Once it had been the "party" that was the active agent, and the "theoretical journal" the passive commentator on events; now it was the party that did nothing but sit around and talk. The journal at least retained one practical task to complete—its own publication—and a chance of influencing a wider circle. Shachtman, whose only profession was that of revolutionary, retained his authority as past master of the political maneuver; Howe, who combined political interests with a career as a literary critic, chose instead to perfect his own mastery of the political word.

Words were a problem for radicals in the 1950s. The grand phrases of the 1930s—"class consciousness," "proletarian internationalism," "revolutionary struggle"—had spent their force, having been called upon too often to explain the unexplainable or to justify the unjustifiable. In the end it almost seemed as if there were only one short word left to rely upon. As a character in *Bread and Wine*, Ignazio Silone's novel of revolution and faith, explained:

In every dictatorship . . . just one man, even any little man at all, who continues to think with his own head puts the whole public order in danger. Tons of printed paper propagate the regime's order of the day, thousands of loudspeakers, hundreds of thousands of posters and handbills distributed free, and stables of orators in the squares and crossroads, thousands of priests from the pulpit, all repeat to the point of obsession, to the point of collective stupefaction, these orders of the day. But it's enough that a little man, just one little man says NO for that formidable granite order to be in danger.[1]

"For Silone," Howe wrote in *Dissent* in the mid-1950s—in a passage that can stand as self-portrait as well as literary criticism—"heroism is a condition of readiness, a talent for waiting, a gift of stubbornness; his is the heroism of tiredness."[2]

Howe's "gift of stubbornness" and "heroism of tiredness" differed from the blind devotion to outworn dogma that was so prevalent among radical sectarians. If the next revival of American radicalism was to avoid the unhappy fate of earlier movements, Howe believed that a new generation of radicals would need to be equipped with something more than the "correct line." They would need to develop the ability to temper commitment with humility, enthusiasm with self-inquiry. This vision of a "heroism of tiredness" was an appealing one for radicals of Howe's generation precisely because they had already gone through a cycle of uncritical commitment and disillusionment. Whatever its intrinsic merits, it proved a difficult vision to pass on to a younger generation as yet ideologically unscarred.

The American Left and the Little Magazine

In his indispensable history of *Partisan Review*, James Gilbert called the little magazine "the public birthplace, the homestead, the prison, and sometimes the rescue mission of . . . contemporary intellectuals."[3] The little magazines were non-commercial ventures, sometimes political and sometimes cultural in inspiration, addressed to select audiences, and without formal affiliation to larger movements or institutions. They required only a small band of devoted editors, writers, and the occasional financial angel to survive—plus readers. During the 1930s, a community of readers for little magazines took shape that was destined to outlive the temporary radical enthusiasms of those years. The history of *Partisan Review*, which began as a publication of the New York John Reed Club and was carried off by its editors, Philip Rahv and William Phillips, into the anti-Stalinist camp in the late 1930s, is not just the story of the enthusiasms and disillusionments of the few dozen people who collectively have become designated the "New York Intellectuals." There could have been no *Partisan Review* had it not been for the existence of an expanding audience of young college graduates (many, though not all of them, Jewish), who because of economic hard times or the still potent ethnic and religious barriers in university hiring never expected to find the kind of academic jobs for which they might otherwise have qualified. Some became full-time radicals or trade-union functionaries; others pursued precarious careers as free-lance writers; and still others sought the security of nonacademic professions, like high school teaching or social work. For such people the little magazines functioned as a sort of continuing post-graduate seminar. Only in its second decade would *Partisan Review* attract significant academic interest, recognition, and subscribers. But in the course of the 1930s it helped define a set of concerns and provide a vocabulary that became the common intellectual discourse of the 1950s. Irving Kristol, who served as an editor of *Commentary* in the early 1950s, found *Partisan Review* an "intimidating presence" when he first encountered it as a young Trotskyist at City College in the late 1930s—intimidating, yet with a seductive intellectual appeal.

Even simply to understand it seemed a goal beyond reach. I would read each article at least twice, in a state of awe and exasperation—excited to see such elegance of style and profundity of mind, depressed at the realization that a commoner like myself could never expect to rise into that intellectual aristocracy.[4]

Kristol himself would make the transition from commoner to aristocrat: most of his contemporaries would not but would remain loyal followers of the debates among the "intellectual aristocracy" of the New York Intellectuals for the next several decades.

The Apprenticeship of Irving Howe

Irving Howe also joined that intellectual aristocracy, though the route he chose was a more roundabout one. Fresh out of the factional wars of the City College cafeteria alcoves in 1940, Howe became editor of the Workers party weekly newspaper, *Labor Action*, and wrote as much as half of each issue under various pen names.

Prolific and cocksure, brimming with energy and persuaded I had a key to understanding the world, I needed only the reams of yellow paper on which I typed and the *New York Times* from which to draw facts. (Blessed *New York Times*! What would radical journalism in America do without it?)[5]

Howe fell into the habit of reading the *Times* while still a student at DeWitt Clinton High School in the Bronx. His neighbors in the East Bronx read the cheaper tabloids or the Yiddish Socialist daily *Forward*. To read the *New York Times* signaled, so Howe later realized, "alien yearnings, perhaps some vision of getting away."[6]

Years later Howe would find in the novels of Henry Roth, Michael Gold, and Daniel Fuchs the "classic pattern of a fierce attachment to the provincialism of origins . . . entangled with a fierce eagerness to plunge into the Gentile world of success, manners, freedom."[7] Joining a political movement regarded by much of the rest of the nation as an alien conspiracy may seem, in retrospect, a peculiar point of entry into the values and promises of that Gentile world, but the universalistic claims of revolutionary socialism obscured the paradoxical character of this commitment to its youthful adherents in the East Bronx and Brooklyn. "The Internationale," they sang confidently at the conclusion of Party rallies, "shall be the human race." In the Trotskyist movement that Howe joined, as in the much larger Communist movement, the taking of a "Party name" was ostensibly a measure of security against the intrusive scrutiny of the FBI and the local Red Squad. It also represented a ritualistic claiming of a new identity. Some young would-be Bolsheviks chose names that echoed those their parents had given them; others chose names that were never heard of in their old neighborhoods. Howe was clearly ambivalent in his choice: "Howe" is itself the most blandly American name imaginable, whereas the decision to retain his given name of "Irving" negates whatever intent he might have harbored of disguising his ethnic origins.

Howe looked to a number of older intellectuals for inspiration in the 1930s, among them Edmund Wilson, Morris Raphael Cohen, and Sidney Hook. But his true mentor would be Max Shachtman. While still a teenager he struggled to perfect an imitation of Shachtman's platform mannerisms, though it cost him some effort to overcome an innate shyness. Irving Kristol would later describe Howe at City College as

a pillar of ideological rectitude. Thin, gangling, intense, always a little distant, his fingers incessantly and nervously twisting a cowlick as he enunciated sharp and authoritative opinions, Irving was the Trotskyist leader and "theoretician."[8]

The war years that Howe spent at an Army base in Alaska (the fate of more than one radical draftee in the Second World War) matured Howe in many ways: removing him from the parochial world of New York radical politics, allowing him to accomplish the equivalent of a graduate education's worth of reading, and giving him a measure of self-assurance to which he had previously only aspired. Lewis Coser met Howe for the first time shortly after his own arrival in the United States, in 1941, and got to know him well after the war when they were both associated with Dwight Macdonald's quarterly journal, *Politics*. By then Howe had channeled his nervous energy into an authoritative intensity. He had become, Coser recalled, "quick, smart, impatient. Very impatient with people—he wanted everybody to be as quick as he was." Of his earlier uncertainties he retained only the unconscious habit of twisting a lock of his hair as he faced down opponents in the sharp verbal exchanges that were so regular a fixture of the Shachtmanite movement.[9]

Howe's natural abilities as a writer represented one area of political endeavor in which he quickly surpassed Shachtman (Shachtman's own gift for language was no longer apparent once he sat down at the typewriter, and he found it increasingly difficult to write in later years).[10] Writing opened doors for Howe that remained closed to Shachtman. Before being drafted Howe had been content to pour his talents into *Labor Action* and the *New International* and could not understand why others might tire of the familiar confines of the radical press. When Dwight Macdonald broke with the Workers party, Howe chastised him in *New International* for associating with people on the *Partisan Review* editorial board who refused to condemn the war. Macdonald responded with his own challenge. If his former comrades didn't like the articles currently appearing in

Partisan Review, then why didn't they submit some of their own for consideration and for once drop the pose of ideological purity?

It seems that in this as in other fields, my dear ex-comrades, you conceive your function to be that of critical by-standers purely, commentators on the struggle looking down from the lofty heights of Marxistical illumination.[11]

Howe had plenty of time to think about Macdonald's challenge as the months of Alaskan exile slowly passed. While he did not hesitate to take up his old responsibilities in the Workers party upon his return from military service (among other contributions, composing an ideologically bristling pamphlet on tenant organizing for the Workers party in 1947 entitled "Don't Pay More Rent!"), he also began to look for new outlets for his writing. Perhaps Macdonald's challenge had hit home, or perhaps Howe just had more to say by this time than could be accommodated in the pages of *New International* and *Labor Action*. He also had to consider the problem of earning a living once his GI Bill benefits ran out. He began submitting articles to *Partisan Review*, *Commentary*, and the *Nation*. And, swallowing his pride, he took a reviewing job at *Time*, a publication whose conservative bias and role in the shaping of mass culture did not endear it to radical intellectuals—though a surprising number of them would find work at one or another Luce publication over the years. As in his choice of a Party name, Howe displayed a familiar ambivalence in making his way into this new world. In the midst of a free-swinging polemical exchange with Howe in *Partisan Review* in 1954, Robert Warshow recounted with malicious irony an anecdote about Howe's early days at *Time*:

The story is told that during the years when Professor (then Mr.) Irving Howe worked as a writer for *Time*—on a part-time basis—he met one day in the corridors of the Time-Life Building an acquaintance whom he had known only in the less commercialized world. "My God," said Mr. Howe, immediately taking the offensive, "what are *you* doing here?" "Why, I'm working here," said his acquaintance. "*Full time?*" said Mr. Howe.[12]

Politics and the Retreat from Politics

Among other jobs Howe took in the years just after the war was one as a part-time editorial assistant to Dwight Macdonald. In 1944, having failed in an attempt to keep *Partisan Review* in the antiwar camp, Macdonald began publishing his own quarterly, which he initially planned to call *New Left*, but finally named *Politics*.[13]

Politics did not survive the decade. In its evolving concerns, the journal reflected both its editor's and many of its readers' gradual abandonment of radical political involvement for more private pursuits. Although the most memorable pieces in *Politics* were written by Macdonald, he drew upon the talents of a number of other writers, including the core of the future editorial board of *Dissent*. In addition to regular editorial duties, Howe contributed a column to *Politics* under the pen name "Theodore Dryden." Lewis Coser was also a frequent contributor. Other *Politics* writers who would later be associated with *Dissent* in one or another capacity included Meyer Schapiro, Paul Goodman, Frank Marquart, and C. Wright Mills. Howe, like Kristol, had been influenced by *Partisan Review*, but *Politics* was the real inspiration for *Dissent*—though it served Howe as a negative as well as a positive model.

Howe admired Macdonald's journalistic skills but not what he regarded as the theoretical pretensions of his "table-hopping mind." Even while in Macdonald's employ, Howe took whatever opportunities presented themselves to make clear his opinion of *Politics*'s limitations. In one "Dryden" column Howe praised a small English journal called *Polemic*, edited by George Orwell. The journal, he wrote:

has given to English intellectuals . . . a central and unifying discussion platform. At the moment there is nothing comparable in America; seldom before has there been less real contact among intellectuals in this country, and seldom before so little concern about establishing it.[14]

By implication, of course, *Politics* didn't count.

Howe offered a staunch defense of Shachtmanite orthodoxy in response to Macdonald's manifesto, "The Root is Man," published in *Politics* a year after the war ended. Macdonald, having rejected first the orthodox Trotskyism of the Socialist Workers party, then the unorthodox Trotskyism of the Workers party, finally discarded Marxism and the optimistic rationalist tradition of which it was a part. "Scientific progress has reached its end," Macdonald declared after Hiroshima, "and the end is turning out to be the end of man himself." Macdonald continued to regard himself as a "revolutionist," but his was to be a highly individualistic revolution. "We must reduce political action to a modest, unpretentious, personal level,"

Macdonald argued, "one that is real in the sense that it satisfies, here and now, the psychological needs and the ethical values of the particular persons taking part in it." In place of the large-scale collective action advocated, if only rarely practiced, by most radical parties, Macdonald had come to favor the formation of small groups in which

members could come to know each other as fully as possible as human beings . . . exchange ideas and discuss as fully as possible what is "on their minds" (not only the atomic bomb but also the perils of child-rearing) and in general to learn the difficult art of living with other people.

Socialists, he concluded, had to learn to "think in human, not class terms."[15]

"The Root is Man" created a favorable stir among Macdonald's pacifist readers: echoes of it could be heard in editorials and manifestos in pacifist magazines for the next decade. But the article infuriated Howe, who sent in a response dismissing Macdonald's search for some kind of absolute standard of morality to guide human affairs. Morality was determined by "class situation and class conflicts." The problem for the Left, Howe insisted, remained the same as it had been before the war, first "destroying the illusion that Stalinism or Social Democracy can bring Socialism" and then "building a revolutionary party which can." Lewis Coser also wrote in to denounce what he regarded as Macdonald's snobbish hypocrisy. Radicals who shared Macdonald's abandonment of political involvement in the name of some higher standard of morality "have no longer even the strength to live by their own gospel. They talk of human brotherhood at their literary cocktail parties." Macdonald and his followers were only playing at emulating Tolstoy: "They write like the old man of Yasnya Polyana but live like the young Count."[16]

In some ways, Howe and Coser protested too much. Deep in their hearts they no longer looked forward with any great expectation of seeing the arrival of the Socialist millennium, at least as it classically had been conceived. Coser refrained from joining any of the available radical parties after coming to the United States as a refugee. And Howe had already started a more or less unconscious process of gradual withdrawal from the movement. "I would come to meetings only occasionally," he wrote of this period in his memoirs, "I would write a piece once in a while for the paper, I would send a check."[17]

In 1951, Howe and his chief ally in the inner-party wars, Stanley

Plastrik, proposed that *Labor Action* abandon the tone of "sectarian agitation" in which its articles were written:

Let our ideas speak for themselves, with dignity and restraint and sufficient subtlety to show people that we are not merely replaying the old records; and let us consider the possibility that sometimes in a room full of loud and raucous voices, it is the man speaking quietly and earnestly who will be listened to.[18]

In essence, they were asking that *Labor Action* step in to fill the gap left by *Politics*'s demise. But by 1951 the Independent Socialist League had nothing going for it as an organization *except* the tone of millennial expectation sustained in the newspaper. To change *Labor Action* along the lines Howe and Plastrik proposed would be to acknowledge that the ISL itself had outlived whatever useful function it once might have served. Plastrik and Howe next proposed starting a quarterly journal, sponsored by the ISL but open to a variety of viewpoints on the anti-Stalinist Left. Again Shachtman wasn't interested. The ISL already had a "theoretical journal"—why should it sponsor a "little magazine" in addition? Soon after this rebuff Howe and Plastrik sent in their resignations.[19]

As Howe was leaving the world of the radical sectarian, he edged his way nervously into the world of the university intellectual. Lewis Coser had been teaching sociology at Brandeis University for several years, and at his suggestion Howe applied for a position as an English professor in 1953. To his great surprise, he was hired. Brandeis's president, Abram Sachar, was determined to build a first-rate faculty for his new institution in a hurry, and was willing to overlook the lack of conventional academic certification and the equally unconventional political pasts of people like Howe.[20]

Bernard Rosenberg, one of Howe's new colleagues, described him as walking around looking "startled" upon his arrival at Brandeis. He had reason to feel that way. Radicals, not to mention Jews, were still very much a novelty in the academic world in the 1930s when Howe had gone to college. The Communist party counted some professors among its members (most of whom would fall victim to academic witch-hunts in the 1950s), but the Trotskyist movement had few. James Burnham was one of the few exceptions in the 1930s, holding a position in the philosophy department at New York University, under the sympathetic chairmanship of Sidney Hook. Manny Geltman would recall that Burnham was regarded with some astonishment by his fellow Trotskyists.

Hook arranged it so that Burnham had the lightest possible schedule. I remember Cannon being impressed. "Imagine this. They pay a guy to be a professor, who has all the time in the world to come around and be a professional revolutionary." It always impressed Cannon, the things that capitalism would do.[21]

Shachtman had long served as Howe's model of what it meant to be a revolutionary intellectual; he lacked any comparable model for what it might mean to be an independent radical in the academic world. Burnham's example was certainly not a happy one; he had swung far to the right in the years since his split with Shachtman. Howe did not intend to go that route, nor did the prospect of becoming a "pure and simple" English professor have much appeal for him. He wanted his ideas to matter in the world outside of the academy. He hadn't left the stuffy confines of the Independent Socialist League for an equally airless sojourn in the Modern Language Association.

There was some familiar satisfaction to be had in playing mentor to a new generation of campus radicals at Brandeis, as Shachtman had to his own generation at City College in the 1930s. Michael Walzer, who enrolled at Brandeis as a freshman the year before Howe's arrival, took the first class that Howe would offer there. Howe was the first "literary/political intellectual" that Walzer had ever met, and he fell under his sway. "It was very exciting to find somebody with developed views about literature and culture and politics, and how they all fit together somehow." Walzer later remembered Howe's role during a "tempest in a teapot" over the Brandeis dress code.

A whole group of us who thought of ourselves as the Left decided that we weren't going to wear ties to the dining room anymore. Irving told us that there were really more important political issues, and sometimes you have to conform in order to live to fight another day.[22]

Battles over the Brandeis dress code couldn't hold Howe's interest for long. The challenge he faced, in its broadest sense, was one of inventing a new social role for himself, that of the independent radical intellectual. Given the bankruptcy of the old radical parties, what role was left for the radical intellectual? How best could one reach out to others who were moving into unaccustomed milieus and careers? How could a community of thinkers and activists be held together without formal organizational ties? "When intellectuals can do nothing else," Howe would write with some self-depreciation on the occasion of the twenty-fifth anniversary of the founding of *Dissent*, "they start a magazine."[23] That makes the decision to found *Dissent* sound all too easy and automatic. In the early 1950s there were no working models for such an enterprise. *Partisan Review's* radicalism had faded as soon as its editors lost faith in Trotsky's forecasts of impending revolution, and *Politics* had lived out its brief life as a personal vehicle for Macdonald's wandering interests. Paul Sweezy's *Monthly Review* was still stuck in the familiar rut of 1930's fellow-traveling. How could a new radical magazine that neither lived in expectation of the impending arrival of the revolution, nor drew sustenance from some single individual's vision and bankroll, nor cherished any illusions about the existing Soviet bloc nations, hope to survive in a time of political reaction and intellectual retreat? Howe and a few friends decided to find out if it could be done.

Since leaving the ISL, Howe had remained in contact with a network of ex-Shachtmanites, including Plastrik and Manny Geltman. Along with Coser they formed the core of the new journal. Other early members of the editorial board, like Meyer Schapiro, Erich Fromm, and Norman Mailer, primarily lent the prestige of their names to the journal. Howe and Coser did the main editorial work and much of the writing in the early years, Plastrik oversaw the bookkeeping, and Geltman took care of design, lay-out, and other aspects of production.[24]

Volume 1, Number 1 of *Dissent* appeared on a few select newsstands in early 1954, an inauspicious season if ever there had been one for the publication of a new radical journal. The editors found it easier to explain in this first issue just what it was that *Dissent* was *not* proposing to do, than what it actually hoped to accomplish. While reaffirming their commitment to socialism, the editors denied any intention of attempting to create "a political party or group":

On the contrary, [*Dissent's*] existence is based on an awareness that in America today there is no significant socialist movement and that, in all likelihood, no such movement will appear in the immediate future.[25]

What then, readers would have been entitled to ask, was there to be done?

The "Mood" of *Dissent*

By comparison with some earlier little magazines like *Partisan Review*, *Dissent*'s history was uneventful. It suffered through no momentous internal upheavals, schisms, or changes in world view. By the time *Dissent* entered the field, the little magazine had become an institution. *Dissent*'s editors had considerable experience in contending with the problems of financing, editing, and producing such journals. The editors were extremely cautious in their management of *Dissent*'s affairs. Michael Walzer, who would join the editorial board later in the decade, recalled that "the whole thing was run like a little grocery store."[26] *Dissent*'s budget, which depended on the editors' willingness to regularly tithe themselves, scarcely covered the cost of a post office box. There was never a *Dissent* office. The subscription lists were kept in one of the editor's spare bedroom closets, and the editorial meetings took place in various apartments. According to Walzer:

Ours was petty bourgeois radicalism at its best, with a very strong internal ethic of commitment, sacrifice, work. . . . Since you have so little money you have to find a printer who is politically sympathetic and willing to do the job at a slightly lower rate. To make an arrangement of that sort you have to agree he'll set your articles in type between other jobs, which means you have to get everything in much earlier. So your lead time is very long, and you have to press writers very hard.[27]

The system worked as well as it did over the years because Howe, drawing on long experience, made the journal's life the center of his own existence. "Irving was always running the show," Walzer recalled, "he was always alert to a possible contributor, a possible article." He also played a key role in keeping a disparate and potentially contentious group of radicals away from one another's throats.

His leadership was intellectual, political, but it was also diplomatic. He was the person who did the necessary stroking and calming. . . . Having lived through many splits Irving was quite determined to hold this group together. Whatever arguments we had with others, we were not going to destroy ourselves.[28]

At best, *Dissent*'s editors expected to have a modest impact on

American cultural and political life. They may not have been happy with the unassuming role political circumstances had forced upon them, but they were not going to pretend to be doing anything more than they felt was possible in a bad season for the Left. In its first years the "dissent" expressed by the new journal was undertaken for the record, for conscience' sake, and to bolster the spirits of the small number of readers who found their way to the journal.

Even such modest radicalism made *Dissent* suspect in some quarters in 1954. The journal escaped the hostile scrutiny of congressional investigating committees, but not that of the watchdogs of intellectual orthodoxy at *Commentary*. When the first issue appeared, Nathan Glazer reported to *Commentary* readers that it was dangerously muddled in its assumptions and bereft of "program." He charged *Dissent*'s editors with having grossly underestimated the severity of the challenge facing the United States and its allies. If they had had their way over the past decade, Glazer declared, "the NKVD would be comfortably established today in Rome, Paris, and London—at least." It wasn't so much what *Dissent*'s editors had published in that first issue that so incensed Glazer as what they had left out. He told of a conversation he had had with one of *Dissent*'s editors-to-be back in 1951, in which the unnamed editor refused to suggest a policy for the United States to follow to end the Korean War. To Glazer this was a sure indication of the kind of "philistine leftism" that could be expected from *Dissent* in the future.[29]

Glazer's assumption seemed to be that the first responsibility of intellectuals should be to write as if they were in charge of figuring out how to keep the Russians out of Rome, Paris, and London— to discipline their thinking so that they stayed within the mental boundaries appropriate to Army generals, State Department officials, and CIA operatives. For the editors of *Commentary* the worthiest ideas were those that armed the United States in its struggle against a malevolent foe. *Dissent*'s attitude was different. "The danger of Stalinism may require temporary expedients in the area of *power* . . . ," Howe wrote that same year in an article for *Partisan Review*, "but there is no reason . . . why it should require compromise or conformity in the area of *ideas*."[30]

C. Wright Mills had declined Howe's offer to join *Dissent*'s editorial board, less out of political disagreement than a distaste for such collective endeavors. But he swiftly came to the journal's defense in *Commentary*'s letters column. How could Glazer demand that the first issue of a new periodical provide a program capable of solving all the problems of the Cold War?

I suspect, although I cannot know, that what Mr. Glazer really objects to is the *mood* of *Dissent*, and that we are really dealing with two contrasting moods, rather than directly with ideas. In reading *Dissent*'s first issue, one feels, above all, a rejection of the prevailing mood of American liberalism, and the intention to establish an opposition mood.[31]

Mill's choice of words was apt. *Dissent*'s editors *were* suspicious of "programs": they had in the past signed on to too many comprehensive plans for the remaking of the world. "We strongly believe," the editors wrote in the second issue, "that our so-called 'looseness,' the lack of a 'program,' is one of the potential strengths of the magazine. This seems to us a moment for rethinking, reformulation, controversy and openness of ideas." As for *Dissent*'s "mood," it was probably best expressed by the Italian novelist Ignazio Silone, someone not formally associated with the journal but whose writings often appeared in its pages in the early years. Silone had charted his personal disillusionment with communism in the novels *Bread and Wine* and *Fontamara*. In an article entitled "The Choice of Comrades" that appeared in *Dissent* in 1955, Silone wrote: "Our number is an ever-swelling legion: the legion of refugees from the International." Refugees, the huddled groups one saw in newsreel shots of European displaced persons camps, were marginal men and women. They were victims. They were powerless. But they were also innocent, which was an attractive state of mind and being to those who had witnessed the great deceptions and grim massacres of the preceding two decades. *Dissent* chose to function in the early 1950s as a journal for political refugees—for some, like Coser, who had actually fled their homelands, and for others, like Howe, who had simply fled the prevailing political orthodoxies. "Keeping faith," Silone concluded in *Dissent*, was "a better rule than any abstract program or formula."[32]

Howe by this point had come around to a position he had once scorned: Dwight Macdonald's insistence that some kind of transcendent morality unbound by political ideology or expediency had to determine political behavior and loyalties. For Macdonald, a belief in the value of expressive individualism had replaced any concern for collective action. Howe still believed in the latter as much as in the former. But political commitments always needed to be tempered by the knowledge of what earlier commitments had led to. It was a question of emphasis and balance: which evils and which dangers were greatest at any given moment? In Silone's *Bread and Wine*, a Communist organizer in Mussolini's Italy disguised himself as a priest and gradually abandoned political for ethical radicalism. Howe commented in *Dissent*:

Silone has here come up against a central dilemma of all political action: the only certain way of preventing bureaucracy is to refrain from organization, but the refusal to organize with one's fellow men can only lead to acquiescence in detested power or to isolated and futile acts of martyrdom and terrorism.[33]

Silone, on balance, would probably opt for individual conscience; Howe, on balance, for political organization. Howe's intent was to keep the choice always visible.[34]

Dissent's "mood," then, was sober and introspective. "We had to turn in upon ourselves," Howe would later write, "questioning first principles (mostly our own) yet fighting hard against opponents who wanted summarily to dismiss those principles." Some critics of the journal accused it of living entirely in the past. Other than attacking *Partisan Review* and *Commentary* for not being sufficiently radical, Daniel Bell complained later in the 1950s, *Dissent* had little to offer: "It has not been able, especially in politics, to propose anything new."[35] But if *Dissent* often seemed preoccupied with the past, it was so precisely because its editors hoped to make the experience, outlook, and practical lessons gained from the radical defeats of the past available to the next generation on the Left—however far down the road the appearance of that generation may have seemed in the early days of the journal.

Salvaging Socialism

Dissent's editors generally avoided grand theory; as a group they were not inclined to that sort of exercise, and did not feel that it contributed much to understanding the Left's dilemmas. They had sat through too many arid theoretical debates in the past. "We didn't know whether we believed in the labor theory of value," Howe would recall of the early days of *Dissent*, "but we found it quite possible to live without that."[36] What they found more important to understand were the actual dynamics of living movements, particularly the causes for the Left's habitual self-deception. Was it possible to create a movement that could live securely in the present without forgetting the grander goals that formed its initial inspiration—to use Daniel Bell's terminology, a movement both *in* and *above* the world? And what about those dreams of the glorious future? Too many crimes had been committed in the here and now in the name of "tomorrows that sing." What should be the connection between immediate practical behavior and concerns and the ultimate aims of the socialist movement?

Howe and Coser grappled with these issues in an article in the second issue of *Dissent* examining the utopian tradition in socialism. Since the early nineteenth century the tendency had been for socialists, mindful of Marx and Engels's contemptuous treatment of St. Simon, Fourier, and Owen and their "castles in the air," to postpone any serious examination of how socialism would work until after the revolution. This tendency was unfortunate, because it left socialists only a blurred vision of "lifeless 'perfection' '' as the goal toward which all their efforts ultimately were supposed to lead. Socialists had to abandon the comforting notion that "History" will somehow resolve all problems once the Socialist millennium is at hand. Socialism would have its own disputes to settle, and socialists had to be prepared to devise means by which they could be resolved democratically.

Today, in an age of curdled realism, it is necessary to assert the utopian image. But this can be done meaningfully only if it is an image of social striving, tension, conflict; an image of a problem-creating and problem-solving society.[37]

Practical models of movements combining such pragmatic and utopian impulses were hard to find; the closest was the British Labour party, whose political fortunes *Dissent* editors followed with an almost proprietary interest.[38] Even if *Dissent*'s evolving political outlook was of little immediate practical importance, the editors felt that an enlightened radical intransigence had some value in its own right. The word "socialism" was a valuable property, Howe argued, given American culture's ability to absorb virtually all other ideas into its own "stew."

But if you so much as mention socialism, then you are likely to be considered dangerous (by the readers of *Life*, whose minds seldom change) or absurdly old-fashioned (by the readers of *Partisan Review*, whose minds have been nourished on a diet of novelties). And that may be a good reason . . . why those of us whose Marxism is vestigial and whose socialism is primarily a commitment to a value and a problem, should continue to regard orrselves not merely as radicals but also as socialists. If nothing else, it helps suggest that we do not wish to be accepted as members of the Establishment.[39]

Or as Harold Rosenberg, the art critic and one-time Trotskyist put it in one of his frequent contributions to *Dissent* in the 1950s: "The weapon of criticism is undoubtedly inadequate. Who on that account would choose to surrender it?"[40]

Challenge to McCarthyism

Dissent's liveliest moments in its early years came in the course of its challenge to the capitulation of American intellectuals to McCarthyism. The editors' assumptions on questions of civil liberties stemmed from a stubborn resistance to changes in political fashion—to that extent, Daniel Bell's charge that the journal lived in the past was justified. Howe was proud to count himself within the ranks of anti-Communists, but the kind of anticommunism that was coming to the fore in the postwar era held few attractions for him. He had attended the Communist party's Waldorf-Astoria peace conference in 1949 as part of the anti-Stalinist contingent. Instead of gloating over the debacle that the conference was reduced to, partially through the efforts of his friends, Howe afterward asked the uncomfortable question why "scores of intellectuals who had been politically mummified for years suddenly [sprang] to excited life" for this particular confrontation? How many of them could have been roused to similar activity on behalf of other causes, such as opposition to Jim Crow or defense of civil liberties? "Only Stalinism rouses their feelings, only Stalinism can jolt them into making an occasional political response."[41]

The American Committee for Cultural Freedom (ACCF), which counted many of the most prominent intellectuals of the time within its ranks, became one of *Dissent*'s favorite targets. The only "cultural freedom" the ACCF was prepared to defend was that threatened by the Soviet Union and its supporters, as it proved in its attacks on those who maintained that there was a crisis of civil liberties within the United States.[42] When Robert Gorham Davis, an English professor at Smith College and president of the ACCF, wrote in the *New Leader* that "those most opposed to 'informers' are often intellectuals whose profession it is to inform and be informed, and who fight for freedom of inquiry in every direction but this," Lewis Coser was quick to take exception. "Surely Mr. Davis must be aware," Coser wrote in *Dissent*, "that there is a world of difference between asking a man for information and reporting one's knowledge of a man's opinion to the police." Informers had existed throughout history but had generally been scorned by those who used them. "What distinguishes our age . . . is that the informer has now, for the first time, been extolled as a model whom others should emulate."[43]

Harold Rosenberg's "Couch Liberalism and the Guilty Past," which appeared in the Autumn 1955 *Dissent*, was the most celebrated of the journal's attacks on the intellectuals' abdication to McCarthyite assumptions. (Rosenberg was one of the few contributors *Dissent* could count on whose writing abilities compared with Dwight Macdonald's.) "Couch Liberalism" attacked Leslie Fiedler's collection of essays, *An End to Innocence* and—by implication—the journals in which Fiedler's essays originally appeared, including *Commentary, Encounter,* and *Partisan Review*. Fiedler argued that American liberals had to put aside their residual distaste for informers, like Whittaker Chambers, and their sympathy for those pursued by the House Un-American Activities Committee, like Alger Hiss, and recognize their own responsibility for having helped clear the path for Soviet subversion and aggression. Every liberal had been implicated in Alger Hiss's conviction for perjury, Fiedler reasoned, because "who that calls himself a liberal" had not "in some sense and at some time shared [Hiss's] illusions?" American liberals had to face up to the "unpalatable truth" that "buffoons and bullies" like McCarthy and Nixon, "those who *knew* really nothing about the Soviet Union at all, were right—stupidly right, if you will, accidentally right, right for the wrong reasons, but damnably right."[44]

To Fiedler's anguished question, "Who is exempt?" Rosenberg had a curt response.

I raise my right hand and reply that I never shared anything with Mr. Hiss, including automobiles or apartments; certainly not illusions, if my impression is correct that he was a typical government Communist or top-echelon fellow traveler. . . . It was Chambers who shared with Hiss, not 'all liberals'; Chambers who was never a liberal, who in his book gives no hint of having ever criticized the Communist Party in his radical days from a libertarian position and who after he broke with Communism became something quite different from a liberal.

It was "Couch Liberals" like Fiedler, Rosenberg argued, with their self-dramatizing anguish, who had done the most to suppress the memory "of the struggle that raged on the Left during the epoch of Communist influence in America." The sins of Stalinism discredited those who had apologized for them, not liberals or the Left as a whole. It was the anti-Stalinist Left that had defended cultural freedom and debunked the Soviet myth in the 1930s, not "Fiedler's bullies" of the Right. In the 1930s the men who would later make headlines as anti-Communist congressional investigators had been "more concerned with what they could sweat out of a Federal road-building contract than with the truth about the USSR."[45]

Dissent argued that McCarthyism should be understood as more than the product of one man's ambitions and demagogic skills. Democrats and Republicans had contributed to the system of political and intellectual intimidation that McCarthy symbolized. After Senator Hubert Humphrey, the rising star of Democratic liberalism, introduced the Communist Control Act (a bill that made membership in the Communist party a crime punishable by imprisonment and fines) into the Senate in 1954, Howe wrote in disgust: "American liberalism [can] never again speak, except with the most vulgar of hypocrisies, in the name of either liberty or liberalism."[46] And when McCarthy overstepped himself in the Army-McCarthy hearings and the Senate finally worked up sufficient courage to pass a motion of censure, Stanley Plastrik warned *Dissent*'s readers not to assume that McCarthyism was dead and buried. McCarthy himself might be "retreating into his cave, grunting, slobbering, bitter," but the threat to civil liberties remained acute. Just look, Plastrik insisted, at who currently occupied the office of the vice-president.

I hold with those . . . who insist that Vice President Richard Nixon may be a far greater danger to the Republic than Joe McCarthy. . . . Nixonism is McCarthyism with its nails pared and cleaned, its 5 o'clock shadow shaved off. It is McCarthyism systematized, made palatable for the respectable and decent.[47]

Mass is a Four-Letter Word

How was it possible that large numbers of Americans could regard Joe McCarthy and Richard Nixon as desirable leaders in the first place? It was a troubling question for *Dissent*'s editors in the 1950s— the more troubling because they had a pretty good idea of what the answer was and didn't like it. Not every historical inquiry lends itself to quantification, but one can chart the level of disillusionment with Marxism among American intellectuals from the 1930s through the 1950s with reasonable accuracy by keeping track of the number of times that the phrases "mass society" and "mass culture" appeared in articles in little magazines during those years. As faith in the inevitability of working-class revolution faded, once-radical intellectuals cast around for explanations for the political disappointments of the recent past.

By the end of World War II the discussion of mass culture already had more than a decade of history behind it. The debate paralleled the popular discussion of the "man in the gray flannel suit," the "organization man," and the "hidden persuaders," but took part in a much more rarefied intellectual atmosphere and, at least in the beginning, had a much more radical edge. The discussion drew upon various sources, from leftist political theorists like Theodor Adorno and other refugee intellectuals associated with the neo-Marxist "Frankfurt school," to mainstream academic sociologists and psychologists studying media influence, to conservative cultural critics like Ortega y Gasset. Articles by Dwight Macdonald and Clement Greenberg in *Partisan Review* at the end of the 1930s were especially influential in developing a political interpretation of what might otherwise have remained a purely aesthetic question.[48] At first, such articles were written from a perspective that suggested that politics could assume ascendancy over culture in times of revolutionary breakthrough: at least some hope was held out that the deadening grip of mass culture on working-class consciousness could be shattered once political illusions about Stalinism or New Dealism were dispelled. But by the end of the war the emphasis within the discussion had shifted to assert the more or less unshakable dominance of culture over politics. Macdonald had left *Partisan Review* to start *Politics* because he felt the former to be no longer sufficiently revolutionary in outlook, but his own rapidly dwindling belief in the possibility of a postwar revolution was evident in an article on mass culture he wrote in February 1944 for the first issue of his new journal.

The masses are exploited culturally as well as economically, and we must look to Popular Culture for some clue as to the kind of response we may expect to socialist ideas. The deadening and warping effect of long exposure, to movies, pulp magazines and radio can hardly be overestimated.[49]

If mass culture led only to the political quiescence of the working class it would be cause enough for concern, but the debate took on added gravity once the full horror of the consequences of Nazism was revealed at places like Auschwitz and Dachau. Barbarism rather than reason, totalitarianism rather than socialism, had benefited from the collapse of traditional folk and élite cultures. Not only did culture dominate politics, but irrational psychological impulses decisively shaped the culture of modern societies. Hitler and Stalin understood the fears, resentments, and desires of the new mass man; liberals and democratic socialists did not. Learning to understand mass culture thus seemed to many intellectuals a matter of political self-defense, even of survival: the analysis of the trivial was linked to the struggle against the monstrous.

Though Howe was a latecomer to the discussion, his first contribution retained some of the revolutionary fervor of the prewar analysis of mass culture. Like many other intellectuals, Howe believed that mass culture revealed disturbing aspects of the collective unconscious of contemporary Americans: in an article entitled "Notes on Mass Culture" appearing in *Politics* in 1948, he went so far as to portray Donald Duck as "a frustrated little monster who has something of the SS man in him." But for Howe mass culture remained the product of a particular historical moment and social system. In "class society,"

leisure time must be so organized as to bear a factitious relationship to working time: apparently different, actually the same. It must provide relief from work monotony without making the return to work too unbearable; it must provide amusement without insight and pleasure without disturbance.[50]

When the first issue of *Dissent* appeared a half-decade later, the mass culture discussion remained in full swing. The rise to political prominence in the early 1950s of yet another frustrated little monster, this time in the person of the junior senator from Wisconsin, did nothing to defuse interest in these matters. *Dissent* regularly featured in its pages the writing of critics of mass culture, most of whom offered gloomy prognoses. In *Dissent*'s second issue, contributing editor Erich Fromm described the increasing number of psychological "automatons" to be found in America, the kind of person who

never experiences anything which is really his, who experiences himself entirely as the person he thinks he is supposed to be; whose smiles have replaced laughter; whose meaningless chatter has replaced communicative speech; whose dulled despair has taken the place of genuine pain.[51]

A society of automatons offered few prospects for the socialist revival that was the long-term goal to which the journal was devoted. Fromm's despair was shared by other *Dissent* editors. Bernard Rosenberg, who edited an influential collection of essays on mass culture, complained in an article in *Dissent* that the quality of political understanding and belief of most Americans now resembled "processed cheese"; into the "mass mind" of the American public, "new attitudes are pumped overnight."[52]

If mass culture, as portrayed in *Dissent* in the 1950s, was not the cold, dark dungeon of Stalinist-style totalitarianism, it offered only the dubious advantages of being stuck between floors in a brightly lit elevator with piped-in muzak. Americans were being psychologically manipulated in ways they could not understand, their deepest anxieties deliberately exploited by politicians, propagandists, and advertisers. "We are more alike than ever" (Rosenberg wrote in 1956), "and feel a deeper sense of entrapment and loneliness."[53]

The mass society thesis was not without its critics, from both the Right and the Left. Edward Shils, a conservative sociologist at the University of Chicago, took on Macdonald, Howe, Rosenberg, and others in an article in the *Sewanee Review*, in 1957. Noting their past radical affiliations, Shils commented:

They criticize the aesthetic qualities of a society which has realized so much of what socialists once claimed was of central importance, which has, in other words, overcome poverty and long arduous labor.[54]

If *Dissent* was not as sanguine as Shils about the material triumphs of American capitalism, some of its editors and contributors did have their own reservations about the mass culture debate. As intellectuals' fears of the coming triumph of totalitarianism faded in the mid-1950s, their preoccupation with mass culture was sustained more by force of habit than force of argument. The essential case regarding mass culture had been made by the end of the 1930s, and little written on the topic since then had done anything but provide still more examples of its deleterious effects. Something more than the intrinsic merits of the discussion helped to sustain it over three decades: particularly toward the end of its run, it filled a void in the intellectual and political discourse of the era. Formerly radical intellectuals did not easily shed their adversarial stance even when they had grown reconciled to the idea of living out their lives under capitalism. They could continue to think of themselves as rebels simply by shifting their animus from Wall Street to a target further uptown. "If you couldn't stir the proletariat to action," Howe would write in a retrospective look back on the evolution of the New York Intellectuals, "you could denounce Madison Avenue in comfort."[55] As the intellectuals left Greenwich Village for the Upper West Side or the suburbs, as they collected regular paychecks from substantial if not mass institutions like universities and publishing houses, they renewed their subscriptions to the old journals in lieu of renewing their commitment to their old political ideals. In the 1930s mass culture was denounced as the opiate of the working class; by the mid-1950s the debate on mass culture had become the opiate of formerly radical intellectuals.

Henry Pachter, another left-wing German refugee who found his way to *Dissent*'s editorial board, led the counterattack in the journal's pages against the mass culturalists. "The newest fashion in mass culture," he wrote irritably in 1956, "is to scorn mass culture. Everybody does, nowadays; those who don't either are writing a book on mass culture or collect early jazz records." Harold Rosenberg admitted he was tired of reading articles by people "who can't switch to Channel 4 or roll over with a paperback without beholding hidden patterns of the soul and society of contemporary man." The way to defend high culture was to immerse oneself in it, rather than spend any more time deploring mass culture. Besides, he added, "I dislike Ortega more than I do crowds."[56]

Howe's sympathies by this point were with Pachter and Rosenberg. It wasn't so much that he disagreed with the analysis of mass culture advanced by Macdonald and the others, but he was always of a more practical turn of mind, and he found it an inconvenient doctrine. Although he refrained from lengthy comment on the issue, he did manage to get in just about the last word in a brief aside in an article otherwise devoted to celebrating the gains made by liberal Democrats in the 1958 congressional elections. It was time, Howe suggested, to stop believing the "nonsense that the American population consists merely of a mass of obedient automatons."[57]

Dissent and the Labor Movement

For some mass culture critics, like Dwight Macdonald, the labor movement provided just another illustration of the general vapidity of American life. Labor had bought in to the "American Way of Life," Macdonald argued irreverently in *Dissent*; if anyone doubted it, they should take note of the fact that the AFL-CIO was now embarked upon a program of teaching social work techniques to union bartenders. Yet another potentially "disruptive force" in mass society, he concluded, "has been neutralized."[58] Howe had come around to Macdonald's perspective on a number of issues since their polemical exchanges in *Politics*, but this was not one of them. Like another one-time Shachtmanite, the novelist Harvey Swados, Howe devoted considerable energy in the 1950s to challenging "the myth of the happy worker." In an introduction to a special issue of *Dissent* in 1959 devoted to the state of the labor movement, Howe wrote, perhaps with Macdonald in mind:

If, a few decades ago, American intellectuals often deluded themselves by contriving an image of the American worker as a potential revolutionary, today they are inclined to accept an equally false image of him as someone whose socioeconomic problems have been solved and who is joining the universal scramble for material luxuries.[59]

Dissent found a small but loyal readership for itself within the labor movement, particularly in the United Auto Workers (some educational directors of locals in the union even ordered bulk subscriptions for their members). Howe had made a name for himself in the UAW with the book he coauthored with B. J. Widick in 1949, *The UAW and Walter Reuther*.[60] The book offered Reuther the kind of "critical support" in his battle against the Communists that was the hallmark of the Shachtmanites in the late 1940s. Howe retained his UAW contacts and his interest in the labor movement after his departure from the Independent Socialist League, and in the 1950s *Dissent* was the only intellectual quarterly to pay serious attention to the labor movement and to issues pertaining to the workplace.[61]

Frank Marquart, a veteran Detroit Socialist and labor educator, proved an especially valuable contact for the journal. He was one of the original contributing editors of *Dissent* and wrote for it frequently in the 1950s. He provided a sympathetic and well-informed running account of the plight of auto workers, who he felt suffered in equal measure from the insecurity of their employment and the quality of their worklife. "In this age of 'people's capitalism' and 'social unionism,' " Marquart complained in *Dissent* in the summer of 1957, too many erstwhile liberals accepted the stereotype of the auto worker as "a contented workman who earns well over two dollars an hour plus substantial fringe benefits." It was true that the UAW had won relatively high wages for its members, but those wages were still poor compensation for the "repetitive, monotonous, physically exhausting" kind of labor they had to perform in return. It was no wonder that most workers looked elsewhere for the satisfactions denied them during their working day: "When working in his basement on some repair job, [the] auto worker finds a sense of satisfaction such as he never derives from his job in the factory assembly line." Nor were the two dollars an hour enough to keep workers out of debt, particularly given the recurrent layoffs to which the industry was prone.[62]

Unlike some radical observers, Marquart did not sentimentalize the workers. They might have been victims, but they also victimized one another. Loan sharking, gambling, and other forms of racketeering were rampant on the shop floor. In one plant, Marquart reported, "a whiskey salesman goes to work on the afternoon shift wearing an 'ammunition belt' ringed with 3-ounce plastic cups of whiskey selling for a dollar apiece. He never has trouble selling out his stock."[63] But Marquart did not blame workers for failing to display the idealism and militancy of their 1930s predecessors. The problem was that nobody was asking them to develop and display their best qualities. Auto workers were poorly served by a union leadership preoccupied with bread-and-butter issues, unconcerned with the quality of work or other broader social concerns. The generally conservative rhetoric of labor leaders, the absence of any ambitious union strategies for organizing the unorganized, and the long-term contracts signed in many industries obscured the discontent brewing on the shop floor to all but the most careful and knowledgeable observers like Marquart, Swados, and the sociologist Ely Chinoy. Here again, what may have seemed evidence of *Dissent's* preoccupation with the past was really an anticipation of an issue of future importance. It was not until the early 1970s, when sufficient media and academic interest was sparked by the combination of the Lordstown, Ohio, auto workers' strike, the publication of Studs Terkel's *Working*, and the release of an HEW report on the quality of worklife, that the existence of the "blue collar blues" was widely—if only briefly—acknowledged. And there was surely a prophetic note in one anonymous piece in *Dissent* in 1956 that declared:

People and activities are leaving the cities along with industry. Whites are fleeing to restricted suburbs, shopping centers are emanating quanta-like onto rural land two and three rings beyond urban boundaries. The concurrence of these movements suggests the possibility that displaced workers may become the unemployed inhabitants of economically gutted cities.[64]

Despite its pessimistic analysis of the current state of the labor movement, *Dissent* remained on the lookout for more hopeful signs. The editors hoped that the unions—perhaps through the infusion of the crusading spirit provided by the newly emerging civil rights movement—again could play a major role in remaking American society. The word "poverty" began to appear with increasing frequency in *Dissent* articles in the late 1950s, and the journal linked the solution to the problem of poverty with the future of the labor movement. Dan Wakefield contributed an article on the 1959 hospital workers strike for union recognition led by Local 1199 in New York City. The mostly black and Puerto Rican workers displayed "the kind of militant spirit that has rarely been seen in labor since the thirties." In one memorable incident, strikers with picket signs attempted to join a parade up Fifth Avenue alongside a class of medical students, until they were dragged off by the police. "How messy and disturbing it is," Wakefield concluded, "when the poor people spoil our parades and demand their own place in the affluent society the magazines tell them they live in."[65]

A Second and a Half Camp in Foreign Policy

The issue that first separated the future editors of *Dissent* from their more orthodox comrades in the Workers party concerned the WP's traditional "third camp" position which held that revolutionaries could not choose sides in a conflict between imperialist powers. As the Cold War mounted in intensity, Howe and Plastrik argued for "critical support" of at least some aspects of American foreign policy, particularly the Marshall Plan. It was no time to cling to militant-sounding abstractions when there was, in reality, no third camp of revolutionary socialists to intervene in Europe's political future and when American economic aid might save Western European socialists and trade unionists from suffering the fate of their Eastern bloc counterparts. But Howe and Plastrik's identification with the West stopped well short of the hard anticommunism of other New York Intellectuals as expressed in the 1950s by *Commentary* and *Partisan Review*. They had rejected the third camp position with its "plague on both your houses" attitude; Stalinism, they insisted, posed a greater threat to the values they cherished than Western capitalism. But when they said "critical support," they meant just that. Instead of taking their place among the ranks of intellectual Cold Warriors, they continued to search for what might be called a "second and a half camp" in foreign affairs. Like Dwight Macdonald, they would "choose the West," but they sought to do so on their own terms.[66]

In an early issue of *Dissent* Howe wrote on "The Problem of American Power."

The central fact is that we continue to live in a revolutionary age. . . . Everywhere except in the United States, millions of human beings, certainly the majority of those with any degree of political articulateness, live for some kind of social change. The workers of Europe are consciously anti-capitalist, the populations of Asia and South America anti-imperialist.

The most positive contribution the American government could make to the containment of communism was not to set out on military adventures but to try instead "to undercut the hold of Stalinism by a genuine appeal of radical democracy." That did not simply mean exporting the American status quo to the unwashed masses of the world. The United States could not approach other nations in the role of political "savior" and expect to reap the admiration and support of the newly converted. Rather, Americans needed to abolish the injustices that marred their own society; they had to be willing to share their material resources with the less fortunate; and, most difficult of all for a missionary-minded society, they needed to make a "profound and humble effort to grasp the outlook" of peoples different from themselves.[67]

Howe *wanted* to be able to endorse American foreign policy in good conscience—in the abstract, he saw no problem in supporting the United States against the Soviet Union—but when it came to specific instances he found himself forced again and again into opposition. He could not warm to the Cold War "triumphs" of the early Eisenhower years. When the CIA overthrew the radical Arbenz government in Guatemala in 1954, Howe wrote indignantly: "For some years now writers like Sidney Hook have been saying that a fundamental ground for objection to Communists and fascists is that they do not stick by 'the democratic ground rule,' but believe in the use of armed coups by minorities." Now it was America that was the sponsor of such acts, and Hook was silent. Howe would not be. He dismissed the rationales that liberals had used in their acquiescence to CIA covert actions in Guatemala. The argument that the Arbenz government was "on the way" to becoming a dictatorship was no justification since "the United States shows no alarm whatever over the regimes in numerous Latin American countries which are already absolute dictatorships (Nicaragua, Paraguay, etc.)." As for the argument that the failure to intervene by the CIA would have delivered Guatemala into the hands of the Soviet Union, such "crass expedience" would only corrupt "whatever remains in this world of democratic principles" and add to the appeal of Stalinism in Latin America.[68]

There was a certain amount of wishful thinking involved in *Dissent*'s search for what it chose to call a "third force" rather than a "third camp": hovering just beneath the surface in many of the journal's editorials and articles on foreign policy was the notion that the State Department might someday be led to support genuinely revolutionary movements if only they displayed a sufficiently anti-Stalinist and indigenous pedigree.[69] In Howe's writings in the 1950s there was no suggestion that American foreign policy was flawed by anything more fundamental than the stupidity and ill will of current policymakers. The "problem" of American power for Howe was a series of bad decisions independently arrived at, or at most having in common the fact that they all reflected the same bad attitudes on the part of American policymakers. Howe's critique of American foreign policy was "radical" in that it was out of step with the dominant tendency among intellectuals to acquiesce or apologize for such actions as the Guatemala coup; it was not so radical in the sense of "going to the root" by attempting to understand why all these bad decisions were constantly being made, and giving a name to the system that produced them.

The one occasion when a writer in *Dissent* decided that the State Department had actually thrown its weight behind a genuine "third force" does not, in retrospect, inspire much faith in the journal's judgment on such matters. In 1954, Joseph Buttinger had traveled to Vietnam to help resettle refugees from the new Communist zone in North Vietnam (Buttinger, an Austrian Socialist refugee, had a longstanding concern for other political refugees and was a major financial backer of the International Rescue Committee; he had also over the years given steadily, if not spectacularly, to *Dissent*).[70] Buttinger grew fascinated with Vietnam while on his mission and formed close ties with South Vietnamese leader Ngo Dinh Diem. For a number of years he functioned as a kind of freelance volunteer publicist for Diem in the United States, and in 1958 published a book on Vietnamese political history entitled *The Smaller Dragon.*[71] He returned to the subject the following year in *Dissent* in a review of William Lederer and Eugene Burdick's caustic fictional portrayal of the ineptitude of American diplomats in Asia, *The Ugly American.*[72] Lederer and Burdick were as anti-Communist as Buttinger, but felt that current American policies in Southeast Asia were doomed to fail. Buttinger dismissed the book as a reactionary tract that lent ammunition "to the enemies of foreign aid." In "Free Vietnam," he argued, United States aid policies *were* succeeding: "Vietnam . . . is the first country in Asia where the West, by replacing imperialism with policies of aid, has stopped the 'Russians' without firing a shot." Not every article appearing in *Dissent* reflected the thinking of the editors, but Howe lent his own authority to the views expressed in the review with an introduction in which he praised Buttinger's "deep concern" for the struggle of the Vietnamese to secure their freedom "from both French and Communist imperialism."[73] In 1954, Howe had warned against the dangers of military intervention in Vietnam, but he seemed oblivious to the possibility that political and economic intervention might serve as the prelude to the "long bleeding war" he had foreseen earlier.[74]

Of *Dissent's* founders, Coser maintained the most consistent skepticism about the benevolent potential of American foreign policy.

"The least a radical can do in these years of the locusts," Coser wrote in the first issue of the journal, "is to try not to be a dupe." It was no longer fashionable to use the term "imperialism" when referring to American foreign policy, but Coser still believed that both the United States and the Soviet Union deserved the label. The former might exercise its power in less murderous ways than the latter, but there was no sense in pretending that it did so with any greater respect for the rights of self-determination of weaker nations.[75] Coser also took a more radical tack than his fellow editors because he did not assume, as they seemed to, that those "third force" countries who had managed so far to remain unaligned with the competing Cold War blocs would or should have any interest in siding with the United States against the Soviet Union. In an article in 1955, Coser wrote enthusiastically about the recent Bandung Conference of African and Asian nations. Notwithstanding the prominent role played by the Chinese Communists at Bandung, he found something new and exciting at work in the gathering that could only be understood outside the framework of Cold War assumptions.

The Asian and African powers gathered in Bandung were deeply divided along political and ideological lines ... yet they were able to express a yearning which in recent years has found little official expression: the yearning to live in a peaceful world, *the yearning to be left alone.*[76]

Howe and Coser both offered radical critiques of American foreign policy in the 1950s: Howe's stemmed from his disappointment that the State Department and CIA failed to live up to the high standards of international morality he set for them; Coser's stemmed from the fact that the foreign policy establishment's actual behavior only confirmed his low estimate of its intentions and capabilities.

Early Stirrings

Dissent began its existence with an editorial statement that virtually wrote off the possibility of a rebirth of the American Left; almost immediately the journal began to take that statement back. Before its first year of publication was out, *Dissent* was lending its pages to those who were trying to spark a revival of the campus Left. George

Rawick, a member of the YSL, challenged the stereotype of the "silent generation" on campus. Without much evidence, but with considerable faith, Rawick wrote:

History has not come to a dead stop; times of crisis and confusion have been weathered before; the energies and emotions of social rebelliousness have not yet been rendered superfluous.[77]

Events in Eastern Europe persuaded *Dissent*'s editors that their earlier tendency to regard the spread of Stalinism as the "end of history" had been premature. Horst Brand, another one of the former Shachtmanites Howe brought over to *Dissent*, wrote an article in the journal's first issue celebrating the 1953 East Berlin uprising. Contrary to what theorists of totalitarianism like Hannah Arendt had predicted, twelve years of Nazism followed by seven years of Stalinism had not destroyed the tradition of working-class self-organization among German workers:

The events of June 17 have furnished . . . an object lesson to those people who have been blandly declaring that the working class was "finished," that it no longer had any resources of activity and rebellion.[78]

And when full-scale revolution broke out in Budapest in the fall of 1956, Howe responded with rapturous words of praise in *Dissent*.

Many revolutions have been defeated in our century, but can anyone remember a revolution in which the spirit of the vanquished remained so high as in Hungary today? It is unbelievable; sublime.[79]

The wheels of change were beginning to turn again, in Berlin and Budapest, and closer to home as well. Lawrence Reddick, a black historian at Alabama State College (soon to be one of the founders of the Southern Christian Leadership Conference), wrote in *Dissent* in the spring of 1956 that Montgomery, Alabama, had suddenly "become one of the world's most interesting cities." The black bus boycotters led by Martin Luther King were providing "a magnificent case study of the circumstances under which the philosophy of Thoreau and Gandhi can triumph." In the same issue Howe predicted that in "a few decades" the bus boycott would be "looked upon as a political and social innovation of a magnitude approaching the first sit-down strikes in the 1930s."[80] Just as the labor movement had contributed to reshaping American politics in the 1930s, so it was possible that the civil rights movement might have a similar impact in the years to come.

Michael Walzer played an important part in shaping *Dissent*'s response to the emerging civil rights movement. After completing his undergraduate studies at Brandeis and serving a stint as a research assistant to Howe and Coser for their history of the American Communist party, Walzer went on to graduate studies at Harvard. He became a frequent contributor to *Dissent* in the late 1950s, writing on topics ranging from the Chinese "Hundred Flowers" episode to the British "Angry Young Men," and officially joined the editorial board in 1959.[81] Walzer had had some peripheral contact with the civil rights movement as a supporter of the Montgomery bus boycott while still at Brandeis, and when the sit-in movement began in Greensboro, North Carolina, in the spring of 1960, he became involved in support efforts in Boston, helping to coordinate the picketing at Woolworth's stores. That spring Howe asked Walzer to go South to report on the sit-in movement for *Dissent*—a request that in itself was an indication both of changing times and of the importance Howe attached to the new movement. It was the first time since its founding that *Dissent* had ever dispatched a correspondent to cover a distant story. Radical analysis could now, at long last, be supplemented with radical news.

"The most remarkable thing about these students," Walzer reported of his visit to North Carolina College, in Durham, "is their self-confidence." Walzer felt that the kind of mass nonviolent civil disobedience being practiced by the Southern civil rights movements could serve as a guiding example for a revived American Left. At the very least the Southern student rebellion should help dispel the defeatist mood prevailing among American intellectuals in the 1950s. For too many years intellectuals had viewed politics through an "apocalyptic haze" in which "every spark of enthusiasm in their hearts and every utopian dream in their heads" was fearfully put aside for fear they would prepare the way for totalitarianism. The civil rights movement proved that it was possible to "step outside the realm of conventional politics" and do so *in defense* of democratic rights and values.

In the West today what we must look for in politics is the defense of standards, the protection of rights and liberties, the maintenance of life. . . . Each of them is endangered and threatened by those historical trends whose conclusions have become contemporary cliches: mass society, garrison state, totalitarianism. Against all these, the forms of resistance are appropriate. . . . When consent becomes a platitude and a myth, resistance is the proper activity of citizens.[82]

Walzer was a little vague about just what he meant by the concept of "resistance" and just how fruitfully it might be employed against, for example, "mass society." More important in his analysis was his insistence on the need to understand what was going on in the South in its own terms. "For some of the people I knew then on the Left the crucial task of intellectuals was to identify the forces that were going to make the revolution. If it wasn't going to be the working class it was going to be the blacks. I was trying to say, that's not what's happening here." Walzer insisted that something new, important, and unprecedented was taking place in the South. Far from approaching the civil rights movement in the role of instructors, radicals could learn from the example set by the civil rights movement. The black struggle in the South represented a new indigenous American radicalism, democratically organized, drawing on the creativity and spontaneity of ordinary people, dealing with issues of immediate concern and of transcendent values.[83]

From Mood to Movement

The Spring 1956 issue of *Dissent* featured an article by Lewis Coser entitled "What Shall We Do?" its title no doubt intended to be reminiscent of one of Lenin's most famous pamphlets. Coser admitted that in recent years, when approached by young radicals, *Dissent* had not had much advice to offer beyond that of "patience." That advice led some impatient readers to charge, with what Coser seemed to suggest was some justification, "that our patience is founded on our political defeats of the past few decades and that it is difficult to imitate attitudes which are the fruits of defeat." This posed a quandary for *Dissent* that Coser felt had to be confronted. Was the journal so hopelessly enmeshed in the past that when a new radical movement finally emerged it would have nothing useful to contribute?

We who prided ourselves on our secret knowledge of the workings of history, suddenly became aware of our ignorance. We have thereby gained in humility and, perhaps, humanity, but we have lost in persuasiveness.

Coser still had no program to offer socialists, but he did have some suggestions about themes that might emerge in the coming radical movements. He predicted that "one of the most significant contributions of a radical movement of the future will be to allow at least some men to fight their way to personal autonomy." The labor movement, at least in so far as its past concerns went, might not necessarily be at the center of future radical organization. "Political and social struggles of the future may revolve not so much upon the quest for adequate 'standards of living,' but rather around the fact that even though immediate material problems may be near solution, many have no control over their social lives." A strategic preoccupation with power and class was less important, at least in the short run, than finding ways to revive a radical spirit in American life, and here the civil rights movement was more likely than the labor movement to play the central role. "To struggle for the civil and human rights of an obscure Negro in Mississippi may be as meaningful a social act as the more spectacular involvements that marked an earlier period." Coser was looking forward less to the "coming struggle for power," as the phrase went in radical circles in the 1930s, than to the coming struggle for radical personal and social values. In a future American radicalism, "responsible determination of one's personal life may perhaps be linked with responsible codetermination in public life"—or, as a slogan adopted in the 1960s would put it, "the personal is political."[84]

With that same issue, *Dissent* ceased to reprint its initial editorial statement swearing off political organizations. *Dissent* editors were no longer feeling quite so isolated as in the past and were beginning to explore the possibilities for renewed political involvement. "Our main difficulty," Howe wrote in *Dissent* in the winter of 1960, "is that we are not related to a living movement about which we could steadily and with loyalty complain." But for at least a year previously *Dissent* had been sounding like a journal that did have a movement, or at least a "mood" to which it could relate.[85]

Dissent's editors, divided among themselves on the proper course to follow in national electoral politics, had refrained from endorsing a political candidate in 1956. The old inhibitions against supporting a "bourgeois" candidate were still strongly felt on the journal's editorial board, while the prospect of voting for the candidate of one or another socialist sect stirred little enthusiasm. The faintheartedness of the leading Democratic liberals in the 1950s in defending civil liberties and civil rights stirred Howe to some of his most caustic characterizations: in 1956 he suggested that the reason liberals found Adlai Stevenson attractive was "because he so neatly typifies [their] mood of somewhat weary accommodation to things as they are, with a strand of aspiration toward a new manner of elegance."[86] But in the aftermath of the 1958 elections, Howe underwent a change of heart. Whether *Dissent* readers liked it or not, he now argued, "the decisive political struggles during the next few years will occur in the Democratic party. . . . [We] would prefer, no doubt, some American version of the British labor party; but there it is: take it or leave it, a fact." Howe favored cooperating with liberals when possible, while continuing to offer a "long range socialist perspective." The general hostility to any display of radicalism that had characterized the political climate during *Dissent*'s first years no longer prevailed, and that moved Howe to propose yet another change in the journal's outlook.

Five years ago we felt beleaguered; now there is no reason to. We began by being suspicious of "programs," in the sense of prefabricated ideologies advanced by left-wing sects; we should continue to remain indifferent to these, but let us also realize that when young people today ask about our "program" *they mean something else.* They mean what we would propose for America today. . . . Our first five years were devoted to cleaning up a little [of] our own intellectual heritage; let the next five be devoted, in part, to seeing what we can say usefully about American society as it operates today.[87]

In the Spring 1963 issue of *Dissent*, Howe wrote that "as a mood, if not a movement, radicalism is beginning to revive." Where once discussion of poverty was confined to the radical press, today it was a commonplace in mainstream publications, as shown by Dwight Macdonald's long review of Michael Harrington's *The Other America* in the *New Yorker*, which attracted the attention of the general public and key figures in the Kennedy administration.[88] Even though radical expression could now find other outlets, Howe still saw a good reason to continue publishing the journal. "If, say, a *Dissent*ish article is lost to us and appears in another magazine, this may cause us a bit of journalistic chagrin . . . but such difficulties . . . ought to stimulate us to greater effort, for they are caused by an improvement in the political climate." *Dissent*'s reason to exist now was not simply to present dissenting opinions; what distinguished articles in *Dissent* from pieces like Macdonald's was that the latter was "unrelated to any concern for *rebuilding a radical political community*." There was a time in *Dissent*'s history when the only sure way to break with the sectarian tradition seemed to be to give up on radical organizations entirely; now Howe wanted to see *Dissent* play a direct role in furthering the growth of a new radical movement: "One of our essential tasks is to nurture the point of view of the democratic left as a coherent intellectual *tendency*, because we wish to exert an influence . . . as a political group or community." What distinguished *Dissent* from radical journalism of the sort that Macdonald had brought to the pages of the *New Yorker* was that *Dissent* remained Socialist in outlook rather than simply being concerned with "one or another social evil." Howe now wrote with an ambitious and optimistic tone new to the journal: "Perhaps we should venture a little into hypothetical 'program-making'—what we would say if there were a significant socialist movement in the U.S."[89]

Dissent Meets the New Left

Dissent's initial response to the New Left was one of enthusiastic praise and support. Arthur Mitzman reported to the journal's readers that "The Campus Radical in 1960," avoided the "windy appeal to theory through which in the past simon-pure revolutionists kept themselves from radical action." Mitzman found "wonderfully few 'apparatchiks' among the new radicals."[90] The general tenor of *Dissent*'s reporting on the New Left was that here at long last was a movement that could take the best that the Old Left had to offer while avoiding its mistakes. Michael Walzer reported in the Spring 1962 issue of *Dissent* on a large Washington, D.C. demonstration organized by the Student Peace Union against nuclear testing. He noted that Norman Thomas was the speaker who most impressed the young protesters at the rally. "The students have made the socialist leader a hero of their own, perhaps knowing only vaguely that he represents a continuity with the past they would do well to explore."[91]

Walzer displayed a sense of generational identification with the New Left in his writing in *Dissent* that distinguished him from the other editors: "What is most engaging about the activities of the sixties," he wrote in the introduction to a symposium on "The Young Radicals" in 1962,

is the keen sense of pleasure in our politics, the desire for personal encounter, the organizational naivete. The false sophistication and largely vicarious weariness of the fifties is gone, while the surrender of self to history or party, which so often characterized the men of the thirties, has not reappeared.[92]

When Walzer enrolled at Harvard as a graduate student in the late 1950s, he became involved in a discussion group that called itself the "New Left Club," in conscious emulation of the newly emerged British New Left. Gabriel Kolko, Stephen Thernstrom, Gordon Levin, and Norman Pollock were among other young radical graduate students involved. Walzer, who had spent the 1956 to 1957 academic year in England, had discovered *Universities and Left Review* (one of the forebears of the *New Left Review*) while there and gone to some meetings organized by the journal. The discussion circle closely followed debates in the British New Left and read theorists like Herbert Marcuse. The New Left Club was not an activist group but did influence some of the leaders of the next generation of Harvard undergraduate activists, like Todd Gitlin, who would play formative roles in activist organizations such as Students for a Democratic Society and the Harvard-based antiwar group TOCSIN.[93] So when Walzer spoke of "our politics" in 1962, he did so with some authority.

But significantly few of Walzer's acquaintances who were his own age or younger would come to share his commitment to *Dissent*. Throughout the 1960s radicals of Howe's vintage, not of Walzer's, would dominate the editorial board. For Walzer, a large part of the attraction of his initial involvement with *Dissent* was that it offered "a foot outside of graduate school" and the chance to avoid being "only an academic." But for most young intellectuals of radical persuasion coming of age in the universities in the early 1960s, academia seemed a more natural habitat than had been the case for Howe's generation or for Walzer individually. Walzer would recall

a whole group of people, many of them students of mine, who have written once for *Dissent*. They had an idea, an experience, a spin-off from their dissertation, and then never wrote again. They became focused on the academic world, "professional" in a way that I never had any inclination towards, reading the [academic] journals, writing for the journals, wanting to be on the editorial boards of the journals. That happened to a group of my contemporaries too. Academic life welcomed them. The place was wide open.[94]

When Howe had attended City College he had done so with the "certainty" of never getting an academic job. By the time Walzer was finishing graduate school at Harvard in the early 1960s, "the only question was where were you going to get tenure." New Leftists paradoxically would adopt a much more hostile political stance toward the universities than Howe ever had and yet, at the same time, feel much more at home and less ambivalent about making a career within the confines of those same universities. The transformation of the intellectual class from a marginal, adversarial role to a securely institutionalized one went on apace in the 1960s regardless of the momentary radical ascendancy on the campuses. The phenomenon of what Howe and Walzer called the "missing generation" at *Dissent* made communication between two generations of radicals all the more problematic after the initial attraction wore off.

Collision

"Perhaps I should not have gotten so emotionally entangled in disputes with the New Left," Howe later wrote, in what could not have been an easy admission. "I overreacted, becoming at times harsh and strident. I told myself that I was one of the few people who took the New Left seriously enough to keep arguing with it. Cold comfort."[95]

Howe's initial quarrel of the new decade was not with the New Left per se, but with one of its older mentors who, he feared, might lead the young movement astray. It proved an especially bitter exchange, because C. Wright Mills had been both a close friend to Howe and a valuable asset to *Dissent* in its early days. A few years after Mills's death, Howe would refer to him as "a marvelous intellectual ally, a native American radical who could speak both with indigenous accents and high sophistication."[96] A Texan, Mills was an exotic bloom among radical New York intellectual circles, and when he spoke on domestic matters his authority seemed unimpeachable. But in foreign policy and particularly in relations with the Communist world, *Dissent's* editors tended to suspect that those from outside their own milieu did not understand the issues involved, were too prone to enthusiasms and illusions, and too ready to blur important distinctions. Mills's break with *Dissent* dated from the time he began to grow preoccupied with foreign policy issues. In 1957 he returned home from a trip to the Soviet bloc, and Howe found him in a "state of manic exaltation . . . he had discovered reasons for hope in the Eastern European world, he was impressed by the industrial achievements of the Communist nations, he regarded the intransigent anti-Communism of his old friends as obsolete."[97] These were issues upon which Howe would not tolerate backsliding.

Two years later, reviewing Mills's *The Causes of World War III* for *Dissent*, Howe argued that Mills had turned the proposal for peaceful coexistence between the United States and the Soviet Union— which Howe agreed was "indispensable"—into a call for a "moral coexistence" that meant abandoning criticism of the character of the Soviet state, which Howe regarded as totally unacceptable. Differences in estimates of international affairs led Howe to question Mills's analysis of domestic questions as well. In focusing on the role of the respective American and Soviet "power elites" in the formation of foreign policy, Mills had obscured the essential difference between the two nations' political orders. For Howe the problem with America was that it was not democratic *enough*; for Mills the problem was that America wasn't democratic *at all*. Howe insisted that "there is a crucial difference between America, a democratic country that shows some signs of drifting toward authoritarianism, and Russia, which for decades has been something considerably worse."[98] Mills responded with an angry letter addressed "Dear Irving" in the next issue: "I had thought you had abandoned the foot-dragging mood of the Cold War and were trying to make a new beginning. . . . To dissent is lovely. But Irving, as regards foreign policy, from what, tell me, do you dissent?" Howe responded in kind: "Better an 'old futilitarian of the dead American Left' [a phrase Mills applied to Howe in his letter] than a surf-rider on the Wave of the Future."[99]

If Howe displayed little patience with the ideological transgressions of old friends and allies, how much tolerance could he be expected to summon up for those committed by the New Left? *Dissent's* editors had spent most of the preceding decade waiting for a new generation of radicals to appear. They imagined that their own writing would contribute to the emergence of that new generation and would help the young to avoid the mistakes of their elders. Their writings anticipated many of the political themes that would characterize the early New Left: an emphasis upon values, decentralization, and discovering the link between personal life and the larger political order. They may have written like old, wizened veterans (in Wallace Markfield's *roman à clef* of the early 1960s, *To An Early Grave*, someone very much resembling Howe makes a brief appearance as the editor of a journal called *Second Thoughts*, exuding "the air of the oldest of men, as if he had been through the Hundred Years' War, taken down Sacco and Vanzetti's last words and seen all movements turn into failure and fiasco"),[100] but they were, in fact, scarcely out of their thirties, much younger than some others destined for influence in the coming decade, like Herbert Marcuse. They could write with humility about their own experience, and self-consciously avoided the error of trying to foist a program or an organization on the new generation. On many issues they were willing to let the New Left find its own way, providing whatever avuncular advice seemed appropriate. But there was one issue on which they would not bend: their attitude toward communism. In the editors' formative political years the Russian Question loomed above all others in importance. And in a mostly mistaken reading of the temper of the early New Left—which was less infatuated with communism than bored by anticommunism—they lost the political opportunity for which they had been waiting a lifetime.

Dissent offered its first direct—though still relatively mild—challenge to the New Left in the fall of 1961, in a brief piece by Howe and Coser entitled "New Styles in Fellow-Travelling" (an excerpt from the epilogue to the paperback edition of their history of the American Communist party). Among younger radicals as well as among some older "progressives" who formerly might have been in or near the CP, Howe and Coser detected a new and disturbing "mood" that they feared might ultimately redound to the advantage of the Communists. Weary of Cold War propaganda, uninterested in ideological abstractions, and attracted to the "style, initiative and flavor" of third-world revolutionaries, the new fellow-travellers were "impatient with the claims, no matter who may make them, that the Communist movement is a major enemy of freedom." The younger generation of radicals was "singularly, even willfully, uninterested in what happened before the Second World War." New Leftists were right, Howe and Coser agreed, "in feeling the need to avoid errors of the past"; their error lay in the assumption "that to do so they should also avoid a knowledge of the past."[101]

This was, by the standards of the movements in which Howe and Coser had earned their polemical spurs, a very gentle chastisement. And yet their message, couched as it was in an attack on fellow-travelling and all the invidious connotations that phrase carried, was not one that could be expected to win a receptive hearing from its intended audience. For Howe and Coser the pattern seemed all too familiar: one started by being "soft" on the Russian Question (or, in this case, the Cuban Question) and wound up endorsing the Moscow Trials. But the pattern did not quite fit the New Left, at least not in 1961. Cuba meant something different to young radicals at the start of the 1960s than what Russia meant to their predecessors in the 1930s. In a sense, they were more *genuine* fellow-travellers than had been true a generation earlier. New Leftists looked at Cuba and saw neither a model of the good society they hoped to create at home nor a map to follow the road to power, but, instead, simply saw the confirmation of their hopes that the world could change, that the power of entrenched interests could be overthrown. The substance of the New Left's politics was not derived from attachment to Cuba or any foreign model. Eliminate the Soviet Union and the *raison d'être* of the Communist movement and the fellow-travelling radicalism of the 1930s disappeared. Eliminate Cuba and not much would have changed in the political outlook of the New Left of the early 1960s. Infatuation with Castro's revolution was thus more the ephemera than the inspiration of the new radicalism. But Howe and Coser proved incapable of distinguishing between the two. They complained of the New Left's indifference to the past history of the radical movement and then couched their complaint in terms guaranteed to make that history seem irrelevant to the New Left. They seemed genuinely surprised when they received a critical letter from a young *Dissent* reader: despite the fears expressed in "New Styles of Fellow-Travelling," Anne Parsons doubted that the "mood" of the younger generation could be expected to "throw very many into the arms of the Communist Party." Howe and Coser conceded that the title of their article was "perhaps ill-chosen." Still, Parsons should have realized that they regarded "the emergence of this new generation as among the few hopeful events in recent American political life." Hadn't *Dissent* praised the antitesting protests and the Freedom Rides? But, they insisted, when some New Leftists "display a mindless admiration for Castro's totalitarian bravado, then we believe it our duty to criticize, for we remember the somewhat similar admiration of an earlier generation of young radicals for the 'future that works' in the Soviet Union."[102] The problem was that Howe and Coser for all intents and purposes continued to argue with their 1930s contemporaries rather than with the present generation of young radicals.

Relations between *Dissent* and the New Left soon took a turn for the worse. In 1962, *Dissent*'s editors met with Tom Hayden and other leaders of the newly organized Students for a Democratic Society to exchange ideas. The meeting was a failure, although it seems to have made more of an impression on the *Dissent*ers than on the younger group. The issue once again was that of conflicting attitudes toward anticommunism. The *Dissent* editors saw it as an essential component of a genuinely democratic radicalism, while the New Leftists, though not pro-Communist, saw anticommunism as a vestige of the Cold War that they would just as soon do without. Howe saw the fatal pattern of the 1930s repeating itself and detected in Hayden "the beginnings of a commissar" with the "authoritarian poisons of this century [seeping] into the depths of his mind."[103]

Walzer retained his own ties to the New Left organizationally, and to Hayden personally, until 1968. He tried to act as a mediator between SDS and *Dissent*, soliciting articles from SDS leaders for the journal and encouraging Howe to tone down his criticisms of the New Left: "Just as Irving didn't want there to be fights within *Dissent*, I wanted somehow to extend that relationship to at least some of the people on the New Left."[104] As the Vietnam War escalated, Walzer had his own disputes with his fellow editors. Walzer's sympathies were with the segment of the antiwar movement, including SDS, that advocated immediate withdrawal of United States forces, while Howe and Plastrik sided with the less influential "Negotiations Now" camp—the latter cherishing the increasingly forlorn hope that through the rise of a "third force" of non-Communist nationalists in South Vietnam, some solution short of a complete Communist takeover could be achieved. (In the aftermath of the Tet offensive, Howe reluctantly came around to Walzer's position.)[105]

By the late 1960s, when SDS had actually begun to regard the Communist regimes in Cuba, Vietnam, and China in the "fellow-travelling" spirit that Howe and Coser had read into the early New Left, any possibility of reconciliation between the two generations on the Left represented by SDS and *Dissent* was lost. Most members of Students for a Democratic Society had never even heard of the journal; those who had knew or understood little of its history and regarded it as just another discredited mouthpiece for the liberal establishment. It was for Howe the very worst of times. "I cared too much. I was too close for detachment, too far for engagement. I grew dizzy before the sight of old mistakes renewed."[106] And yet even at the very end of the decade, as SDS splintered into warring Marxist-Leninist factions in what must have seemed sometimes a surrealistic parody of the worst ideological excesses of the Old Left, Howe still refrained from an absolute and total denunciation of the New Left. When Shachtman's young lieutenant, Tom Kahn (who joined *Dissent*'s editorial board in 1966 when the journal began a brief period of affiliation with the League for Industrial Democracy), asked Howe if he would be willing to cosponsor a conference denouncing the New Left as a threat to academic freedom, Howe declined and chose to make clear his distrust for Kahn's motives.

The desperation of the students is one I try to understand; and I share at least some of its motivations. That the tactics of the New Left segment of the students are appalling I haven't exactly been negligent in saying publicly. But I say that from premises radically different from those of [Milton] Sacks, [John] Roche and I fear, you—I say it because I am against the war, because I fear their tactics are self-defeating (I also give the students—who represent far more than the New Left—a lot of credit for getting opposition to the war going . . .).[107]

Despite the estrangement between *Dissent* and the New Left, the fortunes of the two rose and fell in tandem. With circulation steadily increasing and manuscripts pouring in, *Dissent* switched to a bimonthly publication schedule in 1966, a year after SDS' membership began to grow dramatically; the journal was forced to return to a quarterly schedule with the Winter 1972 issue, when SDS was dead and gone and the remnants of the New Left were dragging themselves through one last round of antiwar and anti-Nixon protests before (for the most part) collapsing into exhaustion and disenchantment. Michael Walzer, in a political obituary for the 1960s generation of radical activists that ran in the Spring 1972 *Dissent*, acknowledged that for all *Dissent*'s criticisms of recent years, its own political aspirations had been tied to the success of the New Left enterprise: "In the New Left fall/We suffered all." Some years later Walzer would comment:

What you need to see about *Dissent*'s reaction to the New Left is that the

New Left was something long hoped for and worked for, and when it came it came in forms that were sometimes quite wonderful, as in the early civil rights movement, and then progressively more and more difficult for us to connect with.[108]

Dissent's editors had known one great chance in their youth to create a radical movement and lost it in some significant measure through their own mistakes; now, in middle age, they saw their long-dreamed-of second chance slipping away owing to the mistakes of others of whom they were incapable of influencing. A sense of disappointment, of hurt pride, and toward the end, of ironic resignation flavored *Dissent's* attitude toward the New Left. As early as 1962, commenting on the "self-absorption" of some of the student responses to a *Dissent* symposium on the new radicalism, Lewis Coser was moved to remark ruefully that "the chickens have come home to roost." After all, it had been just six years earlier that he had called for a radical movement based on the quest for personal autonomy—now that it had arrived, he wasn't quite sure it was what he had in mind. The New Left, Howe charged in 1965, was creating a politics based upon "gestures of moral rectitude" rather than "common action." But who had spoken more eloquently for such gestures—"it's enough that . . . just one little man says NO for that formidable granite order to be in danger"—than *Dissent's* hero of the 1950s, Ignazio Silone? The New Left, according to Howe, was guilty of *"extreme, sometimes unwarranted, hostility toward liberalism."* But who had spoken more scathingly of the shortcomings of liberalism in the 1950s—"a mood of somewhat weary accommodation to things as they are, with a strand of aspiration towards . . . elegance"—than Howe himself? The New Left, Howe declared, had concluded that American society was made up of "zombies," conditioned by mass culture and bureaucracy to utter passivity, and thus "the only remaining strategy of protest is a series of dramatic raids from the social margin, akin to the guerrilla movements of Latin America." But could one turn to a better source than the pages of *Dissent* in the 1950s—"meaningless chatter . . . dulled despair . . . processed cheese"—for the raw materials needed to come to just such a political conclusion?[109]

As Murray Hausknecht wrote in *Dissent* in 1968, "there are ironies here." In the course of the 1950s, *Dissent's* editors crafted a politics of subtlety, depth, and patient commitment. If a generation of nineteen-year-old Howes and Cosers had come along at the start of the 1960s stripped of years but retaining the instincts and sensibility of their elders, then *Dissent*'s politics and those of the New Left might have been identical. *Dissent*'s editors offered ideas to the new movement—but could offer no organized political framework in which those ideas could be absorbed, tested, or modified to fit the requirements of the moment. No process of political socialization linked the experiences of the elder generation with the needs of the younger generation. In these circumstances, a "heroism of tiredness" could have but little appeal or meaning to the younger generation. They weren't tired just yet—they could not even imagine what it meant to be "tired" in the particular way that Howe and his generation were—and they found other and less complicated images of heroism more appealing. "Perhaps it is inevitable that young people come to the radical movement with the fervor of catechumens," Michael Harrington acknowledged in his introduction to an anthology of *Dissent* articles, published in 1967, "and always believe that the veterans of past struggles are tired and going soft."[110] There would come a time when a politics like that offered by *Dissent* at the start of the 1960s would have more appeal to some veterans of the New Left, but not until yet another cycle of revolutionary fervor and disillusionment had played itself out.

4

Radical Pacifism,
The Americanization
of Gandhi

Resistance to something was the law of New England nature; the boy looked out on the world with the instinct of resistance; for numberless generations his predecessors had viewed the world chiefly as a thing to be reformed, filled with evil forces to be abolished, and they saw no reason to suppose that they had wholly succeeded in the abolition; the duty was unchanged. That duty implied not only resistance to evil, but hatred of it. . . . Politics, as a practice, whatever its professions, had always been the systematic organization of hatreds.

—HENRY ADAMS
The Education of Henry Adams

The skipper and crew of the *Golden Rule*:
Captain Albert Bigelow, second from left.
(Courtesy of Honolulu Star-Bulletin)

ALBERT BIGELOW, born into a Boston patrician family of a later generation, rejected Adams's equation of politics and hatreds. In 1958 he and three other members of a pacifist group sailed a small boat named the *Golden Rule* into the Pacific Ocean. Their destination was an area of the Pacific near the Eniwetok atoll in the Marshall Islands that had been designated by the American government as an H-bomb test area. The purpose of their voyage was to force the government to choose between either halting the tests or showering them with a potentially lethal dose of nuclear fallout. "I am going," Bigelow wrote shortly before his departure, "because however mistaken, unrighteous, and unrepentant governments may seem, I still believe all men are really good at heart, and that my act will speak to them."[1]

Albert Bigelow's assumption that an act of conscience could speak to the good in men's hearts seemed somewhat out of place in America in the 1950s; *Life* magazine labeled the *Golden Rule* a "misguided yacht" and dismissed the voyage as a "quixotic sail."[2] Bigelow's assumptions would not have seemed so out of place a century earlier, certainly not in his native Massachusetts. American pacifism in its origins was largely an offshoot of evangelical Protestantism and of the moral reform crusades of the early nineteenth century. Bigelow's beliefs and actions can best be understood as emerging from that moral reform tradition. Despite his willingness to defy the government, Bigelow did not consider himself a radical. Nonetheless, his actions also had implications for the future of the American Left. In the late 1950s a few keener observers understood that there was more to the politics of the coming era than the editors of *Life* ever dreamed of. Martin Oppenheimer, a member of the Young Socialist League in Philadelphia, had been trained in a very different style of politics from the crew of the *Golden Rule*, but he intuitively grasped the significance of their voyage. As he commented in *Dissent* in the summer of 1958:

If, as they admit, their effort may bring no real change, why do it at all? . . .

127

They did it because they could do no other, because no one else did it for them, because politics failed to do it, because the hour was late and because they had to. Effectiveness had little to do with it. This was the individual act undertaken against a state and a condition which seemed omnipotent; above all this was propaganda of the deed, one's physical body thrown into a void where no other bridge seemed to exist.[3]

Conventional politics had failed; the hour was late; one was left with no choice but to throw one's body into the void. Within a few years these would become familiar themes on the Left. Going into the 1960s, pacifism enjoyed distinct advantages over the socialist tradition in its appeal to the newly radicalized young. Pacifists did not have to apologize for their movement's past history; they were not stained with complicity in the crimes of Stalinism nor burdened with a sectarian heritage that was the product of too many years of battling the Communists. All varieties of socialism seemed tired, dated, and "European" in their fixation on program and ideology; while pacifism, with its stress on "values," seemed fresh, individualistic, and in tune with both popular cultural assumptions and the anti-ideological predilections of American intellectuals since World War II. And in their reliance upon Gandhi, pacifists drew from a source of inspiration that seemed far more "American" than Marx, however revised or watered down the latter may have been by his American disciples in recent decades. The politics—or, perhaps more accurately, the spirit—of the new radical movements of the 1960s would owe much to experiments undertaken by a small group of pacifists in the late 1950s, certainly far more than they would to the more conventional political concerns of the Socialists, Communists, and Trotskyists. And yet, as Henry Adams might have predicted, the results were not quite those that the pacifists expected and hoped for.

Pacifism Before the Second World War

The First World War had shaken the pacifist movement's faith in the efficacy of both individual acts of moral witness and the elaborate systems of international law and arbitration promoted by peace groups at the end of the nineteenth and beginning of the twentieth century. It was in this moment of disillusionment that American pacifists came upon the writings and example of the Indian independence leader Mohandas Gandhi. Gandhi's teachings struck a particularly resonant chord with those Americans who shared that strain in American culture derived from New England Protestant dissent.[4]

A word often found in the writings of Gandhi was *Satyagraha*, which literally means "insistence on truth." In Gandhi's teachings *Satyagraha* is both a strategy for nonviolent direct action by a mass movement and an ethical system for the individual. By openly violating unjust laws and maintaining a strict commitment to nonviolence, the *satyagrahi* ("one who holds to the truth") attempts to persuade an oppressive authority of the futility of violence and of the desirability of reconciliation. For a small but influential segment of a generation of American Protestants brought up (at least in the Northeast) to honor the memory of the abolitionists, and living in an age of waning religious piety, Gandhi appeared as the prophet of both a revived spirituality and of revolutionary social change. The Reverend John Haynes Holmes's description of his first encounter with Gandhi could have been lifted virtually unaltered from any nineteenth-century Protestant tract describing the Christian conversion experience. Heartsick at the bloodletting and irrationality of the World War, Holmes providentially stumbled upon "a little paper-covered pamphlet, somewhat the worse for wear," containing Gandhi's writings.

Instantly I seemed to be alive—my vision clear, my mind at peace, my heart reassured. Here was the perfect answer to all my problems . . . [Gandhi] was living in the faith that I had sought. He was making it work and proving it right. He was everything I believed but hardly dared to hope. He was a dream come true.[5]

The 1930s had seen a revival in the fortunes of both the pacifist and the socialist movements, and the lines between the two were not always distinct. In the early 1930s, Norman Thomas, who had served as leader of the religious-pacifist Fellowship of Reconciliation (FOR) before rising to prominence in the Socialist party, considered the possibility that Gandhi's means might serve to attain Marx's ends. As he wrote in the FOR journal, *World Tomorrow*, in 1932:

There is an immense need . . . for men and women capable of applying the spirit and something of the technique of Gandhi to American situations. This is true now in connection with many of our strikes. [In the antiwar movement] I do not think that pacifists will achieve much until they have organized groups of young men who will not submit their consciences and their lives to the dictation of the capitalist state in the event of war. The best guarantees I know for world peace would be such [a] revolution on the part of individuals plus the opposition of war of a genuine solidarity of the workers.[6]

As the Socialists descended into a mire of factionalism and dogmatism in the later 1930s, Thomas dropped that interesting line of inquiry. Other pacifists concluded that it was time to adopt Marxist means to attain Gandhian goals. The marriage between the two did not prove easy to attain, as A. J. Muste's complicated political career would illustrate. Muste, born in the Netherlands in 1855 and brought to the United States by his parents as a child, received his divinity degree from Union Theological Seminary and was ordained a minister in the Dutch Reformed Church. In 1917 he was forced to resign his post as a minister to a Congregational church in Massachusetts because of his staunch opposition to American involvement in the First World War. As had been the case with Thomas, his religious pacifism proved a stepping-stone to more radical beliefs. After helping to organize the Lawrence, Massachusetts, textile strike of 1919, Muste served during the 1920s as the director of Brookwood Labor College, at the same time as he served as the Fellowship of Reconciliation's executive director. With the onset of the Depression he repudiated his pacifist beliefs, founded his own political party, the American Workers party, and then merged the group with the Trotskyists in 1934. The new party that was produced by this merger explicitly repudiated pacifism in its constitution, declaring "The policy of folded arms, passive resistance, 'conscientious objection,' etc. is completely futile as a means of struggle against imperialist war." Muste seemed to have turned his back completely on his old beliefs. But when the Trotskyists entered the Socialist party in 1936, Muste began to have second thoughts about his political allegiances, repelled both by the authoritarian manner in which Trotskyist leaders enforced their views on their own followers and the cynicism with which they set about taking advantage of their new and gullible Socialist party comrades. On a trip to Europe, where he met with Trotsky, Muste had a mystical experience in a medieval church in Paris and soon announced his return to the church and his earlier pacifism. (Trotsky developed a genuine admiration for Muste and uncharacteristically refrained from attacking him after his break with the movement.)[7]

Other pacifists were drawn directly into the Communist movement. Their experience was no happier than Muste's. The Communist party was bigger, better entrenched, and far more organizationally capable than any of its left-wing rivals. The American Student Union (ASU), a coalition of the Communist and Socialist student movements that soon came under the effective control of the Communists, grew to 20,000 members and attracted tens of thousands of others to participate in the antiwar strikes it sponsored each spring on the anniversary of American entry into the First World War. Many future leaders of the pacifist movement in the United States came in close contact with the Communists in the course of the 1930s. Bayard Rustin, a member of the Young Communist League from 1939 through 1941, is the best-known example. Dave Dellinger joined the American Student Union while a student at Yale and came close to joining the Party. Ralph DiGia refrained from joining the ASU while at CCNY, but took part in the antiwar strikes it sponsored and regularly read the *Daily Worker*. Jim Peck dropped out of Harvard and became an organizer for the CP-led National Maritime Union. All of them sought to combine pacifist and revolutionary sentiments and found it difficult to choose between the competing movements and philosophies of the Left. But events at the end of the decade would leave the lines between the movements far more clearly defined.[8]

The coalition of Socialist and Communist students in the ASU began to break down with the start of the Spanish Civil War, when the Communists changed their antiwar stance. In 1938, the ASU dropped the Oxford oath of refusal to serve in the armed forces from the program for its annual spring strike: the Communists in charge of the ASU could now imagine some wars in which they would want college students to fight for "king and country"—and collective security with the Soviet Union. In response, Socialists withdrew from the Popular Front organizations to form their own groups, the Keep America Out of War Committee and the Youth Committee Against War.[9]

The Nazi-Soviet Pact dealt a death blow to the Communists' effort to control the campus antiwar movement. By the spring of 1940 the American Student Union had been reduced to a hollow shell. Neither the Socialists nor the pacifist organizations were able to fill the gap left by the ASU's demise. The Socialists were still reeling from their encounter with the Trotskyists; and pacifists, like the proverbial moss-backed generals, had been preparing to fight the last war. But instead of a renewal of the bloody stalemate that prevailed on the Western Front from 1914 to 1918, the *Wehrmacht* unleashed its blitz-krieg. The solemn piety of the Oxford pledge began to seem like a luxury the world could not afford with Hitler's armies apparently poised to cross the English Channel. By the spring of 1941 most college students, like most of their parents, saw no other recourse than to support Roosevelt's efforts to aid English resistance to Hitler, even if they clung to the increasingly forlorn hope that measures short of war would suffice.[10]

Memories of the official repression and public hysteria that prevailed during the First World War fostered a quietist impulse in pacifist organizations in the closing days of peace. Richard Gregg, a Quaker whose 1934 book *The Power of Nonviolence* more than any other source helped to popularize Gandhi's teachings in America, urged pacifists in 1939 to practice "voluntary restraint" in public opposition to war. His hope was that after the war "liberty will gradually return, and . . . wise conduct by pacifists will hasten the day." The "historic peace churches"—the Mennonites, the Society of Friends, and the Society of the Brethren, along with the Fellowship of Reconciliation and other religiously oriented pacifist organizations—chose to follow the path of cooperation, or "alternative service," rather than resistance to the war. Together they established the National Service Board for Religious Objectors (NSBRO), which undertook the financing and administration of dozens of Civilian Public Service (CPS) camps, to which 12,000 officially recognized conscientious objectors were eventually assigned by the Selective Service System. An additional 6,000 pacifists, who refused any cooperation with draft registration and the CPS camps, were sent to federal prisons.[11]

Conscientious Objectors in the Second World War

Internment in the Civilian Public Service camps or in federal prison was a formative experience for a new generation of pacifist leaders, providing them with the equivalent of a postgraduate education in applied Gandhianism. Many hundreds of conscientious objectors became, in effect, full-time pacifist revolutionaries, supported for the duration of the war—in confined style, to be sure—by camp and prison authorities. Outside they would have found themselves a tiny minority committed to unpopular beliefs and unable to have any measurable effect on national policy. Inside they found themselves surrounded by political comrades, with their opponents equally close at hand. Even if they could do nothing to stop the war, small victories over the injustices of camp and prison life proved to be within their reach.

The conscientious objectors learned useful tactical lessons during the war. Numbered among their ranks in the camps and prisons were veterans of the labor struggles of the 1930s who remembered the direct action tactics that had built the CIO. They looked around for ways to apply those tactics to their own situation. In 1943, eighteen conscientious objectors at the federal prison in Danbury, Connecticut, staged the equivalent of a sit-down strike to protest against the prison policy of maintaining segregated dining facilities. They were confined to their cells for four months, but in the end emerged victorious. Similar strikes against segregation, censorship of reading material, poor food, and stringent parole policies broke out at other federal prison facilities. The resisters learned how to coordinate direct action tactics with more conventional forms of political pressure. Harlem Congressman Adam Clayton Powell lent his support to the Danbury strikers' protest against segregation. Jim Peck, one of the Danbury strikers, concluded:

We discovered that a small number of CO's—totaling not more than 30—could get national and even international publicity for pacifism by means of well-timed public demonstrations of such an unusual nature that the press could not ignore them.[12]

Other lessons were learned as well. Ralph DiGia used his two and a half years in jail to immerse himself in Gandhi's writing.

It filled a gap. Here I was against war, but in favor of revolution. Earlier my idea had been that the workers would rise up and overthrow capitalism, and there would be peace, but only after a lot of bloodshed. That's the way my father thought. But if you were for bloody revolution, when war comes, what's your basis for opposing it? You know that war is wrong but what do you substitute for it? Being in prison with the others led me to deciding that the answer was nonviolent direct action.[13]

Communism lost whatever appeal it earlier may have had for them. Pacifism itself seemed far more radical than the beliefs of the traditional parties of the Left, because it was radical in its means as well as in its ends. "The more violence," radical pacifists now argued, "the less revolution."[14]

Finally, radical pacifists learned to think systematically about the nature of the system that produced wars and the need for a new kind of movement to root out the causes of war. Tom Polk Miller, a conscientious objector who spent the war in the Waldport, Oregon, CPS camp, wrote to Dwight Macdonald's *Politics* in 1945 before he was released:

One of the benefits to CO's from their enforced wartime removal to CPS camps and prisons has been the opportunity to examine some of society's institutions without the fogginess of personal involvement. It has become clear to many men that the war economy and the pre-war economy are all of a piece. . . . Peace [can] only come with the discovery of new patterns of society.[15]

In the months after the end of the war, the conscientious objectors were gradually released from the CPS camps and prisons. Some of them went through a period of feeling at loose ends not unlike the experience of the soldiers who were being demobilized in 1945. The disciplined structure of their daily lives and the close relationships they had formed under adversity were suddenly shaken. Some almost regretted their release. There were no brass bands or ticker tape parades for them, no GI Bill providing jobless benefits or scholarships. The newly released conscientious objectors huddled together for companionship, and some began to apply the lessons they had learned in prison to the outside world.[16]

Postwar Experiments

In the years just after the war, hundreds of conscientious objectors joined utopian or, as they preferred to call them, cooperative or intentional communities. They wanted to retain the close bonds they had formed during their imprisonment; they sought to withdraw from the compromises of living and working in a militarized economy; and they hoped to create a working model of a better society. By keeping their incomes down and providing themselves with as many of their own necessities as possible, they avoided paying taxes to support the government's military programs. And if it did become necessary for some of the conscientious objectors to return to prison for resisting future wars, the communities could provide their families with a measure of security. Perhaps the best-known and most long-lasting of these postwar cooperative communities was the Macedonia community, located in the foothills of the Blue Ridge mountains in Georgia. Macedonia originally had been started by a local college teacher who settled a number of poor farmers on the land to prove the value of scientific subsistence farming and cooperative principles. The local people left during the war for better-paying jobs, and were replaced after the war by a group of conscientious objectors and their families who supported themselves with a dairy and a woodworking shop. The community was not without its problems. As one member admitted, "when a number of individualistic pacifists are gathered together, what you get may be something other than sweetness and light." But Macedonia survived its internal squabbles. A decade after the war, a half dozen intentional communities provided homes to several hundred pacifists, including Dellinger and DiGia.[17]

Just as the conscientious objectors were unwilling to return to old ways of living after their imprisonment, so, too, they proved unwilling to return to old forms of political organization. During the war radical conscientious objectors in prison and in CPS camps had grown disillusioned with the traditional pacifist organizations. The Fellowship of Reconciliation had come under particular attack. The FOR was cooperating with the government in running the CPS camps, and until late in the war A. J. Muste attempted to discourage resistance to camp and prison authorities. In 1944 eight conscientious objectors imprisoned in Lewisburg, including Dellinger, resigned from the Fellowship. In their letter of resignation they challenged Muste to join with them in a "working-class, revolutionary, socialist movement which will be true to the best emphases of religious pacifism." Muste declined their invitation. Still recovering from his own disenchantment with Trotskyism, Muste warned them that if they continued along their present line of thought they would eventually wind up espousing "revolutionary violence." But the radical conscientious objectors were still determined to go their own way.[18]

In February 1946, Dellinger, Peck, DiGia, and other veterans of prison and CPS camps (along with a few others, like Dwight Macdonald) founded the Committee for Non-Violent Revolution (CNVR). They adopted a program calling for "decentralized democratic socialism," draft resistance, the nonviolent "seizure" of basic industry by workers, and the formation of cooperative communities (with the proviso that they did not "isolate themselves from the world-wide class struggle"). This was the first time that pacifists had organized a group that actually tried to supplant the existing Marxist political parties.[19]

For pacifists as for socialists, the hopefulness of the war years soon dissipated. CNVR led a short and unspectacular life, sponsoring a few public demonstrations in support of imprisoned conscientious objectors, and in opposition to the United Nations (which they regarded as a fig leaf for American and Soviet imperialism). Pacifists, like their Marxist counterparts, were stumbling up against the old dilemma of "What is to be Done?" when they had no one to talk to but themselves. As a dissatisfied member of the Philadelphia CNVR branch described a typically disspiriting meeting of the group in 1946:

We proceeded to get down to the business at hand, the first item of which was an evaluation of the two recent CO demonstrations. . . . All agreed they were damn good demonstrations. . . . The group displayed the greatest interest in a discussion of Dwight Macdonald's recent article, "The Root is Man." Every one agreed it is a damn good article and that the world is in a helluva shape. At 9:45 some intemperate person slipped in the question about "what can we DO"? There was a momentary silence, someone mentioned cooperatives and there was a general agreement that cooperatives were very valuable. Then it was 9:50 and time for the meeting to break up.[20]

Pacifists were not immune to the impulse that would lead Macdonald and many other once radical intellectuals to eschew political involvement for more private pursuits. The CNVR *Bulletin* for September 1947 admitted that the call for nonviolent revolution had found few supporters. Making a virtue of defeat, it went on to argue that "cultural and personal areas" were really more important than the political and economic concerns that had traditionally motivated revolutionaries: "We must break away from the Marxist alternative of dealing with large numbers of people (or large institutions like trade unions) and move towards a concept of working in terms of total life pattern of a few."[21]

As the ranks of radical pacifists dwindled and memories of wartime disagreements faded, Dellinger and Muste agreed it was time to pool resources. Together with about 300 other radical pacifists they gathered in Chicago in the spring of 1948 to found a new group. To radical pacifists only two years earlier, nonviolent revolution had seemed to be looming on the horizon, as reflected in the name of the Committee for Non-Violent Revolution. But by 1948 it was clear that such hopes were misplaced, and the new organization chose the more innocuous name of Peacemakers. Peacemakers laid equal stress on the need for "inner revolution" and active resistance to militarism. The stringent requirements for membership guaranteed that it would remain tiny: members could not register for the draft or serve in the military, and were encouraged to refuse to pay taxes. There were different tendencies within the group: the "New York crowd," centered around Muste, Rustin, and Dellinger, leaned toward the resistance side of the equation; the absolutists, centered around Ernest and Marion Bromley and their community near Yellow Springs, Ohio, were more concerned with "inner revolution." Because Peacemakers ran on Quaker principles of consensus decision making, the activists and the absolutists often found themselves unable to agree on any proposals at all.[22]

The Worst of Times

Even if radical pacifists had been able to sort out their organizational differences, they would have been in for a rough time in the next decade. Twenty years separated the Versailles Peace Conference from the start of the Second World War. Less than five years separated V-J Day from the start of the Korean War, which many Americans in 1950 believed to be the opening battle of the Third World War. Pacifists had not had time to recover from the trauma of the last war and proved incapable of mounting any serious opposition to the war in Korea. Unlike the Second World War, the failure of pacifism had little to do with the popularity of the conflict. The Korean War was undeclared, unwinnable, and located in a remote area in which few Americans had felt any previous interest or claimed any personal ties. But dissatisfaction with the war did not translate into support for or even tolerance of antiwar protests. Public hysteria over communism reached an intense pitch in the months before the start of the war. Joe McCarthy embarked on his well-publicized crusade against alleged Communist infiltration of the State Department four months prior to the North Korean invasion. The Democrats were already reeling from the charges that they had allowed the Communists to conquer China, and "steal" the secret of the atomic bomb. The inability of the United States to impose its will in Korea only seemed to substantiate Republican charges that the will to resist communism abroad was being sapped by subversion at home.[23]

This was the first full-scale war the United States fought against a Communist enemy—and it was a war endorsed by many one-time pacifists, like Norman Thomas, who decided that defeating the Communist menace outweighed any other consideration. American Communists opposed the war but by this time had few political resources to make their opposition count. It took them more than a year to pull together an anemic antiwar group called the American Peace Crusade. Between the government-inflicted wound of the Smith Act and the self-inflicted wound of the "underground," the Communist party was bled dry of money and experienced organizers. The major political consequence of the Communist opposition to the Korean War and of the Party's Stockholm Peace Petition campaign (which focused on the issue of nuclear arms) was to make anyone using the word "peace" suspect as a subversive or potential traitor.[24]

Those pacifists who opposed the Korean War were thus operating on very inhospitable political terrain. The major pacifist organizations once again put their main emphasis on "service," looking after the interests of conscientious objectors and raising money for the relief of Korean refugees. Only the Peacemakers, the Catholic Workers, and the War Resisters League (which had been taken over by radical pacifists in the late 1940s) occasionally ventured out in small public protests. However much they tried to distinguish their own opposition to the war from that of the Communists', radical pacifists could not escape the taint of disloyalty. The Peacemakers' newsletter was banned from the mails for "undermining the morale of the armed forces." Every time pacifists appeared in a public forum to demonstrate they risked harassment and injury. Michael Harrington described a demonstration he participated in along with "a motley little band" in Times Square on the first anniversary of the start of the Korean War. Dellinger, representing the Peacemakers, had begun to speak when

a man came screaming through the curious crowd, yelling that we were a bunch of Commies. . . . Dellinger replied that we were pacifists, not Communists. Then, said the man, come down here so I can hit you and see if you really will turn the other cheek. Dellinger left the stand and walked over to reason with our disturbed critic. The latter planted himself carefully and punched Dellinger in the jaw, knocking him to the ground.[25]

Harrington was embarrassed by the whole episode: "I saw myself shuffling along in that pathetic little parade and I thought I looked like one of those cartoon figures with a placard announcing the end of the world." Years later Jim Peck could remember every one of the dozen or so regular participants in pacifist demonstrations in New York during the Korean War: "There were five stalwarts from the War Resisters League, including myself: and seven stalwarts from the Catholic Worker." One had to be a saint or a masochist or a little of both to keep turning out for such events.[26]

In a time when pacifists could find little else to cheer them, they took what little solace they could in talk. The minutes of a meeting of the Peacemakers executive committee in February 1952 reveal the depths of depression that engulfed the radical pacifists. After dealing with current business—the treasurer reported that the organization had $12.84 in its bank account—Muste spoke on "Non-Violence Prospects in USA." The prospects for the immediate future were less than promising.

It seems altogether likely that building a radical pacifist movement of any size will be a tougher and slower job in the U.S. than anywhere else. A non-violent revolutionary movement will probably be in the same tough spot here as the Communist Party is. . . . Here militarism has recently won a second World War and has fabulous means at its disposal. People who are well off are not likely to welcome change, and by and large the American people are incomparably well off. . . . A non-violent movement here cannot gain the advantage which comes from giving support or leadership to revolt against a foreign oppressor. It must necessarily *appear* to be unpatriotic.

Given these hurdles Muste asked if Peacemakers had any realistic expectation of growth in membership and influence, or whether it would necessarily have to concentrate on preserving a "small remnant . . . a church in the catacombs pattern?" In the general discussion afterward, Muste expressed frustration with the absolutist stance favored by many of his fellow Peacemakers, and admiration for the Communists' ability to combine revolutionary goals with reformist means. Though disagreeing with the Communist doctrine of "ends determining the means," Muste felt there was "nothing inherently wrong with certain of the methods the Communists use. Even though they have a revolutionary approach, they use the political party to spread ideas." Dellinger shared Muste's criticisms of the Peacemakers' sectarianism, citing a proposal recently made by some absolutists "to picket pacifists who don't go as far as we do on tax refusal." This was an example of "action just to satisfy revolutionary ardor." Instead of picketing their fellow pacifists, he argued that Peacemakers should break out of their self-absorption and start picketing military recruiting stations. But Muste, Dellinger, and the others were unable to agree on any common strategy. It was a tense and frustrating discussion, leading Bayard Rustin to complain shortly before the group adjourned, "This is getting us nowhere." When they reassembled a week later to continue the discussion, they found themselves no closer to agreement on solutions to their dilemma. "Today there is no place for rebels to go," Dellinger concluded. Muste's last words in the discussion, paraphrasing those of a distinctly nonpacific leader, were less than heartening: "The nonviolent revolutionist can offer no easy way—just 'blood, sweat, and tears.' "[27]

Peacemaker leaders in 1952 were chafing at the constraints placed on them by political circumstances. They did not know the way out of their dilemma. Had they all been absolutists, fanatics, true believers, the sort of political or spiritual dogmatists who took their own isolation as a sign of grace, they might not have minded their powerlessness. That was not enough for Muste, Dellinger, and some others in Peacemakers. They wanted to build a movement that could be a powerful force for changing the world, and they strained to find some way of breaking out of their isolation. But other than sheer perseverance, "blood, sweat and tears," they had nothing to offer.

The Rebirth of the Movement

Perseverance turned out to be enough, at least in the short run. By mid-decade the movement's fortunes began to revive. In the spring of 1956, a number of people who had been present at that Peacemakers executive committee meeting, including Muste, Dellinger, and Rustin, began publishing a new monthly magazine called *Liberation*. In a "Tract for the Times," in the first issue, the editors decried "the gradual falling into silence of prophetic and rebellious voices" in recent years. Both liberalism and Marxism had failed to "come to grips with war, poverty, boredom, authoritarianism and other great evils of the modern world"—liberalism because it ignored "the inequalities and injustices upon which our present social order is based," and Marxism because of its "tendency to sacrifice the present for the future," treating "human beings . . . as pawns for bringing about something better in a tomorrow that never comes." *Liberation*'s editors were committed to finding a "third way" that would avoid the mistakes of liberalism and Marxism, a nonviolent revolutionary approach representing a synthesis of "the individual ethical insights of the great religious leaders and the collective social concern of the great revolutionists."[28]

The renewed sense of optimism among radical pacifists that led to the publication of *Liberation* stemmed from changes in both the international and domestic political climate. Stalin's death in 1953, the settlement of the Korean War shortly afterward, a cordial summit meeting between American and Soviet leaders in 1955, and Khrushchev's visit to the United States in 1959, raised hopes for the possibility of "peaceful coexistence." Events in Hungary in 1956 had the paradoxical effect of reinforcing the image of Soviet brutality while undermining the image of communism as a unified and invincible totalitarian movement. The United States's restraint during the crushing of the Hungarian revolution indicated that the State Department's then current fondness for the rhetoric of "roll-back" and "liberation" was just that, and nothing more. The Cold War was not over, by any means, but with each passing year in the late 1950s it seemed less likely that hostilities between the two camps would escalate into a major war.

Americans were eager to get off the emotional war footing they had been on, more or less continuously since the start of the Second World War, and enjoy the fruits of the consumer revolution of the

1950s. With Republicans in office, the "politics of revenge" that dominated the first half of the decade lost much of its appeal. Domestic issues like the concern for economic prosperity began to reemerge, and led to a revival in liberal fortunes, as became evident in the 1958 midterm congressional elections. The Democrats, having learned the lessons of the "Who Lost China?" debate all too well, were, on the whole, no less hawkish than the Republicans; but a few dovish Democrats, like Congressman William Meyer of Vermont, were carried into office by the Democratic wave that year.[29]

American pacifists' spirits were also revived by the gains made by their British counterparts. The formation of the Campaign for Nuclear Disarmament (CND) early in 1958 attracted the sympathetic attention of American pacifists. British pacifists had begun to experiment with direct action tactics in the early 1950s, starting with small-scale civil disobedience at the Atomic Weapons Research Establishment at Aldermaston. The surprising size and spirit of the marches organized by the Campaign for Nuclear Disarmament to and from Aldermaston, beginning Easter weekend of 1958 (and memorialized in Doris Lessing's *The Four-Gated City*), helped dispel the political passivity and fatalism of the earlier 1950s on both sides of the Atlantic.[30]

More than any other factor, the rise of the Southern civil rights movement gave new inspiration to the pacifists. Without the civil rights movement it is difficult to imagine the emergence of any of the new radical movements of the 1960s. Like the CND in England, civil rights enjoyed the enormous advantage of being able to present itself as a moral rather than as a political movement, untainted by association with parties or ideologies. And from the beginning there were close links between the civil rights and pacifist movements. Radical pacifists, including many of the founders of Peacemakers, had helped establish the Congress of Racial Equality (CORE) during World War II. CORE played a pioneering role in the use of civil disobedience tactics to challenge segregation in Northern cities and on the South's interstate bus system.[31] While still a divinity student, Martin Luther King had studied Gandhi's writings, attended lectures by A. J. Muste, and read Richard Gregg's *Power of Nonviolence*. Although he had not yet fully developed his own nonviolent philosophy, when King found himself head of the Montgomery Improvement Association in 1955 as it began its boycott of the city's segregated bus system, he welcomed the support that Northern pacifist organizations were eager to provide. If pacifists had accomplished nothing else in the early 1950s, they had kept alive a body of knowledge of how movements were organized, knowledge that they would put to good use when the opportunity presented itself.[32]

Bayard Rustin was destined to play a particularly important role. Rustin had been a participant in the first postwar challenge to segregated buses, CORE's 1947 Journey of Reconciliation. He had been forced to resign from his position with the FOR in 1953, following his arrest in Los Angeles on a morals charge, and had moved on to become executive secretary of the more tolerant War Resisters League. When the Montgomery bus boycott began, he became a liaison between King's movement and the non-Communist Left in the North, having originally gone to Montgomery at the behest of an informal group of radical leaders including A. J. Muste, Norman Thomas, A. Philip Randolph, and James Farmer. Rustin and Stanley Levinson coordinated King's Northern fund-raising efforts. (Levinson, a white lawyer, had been a member of the Communist party, but had drifted away from it by the mid-1950s.) Rustin would go on to become instrumental in the initial organization of the Southern Christian Leadership Conference and remained an important informal adviser to King for many years (he would have been King's first choice for the post of SCLC executive director, were it not for fears that his homosexuality and his brief membership in the Young Communist League would compromise the organization; he had to leave Montgomery in the midst of the boycott when local reporters began to look into his background).[33]

Montgomery proved that nonviolent direct action could work in America, not just as a tactic for use by a small group of highly committed and trained activists like CORE, but as the basis around which a genuine mass movement could be created. As Gandhi and Gregg had predicted, the nonviolent movement was able to disarm its opponents and transform its supporters. The bus boycott began with modest goals of ameliorating rather than ending segregation, but as the struggle endured through month after month of official and vigilante harassment, it took on new meaning to its participants. In an article that Bayard Rustin wrote for *Liberation* in April 1956, and that was published under Martin Luther King's name, Rustin declared:

We are concerned not merely to win justice in the buses but rather to behave in a new and different way—to be nonviolent so that we may remove injustice itself, both from society and from ourselves.[34]

Dave McReynolds could hardly restrain his enthusiasm in a memorandum to Socialist party members:

WHAT IS HAPPENING IN MONTGOMERY IS NON-VIOLENT, DIRECT, MASS ACTION. WHAT WE SEE IN MONTGOMERY IS ESSENTIALLY AND FUNDAMENTALLY A REVOLUTIONARY ATTACK CARRIED ON IN THE MOST DIRECT MANNER AGAINST JIM-CROW. ALL OF US HAVE A LESSON TO LEARN, BOTH IN TECHNIQUE AND IN SPIRIT, FROM THE NEGROES OF MONTGOMERY.[35]

The Civil Defense Protests

The "technique and spirit" of the civil rights movement would find direct application in the Civil Defense protests of the early 1960s. Every spring from 1951 through 1961, residents of New York City were required to take shelter during a mock nuclear attack. When the air raid sirens sounded the initial alert, traffic stopped in its tracks, and anyone caught out on the street was required to take shelter in a subway or nearby building as a supposed measure of protection from nuclear blasts and fallout. According to state law, refusal to take shelter during the ten-minute duration of the test was a misdemeanor punishable by up to one year in prison and a $500 fine.

The 1955 drill in New York coincided with a nationwide Civil Defense exercise dubbed "Operation Alert," during which President Eisenhower and 15,000 other top federal and military officials left Washington for secret control centers from which they would supposedly carry on the business of government in the event of an actual nuclear war. Simultaneous drills were conducted in cities across the country, with the Office of Civil Defense releasing projected casualty figures for each city. It was a macabre and ludicrous exercise. In the Times Square area in New York City an estimated quarter to a half million pedestrians cleared off the streets in the three minutes that the warning sirens wailed. Bus riders were given special coupons to allow them back on the buses after the drill was over. The 17,000 fans attending an afternoon game at Yankee Stadium were not required to leave the stadium, but ground crews brought out water hoses and aimed the nozzles at the stands. Civil Defense officials estimated with imaginative precision that had New York actually suffered a nuclear attack, 695,245 schoolchildren would have been killed or wounded, while 572,277 would have escaped injury. In P.S. 6 on the Upper East Side of Manhattan, schoolchildren settled on corridor floors outside their classrooms during the test, clutching little pamphlets about civil defense. According to the *New York Times* reporter at the scene:

With shades drawn and the children ranged along the walls, teachers explained to the younger pupils that everyone, "all over the country," was "taking shelter." "OK, I take shelter too," one kindergarten boy said, covering his eyes. "They accept this readily," said Leonore Voit, a kindergarten teacher. "They're growing up in a different world."[36]

This proved too much for Dorothy Day, Muste, Dellinger, DiGia, Rustin, Peck, and twenty-two other pacifists to swallow. In the first group act of civil disobedience of the 1950s, they gathered together in the park outside of City Hall and refused to take shelter. They were all arrested, and were treated by the authorities as dangerous criminals. Day and her codefendants were denounced by the judge at their trial as "murderers" responsible for the deaths of millions of New Yorkers who might be killed in a genuine nuclear attack. One woman protester was sent by the judge to Bellevue Hospital for psychiatric observation.[37]

Undeterred, the same group reassembled the following June and were arrested again. The ritual continued for the remainder of the 1950s, with the group never growing much larger, and each year the participants sentenced to longer prison terms. But 1960, the year of the Greensboro sit-in, proved to be a different story. On 3 May 1960, the day set aside for the annual drill, an ad hoc Civil Defense Protest Committee attracted a crowd of more than 600 supporters to City Hall Park, including such notables as Dwight Macdonald and Norman Mailer. The reporter from the *Village Voice* described the crowd as "members of the Catholic Worker organization, the War Resisters League, Quakers, as well as mothers of young children, pacifists, Socialists, and a large scattering of rugged individualists." A reporter asked Mailer why he was there and he replied, "Politics is like sex: you've got to go all the way." The sirens sounded and the crowd remained in the park. A police official climbed on a bench and ordered them to disperse. When the only response was good-natured boos and laughter, he shouted, "Are you Americans?" which drew loud cheers from the crowd. Finally, he announced they were all under arrest, which led to several spirited choruses of "We Shall Not be Moved." Only twenty-six people, none of them pacifist leaders, were taken into custody by the obviously nonplussed police. Dave McReynolds proclaimed that the Civil Defense drill was dead, and the group dispersed in good humor. At the same time hundreds of college students at CCNY, Brooklyn College, Queens College, and Columbia University had stood outside on their campuses while the sirens sounded and refused to take shelter, as did many New York City high school students.[38]

Unlike earlier protests, the 1960 Civil Defense protest did not draw on people with long training in nonviolence. In the days leading up to the protest, radio station WBAI broadcast an interview with Dorothy Day, and the *Village Voice* offered extensive and sympathetic predemonstration coverage, both of which contributed to the turnout of new faces. The *Voice* cover during the week of the protest consisted solely of a Jules Feiffer cartoon strip portraying an increasingly haggard-looking character sitting in the dark and explaining why, even though it had been three days since the Civil Defense drill started, he still insisted no one should leave the shelter:

The *Law* says we *must* wait for the siren. If we leave *before* we hear the siren even if it *is* broken we're as bad as those people sitting out in the park who insist this whole business is insane.[39]

The appeal of the Civil Defense protest was similar to that of the Montgomery bus boycott, a movement that stood above questions of ideology. The Civil Defense protesters were united by the feeling that they had common sense on their side: it was the promoters of the Civil Defense drills who were the "ideologues." What conceivable point was there in descending into the subway or crouching under a school desk when anybody who read the newspapers knew that a single H-bomb would instantly incinerate everyone in New York City and a good portion of Northern New Jersey to boot? One student at New York City's High School of Music and Art was suspended by a teacher for refusing to take shelter but was completely unrepentant. As she told a *New York Post* reporter:

[The teacher] stood in the corridor and told us we were confusing the issue and that what we were doing was mixing up the other students and making the school unorganized. We said it was the only way we knew to let the kids know that hiding under a desk was not the way to avoid getting killed.[40]

Only five years earlier the act of protesting a Civil Defense drill had been deemed evidence of probable insanity. Now, Murray Kempton predicted in the *New York Post*, "We seem to be approaching a condition of sanity where within a year or so there'll be more people defying than complying with the Civil Defense drill." By 1960, the political climate had changed sufficiently so that a growing number of Americans were no longer allowing government authorities to define for them what was sane and what was insane. Individual doubts had prepared the way for collective resistance. Although this was a strictly nonideological protest, the revolution in attitudes toward authority displayed that day in May 1960 would have consequences that stretched well beyond the immediate issue of taking shelter when the sirens wailed. The Peacemakers' newsletter attributed the big turnout to the fact that "many students are now aware of and responding to an atmosphere of action resulting from the Southern sit-ins." The following year the Civil Defense Protest Committee went into action again, attracting 2,000 people to City Hall Park, of whom only 52 were arrested; in 1962, as McReynolds and Kempton had predicted, the drill was permanently canceled. Nonviolent resistance, a concept that in the early 1950s seemed to be the property of a small cult of radical fanatics, was proving in the early 1960s to be an effective means of spreading common sense.[41]

The Formation of SANE and NVAANW

Another Jules Feiffer cartoon strip of the same period told the story of the "Big Black Specks." Feiffer's characters lived under ever-darkening skies that were filled with big black specks of nuclear fallout, while confident-looking government spokesmen assured them that nuclear tests have "added no appreciable amount of radioactive fallout to the atmosphere." Unable to allay public anxieties, the government launches a public relations campaign featuring huge billboards with slogans like "Big Black Floating Specks Are Very Pretty!" and "Big Black Floating Specks are Good for You!"[42]

Radical pacifists had preached the horrors of nuclear war from every available forum since 1945, without measurable impact on public opinion. Pacifist arguments against nuclear weapons were easy to parody, as in "Better Red than Dead": for Americans to give

147

up their nuclear weapons would mean inviting conquest by the Communists. But the narrower issue of nuclear testing stood outside the framework of conventional Cold War assumptions. Linking the abstract issue of nuclear war with the direct and immediate concern for personal health prompted by nuclear fallout offered pacifists the opportunity they needed for a political breakthrough. Once people began to question government policy on nuclear testing, or so pacifists began to hope, they might become more open to reexamining broader issues of military and foreign policy.

Larry Scott, a member of Peacemakers, played a key role in sparking an antinuclear testing movement in the United States in the late 1950s. Scott, born and raised in Missouri, graduated from a Baptist seminary and then devoted himself to civil rights organizing in Kansas City. In 1948 he had gone to Philadelphia as a delegate to the Progressive party nominating convention, but he abandoned the Wallace campaign when he saw the dominant role that Communists played at the convention. "This experience with one form of political action," he later wrote, "helped to convince me of the relevance of another kind of action—Gandhian." Later that year he joined the Peacemakers and the Society of Friends. In the mid-1950s he served as the peace education director for the Chicago American Friends Service Committee (AFSC). He resigned that position in the spring of 1957, convinced, as he wrote in a letter to *Liberation*, that "Words are not enough."[43]

Scott came to New York and persuaded leaders of both radical and mainstream peace groups to consider undertaking a campaign against nuclear testing. Along with Bob Gilmore of the New York AFSC, he organized a meeting of pacifist leaders in Philadelphia in April 1957 to discuss a new pacifist agenda. Despite a personal belief in the need for Gandhian-style direct action, Scott was willing to compromise with more moderate leaders in the interests of reinvigorating the entire peace movement. He insisted that in both tactics and in demands, the movement should operate in a way that would allow the greatest possible participation by the greatest number of people.

Out of that meeting came two new organizations, as yet unnamed, both devoted to publicizing the dangers of nuclear testing. One group, with Gilmore as its principal organizer, would devote itself to a broad effort at political education; while the other, with Scott as its principal organizer, would be smaller, more radical, and oriented toward direct action. In addition, established peace groups like the

War Resisters League pledged to pay more attention to nuclear testing issues than they had in the past.[44]

Gilmore enlisted Norman Cousins, former president of United World Federalists and editor of the *Saturday Review*, and Clarence Pickett, secretary emeritus of the AFSC, to cochair a meeting in New York in June. Out of that meeting came the Provisional Committee to Stop Nuclear Tests, renamed later that year the National Committee for a Sane Nuclear Policy, or as it came to be known, SANE. On 15 November 1957, SANE went public with an advertisement in the *New York Times* that carried the headline "We are Facing a Danger Unlike Any Danger That Has Ever Existed," and that called for immediate suspension of all nuclear testing. Independent efforts by the AFSC, Women's International League for Peace and Freedom (WILPF), the World Council of Churches, and various groups of scientists who opposed nuclear testing helped lay the groundwork for SANE's effort. The *New York Times* advertisement drew a response far beyond the expectations of its sponsor, generating thousands of contributions and letters from people writing in to ask how they could join. Because of that response, SANE, initially conceived as a temporary and élite committee, transformed itself into a permanent, nationally organized membership organization. By January 1958, two months after the appearance of the first advertisement, SANE groups had been set up in fifteen cities, all of them organized by local supporters without any practical aid from SANE's national office. The first national convention was held that spring, and by the summer of 1958 SANE had grown to 130 chapters with an estimated 25,000 members.[45]

Meanwhile, Scott had gone ahead with plans for the small direct action group. In May 1957, radical pacifists formed a group called Non-Violent Action Against Nuclear Weapons (NVAANW), with Scott as its coordinator, and George Willoughby, a World War II conscientious objector, as its chairman. They also decided to organize a protest against an upcoming series of nuclear tests scheduled for that summer in Nevada. In early August NVAANW members made the long journey to Camp Mercury, a test-site about seventy miles northwest of Las Vegas. The Atomic Energy Commission (AEC), displaying a remarkably inept sense of public relations, had scheduled one of the tests for 6 August 1957, the twelfth anniversary of the bombing of Hiroshima (as it turned out, the test was postponed at the last moment for one day because of unfavorable weather conditions). On Hiroshima Day, in the first demonstration ever held at the site of a nuclear test, eleven pacifists, including Scott, Jim Peck, and Albert Bigelow, crossed through the main gate of the camp into a restricted area and were arrested. Though stories on the protest were confined to the inside pages of most newspapers, the organizers considered it a political breakthrough; the protest generally escaped being labeled Communist inspired, and the *New York Times* went so far as to note that the action "marked the unusual employment in this country of the 'civil disobedience' tactics made famous by M. K. Ghandi, the late Indian independence leader." After receiving suspended sentences for trespassing, the eleven returned to the gate of the camp and spent the night outside awaiting the explosion. It came at 5 A.M. on 7 August 1957, lighting up the sky, and providing the pacifists with a dramatic symbol of what they were opposing. "It was," Jim Peck wrote, "a nightmare come true."[46]

The Nevada Project had gone so well that NVAANW members decided to move on as soon as possible to new direct action projects. NVAANW had come into existence because pacifists like Scott and Muste had grown tired of the absolutist sectarianism of Peacemakers, which had mired the group in inactivity. The consensus within NVAANW was that it was now a time for action. Bob Pickus, an associate editor of *Liberation*, wrote that NVAANW's maiden project "demonstrated the power and appropriateness of organized, responsible civil disobedience as part of the democratic process in twentieth century America." And yet he also had a few qualms that kept him from joining the group. NVAANW members had been so entranced with the act of moral witness they were performing in the Nevada desert that they displayed little concern for practical politics. Action was better than inaction, but action that inspired others to think and act should be the real goal of radical pacifists. Pickus hoped that NVAANW would not develop the attitude that "civil disobedience *proves* devotion to peace, the rest is just talk." The problem for pacifists over the next few years, Pickus believed, was to "achieve a marriage between a concern for eternity and the politics of time—between that which compels the single soul and that which speaks to the intelligence of all."[47]

Voyage of the Golden Rule

A month after the NVAANW pacifists returned from Nevada, the United States government announced its intention to hold a series of H-bomb tests in the spring of 1958 near the Eniwetok atoll in the Marshall Islands. The news coming so soon after the Mercury protest seemed to mock the pacifists' efforts. Nevada had been remote enough for a largely New York-based group of pacifists with slender resources to contend with: what could they possibly hope to do about tests in the middle of the Pacific? But this was a moment when the pacifists' self-confidence was beginning to expand in exponential fashion. In November 1957 the NVAANW executive committee held its first discussion about a new venture in direct action, vaguely labeled in its minutes the "Pacific Project." Albert Bigelow, one of those arrested in August in Nevada, played a large role in those discussions. Without him, they could not have taken place.

Bigelow, an architect living in Cos Cob, Connecticut, was fifty years old in 1957. He did not fit the conventional stereotypes suggested by the word "pacifist." He carried himself with the poise and self-assurance provided by comfortable means, a Harvard degree, and years of wartime command of Navy destroyers in the North Atlantic and the South Pacific. His family background was patrician New England of Puritan lineage: his grandfather had been a prominent Boston banker, and his father served as the Republican chairman of the Massachusetts state legislature's Ways and Means Committee for many years. It was not the kind of background that was noted for producing radicals in the twentieth century. But there were other elements at work in Bigelow's background. When he was a child, his mother took him to Boston Common to visit the memorial to Robert Gould Shaw, a Boston patrician of an earlier generation who had achieved a martyr's death while commanding a regiment of Massachusetts free blacks in the Civil War. Although his political beliefs remained conventional for someone of his class and education throughout the period of his military service, something of the crusading spirit of Yankee abolitionism resurfaced in Bigelow. In the mid-1950s he joined the Society of Friends, met Bob Gilmore and Bayard Rustin through Quaker activities, and through them enlisted in the pacifist movement. Bigelow and his family played host for several months in 1955 to two Japanese girls who had survived the atomic blast at Hiroshima and who had come to the United States with a larger group known as the "Hiroshima maidens" to undergo plastic surgery treatment of their radiation scars. His already strong conviction about the immorality of nuclear weapons evolved into a determination to take some kind of dramatic action to oppose their further development.[48]

In November 1957, Bigelow reported to the NVAANW executive committee on certain logistical problems connected with the proposed "Pacific Project." As the minutes somewhat laconically recorded, "it was brought out that such a project might be the final choice for those directly involved and recruiting for it would be a very serious matter." The Pacific Project would be the voyage of the *Golden Rule*. It was, in all respects, a remarkably daring enterprise to be undertaken by such a small group that had, up to that point, always operated on a shoestring budget and numbered its active supporters in the dozens. In December Bigelow reported that a suitable vessel had been located in San Pedro, California, and a down payment made. Bigelow had already recruited one crew member, William Huntington, an architect, Quaker, and World War II conscientious objector, who knew his way around a sailboat and was sufficiently well-off to put up most of the money to pay for the *Golden Rule*. (The philanthropist Stewart Mott was also a major source of funds for the project, which eventually cost NVAANW $55,000.) By year's end, Bigelow and Huntington recruited the two remaining crew members necessary for the voyage, George Willoughby and a young Presbyterian named David Gale, neither of whom had previous sailing experience.[49]

Bigelow and the other crew members took their Gandhianism seriously; indeed, Bigelow described himself as a "fundamentalist Gandhian." Their best chance of actually reaching the test zone in the Pacific would be to keep quiet about their intentions until they neared Eniwetok. But remaining true to the letter of Gandhi's teachings they announced their plans in early January in a message to President Eisenhower. On 10 February 1958, the *Golden Rule* set sail from San Pedro. Seven days and 700 miles later it was forced to turn back by heavy seas and David Gale's persistent seasickness. On 25 March the ketch set out again, with Orion Sherwood, a science teacher from a Poughkeepsie, New York, Quaker school, taking Gale's place. This time the *Golden Rule* reached Honolulu, where it put in for refitting. In the meantime the Atomic Energy Commission, acting on questionable constitutional authority, had declared 390,000 square miles of open sea around the test zone "off-limits," a measure specially aimed at the crew of the *Golden Rule* and carrying a penalty of up to two years imprisonment and a $5,000 fine for violators. NVAANW attorneys would argue that the ruling amounted to a bill of attainder directed against the *Golden Rule* crew.

A complicated legal and political battle ensued. The government obtained a restraining order forbidding the *Golden Rule* to leave port. When the crew appealed, a hearing was set for 1 May 1958. The crew agreed to refrain from any new attempt to sail until after the hearing. Back in New York, NVAANW executive committee members were distressed by what they regarded as an unjustifiable compromise with illicit authority. They refused to authorize the expenditure of project funds for a prolonged legal challenge and urged the crew to use the 1 May hearing to "make it plain that they intend to obey God rather than men." A. J. Muste flew to Honolulu to bring their concerns to the crew.[50]

At the 1 May hearing, as expected, the federal judge reaffirmed the restraining order. An hour later the *Golden Rule* and its crew headed out from port, with Muste casting off the last rope from the dock. They made it two miles before being intercepted by a Coast Guard cutter and forced to return to port. The crew was arrested and, after refusing to post bond, imprisoned. At their trial on 7 May they challenged the constitutionality of the AEC ruling and proclaimed themselves governed by a higher law than government regulations. Such arguments were to no avail: they were convicted and each given suspended sentences of sixty days imprisonment.[51]

Once again, to the distress of NVAANW, the crew waited for the outcome of a legal decision. This time they appealed their conviction and the legality of the initial AEC ruling to the Circuit Court in San Francisco. NVAANW leaders were afraid of losing public and media attention while the case worked its way through the courts. Actually the delay worked to increase public interest and sympathy. The plainspoken dignity with which the crew of the *Golden Rule* defended its actions appealed to Americans, who as a nation combined a deep-seated commitment to "law and order" with an equally deep-seated suspicion of government. "They didn't make believers out of all of us," a shipwright in the San Pedro Boat Works told reporters, "but they won everyone's respect. They've got decent convictions." The obvious religious sincerity of the group, along with Bigelow's war record (reporters respectfully addressed him and referred to him in their stories as "Captain Bigelow") helped defuse the government's attempts to smear them as subversive conspirators. In early May, Atomic Energy Commission chairman Lewis Strauss went on "Face the Nation" and charged that protests against United States nuclear tests were being promoted by "a kernel of very intelligent and deliberate propaganda" and that they "run up a signal which warrants inquiry." Strauss's attack had little effect. NVAANW and other pacifist groups organized demonstrations in cities across the country, attracting large numbers of supporters who carried picket signs with slogans like "Stop the tests, not the *Golden Rule*." In San Francisco over 400 people petitioned the U. S. attorney to prosecute them along with the crew of the *Golden Rule* as supporters or contributors to the voyage; hundreds of others marched in cities across the country. Even those who had no use for the pacifists' cause were stirred by the drama of four men in a small boat confronting both the elements and the government. Shortly before the first sailing, *Newsweek* ran a long story on the *Golden Rule* in its "Religion" section, complete with a photograph of Bigelow standing in the prow of his vessel, and concluded with an admiring paragraph:

At a news conference in Los Angeles last week, a reporter asked Bigelow if he realized that he and his friends might very well be killed by a test-firing. The skipper looked up, surprised, and replied: "Why, of course."[52]

Bigelow's hometown newspaper, the *Boston Herald*, declared editorially, "There is something almost Thoreau-esque in the position of the crew of the *Golden Rule*, who would rather be right than exist in complacent, neutral silence." The Fall River, Massachusetts, *Herald News* summed up its own reaction simply in a headline, "The Seas Are Free, Those People Have a Right to Get Killed."[53]

On 24 May 1958, the crew lost its appeal in San Francisco Circuit Court and on 1 June announced its intention to sail again. In the meantime Bill Huntington, the only crew member other than Bigelow with sufficient navigational skill to command the *Golden Rule*, had returned to the United States to recruit a backup crew. He also wanted time to consider his future actions, being less convinced than the rest of the crew of the value of sailing again. Jim Peck flew to Hawaii to take his place. On 4 June, shortly before the *Golden Rule*'s announced sailing date, federal marshals arrested Bigelow on a "criminal conspiracy" charge. Coincidentally, Huntington arrived back in Honolulu that same afternoon and upon learning of Bigelow's arrest abandoned his earlier qualms about sailing. "What are we waiting for?" he asked the other crew members, and took command of the *Golden Rule*. This time the vessel made it almost six miles out before being apprehended by two Coast Guard cutters. Huntington was arrested and joined Bigelow in jail to serve their original sixty-day sentences in Honolulu city jail, where they were soon joined by the rest of the crew.[54]

The story of the *Golden Rule* might have ended there had it not been for a chance encounter in the Honolulu port. While awaiting the outcome of their appeal to the circuit court, the NVAANW crew became friendly with Earle and Barbara Reynolds, whose sailboat the *Phoenix of Hiroshima* was moored near the *Golden Rule*. Earle Reynolds was an anthropologist who had spent four years in Hiroshima working for the AEC's Atomic Bomb Casualty Commission, studying the effects of the nuclear attack on the lives and health of the children who survived the attack. A week after the second seizure of the *Golden Rule*, Reynolds, his wife, their two teenaged children, and a young Japanese friend set sail for the Marshall Islands determined to carry out the *Golden Rule*'s mission. After two and half weeks at sea they made it several miles into the test-zone before they, too, were boarded by the Coast Guard and forced to return to port.

The *Phoenix*'s voyage attracted even more favorable publicity than that of the *Golden Rule*: the image of a family, alone and beset by the possibility of a horrible death from radiation, evidently touched the public imagination and spoke to many people's fears of the effects of fallout on their own families. The July 1959 issue of the popular woman's magazine, *Redbook*, ran a long and enthusiastic article about the exploit entitled, "A Family's Voyage into Danger," and subtitled, "Why did a scientist and his family risk their lives and reputations to defy the U.S. Government and sail into the H-bomb test zone?" Reynolds and his family received thousands of letters of support and some $12,000 in contributions for their legal expenses. (Reynolds was convicted for entering the test-zone but the conviction was eventually overturned by the San Francisco Court of Appeals, which decided that the AEC regulation prohibiting entrance into the test-zone was invalid, a vindication for both Reynolds and Bigelow's crew.) The *Golden Rule* and the *Phoenix* presented a radical challenge to the government in a conservative decade but had done so in a way that made the government look like the real threat to the nation's liberties and well-being.[55]

From Moral Witness to Confrontation

"EVENTS OF THE PAST YEAR HAVE GIVEN A BASIS FOR HOPE," Larry Scott wrote in an internal NVAANW memorandum soon after the voyage of the *Golden Rule*. But he cautioned against any immediate attempt to duplicate the success the *Golden Rule* had enjoyed in its venture into civil disobedience.

Following the voice that is within oneself without sharing the concern with others is not adequate, not even when one feels that voice to be the voice of God. The beginning of spiritual maturity is the quality of humility. . . . Words of truth may be conveyed to each of us, but the complex union of separate truths which we denote as wisdom is almost always incarnated only by those who seek and share with others. This is crucial before the next step is taken.[56]

As Scott apparently feared, some NVAANW members would soon be found wanting in spiritual—and political—humility. A recurrent problem faced by the pacifist movement in the years to come was how to discipline "the voice that is within oneself," or as Bob Pickus wrote after the Nevada Project, "how to marry a concern for eternity" with practical politics. This problem was in part a legacy of the formative experiences of the present generation of pacifist leaders in the CPS camps and prison in World War II and in political isolation in the early 1950s. Those experiences had forged a strong sense of inner purpose among radical pacifists, which had helped sustain the movement through many bad years. They also had led many radical pacifists to place more value on the display of individual commitment than on the development of effective political influence. Simple, dogged perseverance had seen them through hard times, and to some in the movement it still seemed like the most reliable formula for guiding them through the more opportune era they now had entered. Like the abolitionists 100 years earlier, radical pacifists in the late 1950s had to choose between absolute moral purity and political expediency. The tension within the pacifist movement between "speaking truth to power" and acquiring some power of its own was evident in the next three direct action projects undertaken by NVAANW at Cheyenne, Wyoming; Omaha, Nebraska; and New London, Connecticut.

The Cheyenne Project did not begin as an official NVAANW venture. Ted Olson, a Baptist minister and a veteran of the Mercury

Project, and Arthur Springer, a staff worker in the New York AFSC office, decided, in the face of opposition from some NVAANW members, to launch a civil disobedience campaign against the construction of the first American intercontinental ballistic missile (ICBM) installation at Camp Warren Air Force Base near Cheyenne, Wyoming. For radical pacifists, the Cheyenne Project represented a step beyond the limited issue of nuclear testing that had been the focus of the Nevada and *Golden Rule* projects, toward the larger issue of the American government's preparations to fight a nuclear war. The Cheyenne Project also introduced the use of more confrontational tactics. In the Nevada and *Golden Rule* projects, pacifists had used civil disobedience as a means of accomplishing "moral witness," crossing into a restricted zone and submitting to arrest. When the pacifists had been arrested in Nevada they walked to the police car that took them to court. When the Coast Guard intercepted the *Golden Rule* at sea its crew voluntarily steered the vessel back to port. The Cheyenne Project was designed to go beyond such acts of witness to acts of obstruction. Olson and Springer's plan was to have project participants attempt to block construction of the base by sitting down in the road in front of trucks carrying construction materials onto the site. The only way they would get out of the way would be if they were dragged or carried off—or run over. To more "conservative" Gandhians in NVAANW like Scott and Bigelow, this use of nonviolent tactics for coercion rather than persuasion violated the spirit of Gandhi's teachings. And they feared that such confrontational tactics would detract from the greater public acceptance that pacifists had gained during the voyage of the *Golden Rule*.[57]

The Cheyenne Project realized the worst fears of its opponents within NVAANW. Project participants showed up at the base in mid-August and for a few days tried to win over base construction workers to their cause with vigils and with leaflets that asked, "How do you feel about helping to build a base for weapons that can kill millions of people? . . . No man really believes that a few quick dollars are more important than the future of the human race." Not surprisingly, they found few sympathizers among base workers or local residents, some of whom turned out to taunt and assault the pacifists. An irate woman poured a bottle of soda down the blouse of Erica Enzer, a pacifist from Chicago, and screamed at her, "If you were my daughter, do you know what I'd do? I'd kill you." On 18 August 1958, the group began direct action, waiting by the side of the road, then rushing in to sit down in front of trucks as they approached the base. Dragged off by police or truck drivers, they would wait for the next truck to appear and repeat the process. Ken Calkins, a graduate student of history at the University of Chicago, was struck by a truck on the second day of obstruction and suffered a fractured pelvis. Five of the demonstrators, including Calkins, were sentenced to 100 days imprisonment for trespassing.[58]

At the last minute NVAANW lent its reluctant endorsement to the Cheyenne Project, with the understanding that its role would be to wind up the affair and pay its bills. Larry Scott, who had been skeptical about the Cheyenne Project from the start, was sent from New York to oversee the last few weeks of the vigil. He wrote back to NVAANW headquarters that Olson, Springer, and others were "solid, rational people with deep convictions and a desire to make a moral witness as they see it." Solid and rational as they may have been, they also seemed to "care little about whether this builds a peace movement or has any political relevance or communicative value."[59]

In the aftermath of the Cheyenne Project, NVAANW renamed itself the Committee for Non-Violent Action (CNVA). The group gained one recruit from Cheyenne who would prove to have an important influence over its future direction. Brad Lyttle was thirty-one years old in 1957, a graduate of Earlham College, a Korean War conscientious objector, and Scott's successor as peace education director for the Chicago AFSC. He quit his job to participate in the Cheyenne protest, and afterward came East to work for NVAANW. That fall, Lyttle emerged as one of CNVA's most important leaders, and eventually became its national secretary. Lyttle had no sympathy for those CNVA members who had been disturbed by the nature of the Cheyenne Project. He argued in *Liberation* that fall that pacifists had to be prepared to take dramatic action, and even risk death, to get their message across. Ken Calkins's broken pelvis proved the seriousness of the pacifists' commitment to the issues they were raising.

Pacifists have long been articulate with tongue, typewriter and mimeograph. It isn't misinterpretation from which their cause suffers most; it is from not being listened to. Before non-violent obstruction was used at Cheyenne, the protest was ignored. All the releases and leaflets made little dent on public apathy. Non-violent obstruction shattered the apathy, local and national. Many of the people of Cheyenne may have been made hostile; they were also made *aware*.[60]

Lyttle's militancy appealed to some leading pacifists. Dellinger remembers his arrival in the East as a "marvelous breath of fresh air." Lyttle had drive, imagination, and enormous persuasive abilities, and he was determined to prevent the Committee from resting on the laurels of the *Golden Rule* triumph. Muste would occasionally chide Lyttle for substituting a conviction of divine guidance for more practical considerations—"None of us is God," he wrote Lyttle in 1958—but he also admired his determination, and perhaps saw in Lyttle a reflection of his own youthful militancy. In any case, Lyttle soon gained Muste's ear, and they worked closely together over the next several years. Lyttle's organizational skills and Muste's fundraising abilities insured that CNVA would tackle at least one major project a year for the next half decade.[61]

But Lyttle's energies did not always work to CNVA's benefit. According to Dellinger:

Brad was so convinced that the world was going to end in six weeks or six months unless we dropped everything and did something about it, that you weren't allowed to read a book, climb a mountain, play music, or have a family or anything else.[62]

Lyttle even regarded the growing civil rights movement, a source of inspiration to most radical pacifists, as a distraction from the all-important issue of nuclear war. As CNVA supporter Barbara Deming later summed up Lyttle's view on the matter in an article in the *Nation*: "Would it matter whether we blew up integrated or segregated?" Ted Olson, the initiator of the Cheyenne Project and initially one of Lyttle's admirers, later developed second thoughts. In 1961 he complained in a memo to CNVA members that Lyttle displayed "a strongly-held and winsomely-presented true-Church attitude" and that "Brad is really uninterested in other people's ideas."[63]

With Lyttle and Muste acting as project coordinators, the Committee returned to the fray in the summer of 1959, this time directing its energies against the construction of the Mead ICBM base near Omaha, Nebraska. Once again there was substantial opposition to the project from within the group, but the advocates of the Omaha Project won the day by arguing that their consciences would not permit them to refrain from the action. CNVA projects, Olson would complain two years later, were growing ever wilder in conception because they were no longer subjected to realistic evaluation. "The

159

argument from 'God told me so' is subtly transmuted into 'God is telling you to underwrite my conscience-led action.' In this context, free discussion is difficult to carry on."[64]

The spirit of the Omaha Action, like that of the Cheyenne Project, was deliberately confrontational. Lyttle believed that direct action should act as a "spiritual explosion," jarring bystanders loose from their conventional ideas. Project participants wrote a song called "Nebraska Missile Blues" that embodied Lyttle's philosophy:

> To make them all think about killing
> To sit in the road we'll be willing.
> If they can't kill a few
> Well, what else can they do
> But think of that monster they're building.[65]

Omaha Action combined the tactics of Nevada and Cheyenne: thirteen pacifists, including the seventy-four-year-old Muste, climbed over a fence into the base and were arrested, while two others were arrested for lying down in the road to block trucks going to the construction site. Some of the pacifists, including Lyttle and Karl Meyer (the son of Vermont Congressman William E. Meyer), violated the terms of their probation and returned to the base for a second round of civil disobedience, for which they received six-month sentences for trespassing. Omaha Action found a few local supporters, but many more turned out to heckle and sometimes physically assault the pacifists. Outside of Nebraska the pacifists' actions achieved little notice and less sympathy. Even those Americans concerned with the dangers of fallout from nuclear tests were generally uninterested in the larger issues that CNVA was now tackling. As Bigelow had warned in a letter to Muste before the project began, "Omaha doesn't speak to people 'where they are' like nuclear tests."[66]

Strains within CNVA had by now reached the breaking point. Larry Scott and George Willoughby resigned in 1959 because of their disagreements with the Cheyenne and Omaha Projects. Others would leave the following year in response to the organization's next major enterprise, the Polaris Action Project, based in New London, Connecticut.[67]

Polaris Action represented both a continuation of the tactics developed in the preceding summers and an attempt to overcome some of their limitations. Instead of a small group of pacifists descending on a remote military base and staying for only a short time to make its point, Polaris Action was CNVA's first sustained organizing project, initially proposed for three months, but actually lasting through several years of sporadic activism. In 1959, the U.S. Navy acquired its first nuclear-powered ballistic-missile-launching submarine, the *George Washington*, built in the Electric Boat shipyard at Groton, Connecticut. Three similar Polaris submarines were scheduled for launch by the end of 1960. Pacifists argued that once the submarines were in service the possibility for meaningful arms control agreements would be eliminated, because submarines could not be subjected to the same scrutiny as land-based missiles. They also feared that the missile-launching submarines would place the decision to begin a nuclear war in the hands of individual Navy commanders. CNVA opened an office in New London in June 1960, and its volunteers spent the summer distributing leaflets in New London and at the Groton shipyard, which was located on the other side of the Thames River. As they had at Cheyenne and Omaha, the pacifists urged base workers to quit their jobs and seek employment in non-military industries.[68]

In late August they began civil disobedience, once again waterborne as in the days of the *Golden Rule*. CNVA had established its own flotilla in the Thames River, including a twenty-three-foot sloop named *Satyagraha*, a rowboat named the *Henry David Thoreau*, and a nameless collection of miscellaneous small craft. At first the pacifists sailed or rowed across the river and clambered up onto the boatyard docks next to where the submarines were being built. Electric Boat officials, who had probably learned something from studying the *Golden Rule* events, had guards posted to escort the pacifists off the dock. The protesters were not arrested, and their actions were generally ignored or downplayed by the newspapers. The pacifists then escalated their tactics and began to attempt to board the submarines and to block them as they sailed down the river to open sea. Wild scenes ensued on the normally placid Thames. The navy sent out a tug to swamp the CNVA craft, and sailors on the submarines sprayed hoses at the boarding parties. In November nine pacifists were arrested as they attempted to board the *Ethan Allen*, the latest and most lethal of the Polaris submarines to be produced by Electric Boat. And, as they had hoped, their story finally appeared on the front page of the *New York Times*.[69]

The Committee for Non-Violent Action found some sympathizers in local schools and churches, and a few workers even expressed a willingness to quit their jobs if CNVA was prepared to find them other jobs. But the dominant reaction was one of extreme hostility. The local newspaper, the *New London Day*, invariably noted the number of beards and the "bushy hair" of the pacifists in its news stories, and darkly speculated on its editorial page as to the true identity of the people bankrolling the project: "What organizations and philosophies—or ideologies—they represent is anyone's guess, and the FBI's concern, no doubt." A navy officer walked in to the CNVA office and screamed at a woman volunteer, "When the first Russian soldier rapes you, I hope you remember me!" Leafleters had their leaflets torn up in front of them, and the windows in the New London CNVA office were broken repeatedly. One Groton woman wrote in to the *Day*:

How many of these pacifists have seen their fathers tortured, their wives and mothers raped and beheaded, their children torn from them and placed in cages to die of starvation like animals. . . . This is what Communists are doing every day . . . Polaris subs and other weapons are being built to defend this country from such atrocities.[70]

Some of the angriest reactions came from Electric Boat workers, who during most of the summer of 1960 were expecting to be called out on strike by their union over contract demands. They yelled "Commies" and "Go back to Cuba" at CNVA leafleters. Some CNVA members were not oblivious to their responsibility for this reaction. One of them wrote to Dave McReynolds at the end of July acknowledging that Electric Boat workers may have had good reason for hating the pacifists. The workers feared that "we will become a mass movement which will deprive them of their jobs." In approaching Electric Boat workers CNVA had almost exclusively stressed the immorality of building nuclear weapons, "never the practical, 'enlightened self-interest' angle."

The workers at the bases are asked to resign but they are not told that by living and working at Polaris they are making the town, their wives and families targets which invite attack. They are not asked how long they can work on this kind of work—someday the weapons will be out-dated and they will have to find other employment. . . . The other choice is not their resignation, but rather pressing for adequate planning so that the nation can convert slowly and effectively towards peacetime full employment.[71]

As Polaris Action proved, radical pacifism had traveled quite a political distance since the 1940s. In 1946 the Committee for Non-

Violent Revolution had canceled a planned demonstration at the atomic weapons plant at Oak Ridge, Tennessee, because CIO officials feared the effects such a demonstration might have on the workers they were trying to sign up as union members. "Despite this disagreement," Jim Peck had written at the time to the local CIO organizer, "our committee wishes you the best of luck in your campaign to organize the South." In 1960 CNVA, a lineal descendant of the Committee for Non-Violent Revolution, thought in very different terms about its own political priorities. CNVA activists had either never shared or had long since discarded the Marxist belief in the centrality of the working class to the transformation of society. As far as the pacifists were concerned, the issues in New London, as at Omaha and Cheyenne, were reduced to a question of sin and repentance: workers were accomplices to murder as long as they contributed their labor to building missile bases and submarines. Most of the pacifists came from better-educated and more prosperous backgrounds than the workers they were trying to reach, even if many of them now proudly lived lives of "voluntary poverty." They made no effort to understand why a high-paying union job was not something that workers in New London were likely to quit on the advice of high-minded middle-class strangers. They also seemed completely oblivious to the difficulties that a largely Protestant group necessarily would face in preaching salvation to a largely Catholic working class—another unfortunate legacy of the New England moral reform tradition.[72]

Polaris Action proved to be the last straw for Albert Bigelow. Shortly before the start of the project he wrote to Lyttle, describing a SANE meeting he had recently addressed in Larchmont, New York. Fifty people turned up, double what the organizers had expected, and "numbers of well-to-do, respectable matrons volunteered proudly to go to jail rather than take shelter in the next [Civil Defense] drill." A commitment to civil disobedience no longer confined pacifists to the status of political pariahs. But that made it all the more important that CNVA take no action that might discredit the idea of nonviolence. "Should we not be very careful to 'use the current while it serves' and not risk diverting it to a backwater, or ourselves grounding out in the shallows?" Lyttle was not persuaded. Shortly afterward Bigelow sent in his resignation. CNVA's recent projects, he declared in his letter of resignation, "appear only as attention-getting devices, and not the clear, deeply-concerned, considered appeal to the heart and to the head that *satyagraha* requires."[73]

163

Muste sent back a conciliatory letter. "We cannot always expect a project that is hailed so generally as *Golden Rule* came to be . . . ," Muste wrote, "because we do not always have a person with the background, the special experience, the personality and the intellectual and moral stature of this guy named Bert Bigelow." But he took issue with what he felt was Bigelow's over-literal reading of Gandhi on the prohibition of "coercive" nonviolence.

I don't recognize some kind of eternal, principled difference between climbing over a fence at a missile base and sitting in the road in front of the fence. . . . I think if the *Golden Rule* had gotten within 100 miles of the Eniwetok testing site it would have been doing the equivalent of blocking the road. Those in charge would have had the choice of maiming or killing the crew if they set off the blast on schedule, or waiting and removing the crew.[74]

Bigelow would not reconsider his resignation. And CNVA projects continued to generate internal dissent. While Peacemakers had suffered from an inability to decide to take action, CNVA suffered from its inability to decide *against* taking action. Ted Olson wrote the following summer:

Bert Bigelow and others are right when they suggest that something went out of CNVA when project decisions began to be made in the face of substantial objections on the part of members. When we lost the "substantial unanimity" principle, we lost the only place in the peace action movement in which all sorts of actionists could feel comfortable, where a nonmanipulative atmosphere made possible full mutual confidence and full open discussion. Since that time we have been drifting slowly toward becoming a sect.[75]

Bigelow and Scott wanted to preserve the spirit of 1957, when the pacifists who founded NVAANW and SANE agreed to cooperate in the campaign against nuclear testing. Muste and Lyttle felt constrained by the group's original conception and wanted CNVA to take ever bolder steps in order to guarantee its status as the cutting edge of a radical peace movement. Lyttle's looser tactical approach began to pay results with Polaris Action in 1960, and attracted some youthful recruits to the group. CNVA tactics in New London did not seem shocking to a generation newly inspired by the tactics that black students were using in their fight against segregation; if the civil rights movement had held to Bigelow's stringent ban on "coercive" tactics, there could have been no lunch counter sit-ins that spring.

But if CNVA seemed to be moving with the spirit of the times in 1960, it ultimately proved unable to gain permanent organizational influence in the emerging antiwar movement. As Olson warned the following year, the group was on its way to becoming a sect. CNVA's founding members continued to drop out, and it was unable to win the allegiance of the new generation of antiwar activists. For all of his tactical disagreements with Scott and Bigelow, Lyttle proved to be something of an orthodox Gandhian himself when it came to matters of personal discipline and morality. Gandhi had insisted that self-purification through self-denial was a crucial part of preparations for a campaign of *Satyagraha*. On subsequent projects, like the 1960 to 1961 San Francisco to Moscow Walk for Peace and the 1963 Quebec-Washington-Guantanamo Walk, Lyttle was enraged when younger participants engaged in sexual relations, or smoked marijuana, or in other ways interfered with the purity of their act of moral witness. The Committee for Non-Violent Action remained a kind of cadre organization, consisting of a highly trained, highly disciplined, self-sacrificing élite—an élite increasingly cut off from the mass movements of the 1960s. Rather than the cutting edge, Lyttle's fervor was converting CNVA into the laughingstock of the pacifist movement. During the Quebec-Washington-Guantanamo Peace Walk, FOR's *Fellowship* magazine ran a poem entitled "To a Militant Pacifist" and it was obvious who the poet had in mind:

> Put down your fists and let's be friends
> Take peaceful means to peaceful ends
> I'm inclined to believe in what you say
> Stop beating my head with that olive spray.

In the later 1960s CNVA's existence increasingly centered on its Polaris Action Farm located near Voluntown, Connecticut. The move to the farm in some ways represented a return to the communal impulse of late 1940s pacifism, but it came at a moment when the rest of the peace movement was reaching unprecedented levels of public influence and involvement. Deeply in debt, and increasingly irrelevant, the Committee for Non-Violent Action finally merged with the War Resisters League in 1968.[76]

The Limits of Pacifist Influence in the 1960s

As the war in Vietnam became ever more unpopular, some individual pacifists who had performed lonely acts of moral witness against the Korean War or nuclear testing in groups of ten or a dozen suddenly found themselves in the leadership of political coalitions that were capable of bringing hundreds of thousands of antiwar protesters into the streets. Pacifist leaders enjoyed a popularity among young radicals that far exceeded that of any of the surviving veterans of the Old Left. Writing in the *Nation* shortly after the first large anti-Vietnam demonstration in Washington in 1965, Jack Newfield commented, "The few older figures whom the new generation seems to respect come out of the radical pacifist tradition—men like Paul Goodman and the 80 year old A. J. Muste." Yet the respect paid to Muste had more to do with the example set by his personal integrity and political commitment than his beliefs. Pacifist ideas were only marginally more influential than they had been a decade earlier. Most of those who marched in huge antiwar demonstrations, if they thought about the question at all, would have counted themselves opponents of that particular war rather than of wars in general. Only a tiny minority of protesters understood the principles of nonviolent resistance. Most simply wanted the war to end as soon as possible and accepted the leadership of pacifists and other radicals without concerning themselves with the political beliefs of those leaders.[77]

By the late 1960s, there were other voices being heard in the antiwar movement, particularly on campus, where the political tone was often set by members of Students for a Democratic Society (SDS). SDS' slogans had shifted from "End the War" in 1965, to "Bring the War Home" by 1969. In the summer of 1969, Bill Ayers, a leader of the Weatherman faction of SDS, made an extraordinary speech to a gathering of Weatherman cadre. He acknowledged criticisms that Weatherman's plans for four days of violent demonstrations in Chicago, graphically billed as the "Days of Rage," had received from others on the Left. But Ayers had no problem in dismissing such criticism.

There's a lot of skepticism in some places about whether this action can come off, and that skepticism comes out of one thing, and that is that people have been listening to so-called "Movement people," and these "Movement people" have been telling them that it won't work . . . that it's going to hurt people . . . that we have to build a united front, or some other bull-shit . . . it's all these old people who came into the Movement at a time when pacifism was important, at a time when there was a total conscious-ness of defeat, when the only reasons that we were in it were moral reasons, when there was no strategy for victory.[78]

Ayers's "strategy for victory" consisted of the willingness of him-self and a small group of comrades to take part in bloody confronta-tions with the police: "What we have to communicate to people is our strength, and to show people our strength we have to show them the strength of fighting on the side of the worldwide movement." Ethics and strategy were one and the same for Ayers: white college radicals had to reject their "white skin privilege," by taking the same kind of risks faced by the Viet Cong and the Black Panthers. By showing they were willing to suffer, they would—somehow—con-vince others to join the battle.

On the face of it, there could be no better proof of the limits of pacifist influence over the New Left than the drama enacted a few weeks later in the streets of Chicago when Weathermen, armed with lengths of lead pipe, did battle with the city police. And yet there is a thread that stretches from the last apocalyptic days of SDS back to the pacifist movement of the 1950s. In October 1958, shortly after the Cheyenne Project, Brad Lyttle wrote a letter to Lyle Tatum of the Philadelphia American Friends Service Committee. Tatum had been appalled by the obstructionist tactics used at Cheyenne, and espe-cially by the incident in which Ken Calkins suffered injury when sitting down in front of a truck. Lyttle defended the project in no uncertain terms:

Certain kinds of non-violent action are so deeply spiritual in nature that they should not be restricted to the logical framework of strategy; indeed, they are so powerful that strategy should be shaped around them . . . with the right principle, it seems to me, goes the power. Individual, non-violent obstruction generates spiritual power of immense magnitude. . . . Pacifist leaders . . . would do well to watch for these spiritual explosions and capi-talize on them, not become alarmed and apply dampers. In my judgment, [Ken Calkins's and another of the protesters' acts of] satyagraha were two of the best examples of non-violent action that have occurred in the West-ern World. For an instant, their demonstrations released an immense burst of spiritual power. Had the leaders of the pacifist movement seen this, and capitalized on it, I believe the end of stopping the missile base might have been achieved. . . . I strongly believe the United States' Pacifist movement is entering a stage where God's power will be breaking forth again and again. The old organizational structure [of the pacifist movement] will be shaken. . . . Watch for these bursts of power! . . . The stakes are high! Use God's power to win them![79]

Lyttle displayed a sense of self-righteousness that bordered on megalomania. The Cheyenne Project was not a symbolic protest for him; he believed that a dozen protesters, blocking trucks with their own bodies, could force the United States government to abandon nuclear weapons. To suffer injury was the proof of the authenticity of one's commitment to *Satyagraha*. "Logic" and "strategy" were merely excuses for inaction; the individual deed counted for far more than any bid for mass support. Those who doubted the value of such actions were siding with the enemy. If the old pacifist movement had to be pushed aside for Lyttle to set off his "spiritual explosions," that was a price he was quite willing to pay.

Albert Bigelow undertook the voyage of the *Golden Rule* in the belief that the American people could be inspired to generous and rational acts. Bigelow's commitment to a "higher law" led him to violate Atomic Energy Commission and federal court rulings, but he remained eager to find ways to cooperate with less venturesome Americans who shared or might be brought to share his goals. Brad Lyttle felt that Americans were stained with the sin of complicity in their government's preparations for nuclear war. The direct action projects at Cheyenne, Omaha, and Groton were undertaken to shock Americans out of their complacency. No other movement, no other tactic, was worthy of consideration. Two men in one organization spoke for two very different visions of the politics to come in the next decade.

Although the formal beliefs of pacifists like Bigelow or Lyttle counted for very little with the New Left, a set of impulses, present in the movement since the late 1950s, worked their way out in complicated ways over the next decade and found their final and perverse expression in Weatherman. The politics of most eras—and particularly the 1960s—cannot be understood simply as a matter of formally organized groups and formally adopted manifestos. Less tangible but as important is the spirit of the times, the mood and style in which politics is understood and undertaken. Lyttle's stance in the nonviolent protests of the late 1950s and early 1960s anticipated and prefigured the spirit of the more violent protests of the later 1960s, however much he might have deplored the latter.

The New Left believed in the value of "putting your body on the line." Sometimes this reflected an innocent and gentle idealism, reminiscent of the voyage of the *Golden Rule*. But other impulses were at work in the decade between the formation of the Committee for Non-Violent Action and the formation of Weatherman: a moral urgency that precluded consideration of political effectiveness, an identification with a force larger than the individual, a desire, above all else, to display one's personal commitment to the cause, even (or especially) if it involved the risk of injury or death. All of these impulses were shared by Brad Lyttle and Bill Ayers. Even if Ayers could not imagine that he had anything in common with those "old people" who dated back to the days "when pacifism was important," in a sense, the Days of Rage would be Weatherman's act of *Satyagraha*.

5

Toward a New Left

Now I have a hammer
And I have a bell
And I have a song to sing
All over this land.
It's the hammer of justice,
It's the bell of freedom,
And a song about love between
My brothers and my sisters
All over this land.
                    —PETE SEEGER, LEE HAYS
                                1949

The news that something this *Good* can be as popular
as this is can fill you with a new kind of optimism.
Maybe everything's going to be all right. Maybe
mediocrity has had it. Maybe hysteria is on the way
out. One thing is for sure in any case: Honesty is
back. Tell your neighbor.
                    —LINER NOTES TO PETER, PAUL,
                        AND MARY'S FIRST ALBUM
                                1962

Putting his body on the line: SDS leader Tom Hayden struck by an assailant at a civil rights march, McComb, Mississippi, October 1961. (UPI/Bettmann Newsphoto

B EFORE C. Wright Mills wrote his "Letter to the New Left," before English intellectuals began publishing *New Left Review*, before Tom Hayden enrolled as a freshman at the University of Michigan, before there was anything in the United States that might be considered a "New Left" in the sense that the term would acquire in the 1960s, American radicals began speculating about the character and prospects of the "new Left" they hoped would emerge from the wreckage of the Communist and Socialist movements. Under a headline reading "The new Left: What should it look like?" the *National Guardian* reported in October 1956 on a meeting between Earl Browder and Norman Thomas, held in Thomas's office at Browder's request. The meeting—a source of ironic satisfaction to those on the anti-Stalinist Left who remembered the years when Browder regularly denounced Thomas before throngs of cheering Communists in Madison Square Garden—was apparently quite cordial, as far as can be told from what the two men told reporters afterward.

Thomas said Browder had gone very far in the re-thinking necessary for working together. He denied any thought of starting a new party with Browder, since nothing could be launched by "those of us who bear too many scars of the past.". . . Browder said that in any rebirth of the Left "a key role must be played by Norman Thomas who, over the years, has won a special moral authority among large masses, who has always stood superior to faction, and who spoke for one of the main currents when the Left was strong."[1]

Nothing much came of the meeting. Thomas, though willing to be gracious to his one-time traducer, had no intention of allowing Browder to make use of his "special moral authority" as a stepping-stone back into the political arena. What is of interest is the coverage the event received in the *National Guardian*, particularly its use of the term "new Left" to refer not just to a student or young people's movement but to the future of the radical movement in its entirety, youth and adult. What was expected to be "new" in this new Left were the ideas and organizations it developed, rather than the people it involved. In 1956, the *National Guardian* considered it within the realm of possibility that Earl Browder and Norman Thomas would be among the contenders for leadership of the new Left. Even at the end of the decade, when both words in the phrase began to be capitalized in keeping with British usage, "New Left" referred to the possibilities emerging for a renewed radicalism *off* as well as on campus. Michael Harrington reported to the Young People's Socialist League national executive committee in 1959 that "the prospects for a New Left in the United States are perhaps most immediate on the campus"—but he went on to consider the AFL-CIO's battle against "right to work" laws, the organization of the Committee for a Sane Nuclear Policy, the continued growth of the civil rights movement, and the (largely imagined) stirrings of sentiment among rank-and-file trade unionists for an independent labor party, as further examples of the New Left that was a-borning.[2]

The coinciding of the collapse of the American Communist party with the emergence of new movements for civil rights and against nuclear testing set off a scramble to initiate what many leading American radicals agreed was a long overdue and badly needed regroupment of the Left. Despite much talk of the necessity of setting aside old factional and doctrinal disputes, this regroupment eventually fell victim to some of the same sectarian habits that had done so much to cripple the old American Left. The failure of the older generation of radicals to settle their differences in the "new Left" of the late 1950s and their failure to create new political mechanisms that could function effectively in the coming decade left to its own devices the younger generation of radicals then beginning to emerge as the New Left. By the end of the decade the New Left would recapitulate some of the worst excesses of its predecessors. While many factors shaped the history of 1960s radicalism, one of the most important, and least often considered was the failure of the "new Left" of the late 1950s.[3]

The American Forum for Socialist Education

In March 1957, A. J. Muste took the initiative in the first and most publicized attempt at regroupment. His American Forum for Socialist Education was created to draw together the disparate strands of

American radicalism. The moment seemed right, the initial response encouraging. But through a combination of his own decisions, the still potent power of McCarthyism, and the factional maneuvers of some of those whose support he sought to win, the project proved a dismal failure.

Muste was a complex character; sometimes beloved, sometimes distrusted, and sometimes beloved *and* distrusted by those around him. He had devoted a long life's work to a wide range of radical causes and had probably known and worked with more people in more sections of the Left than any other person in the history of American radicalism. Few would question his dedication. He lived for whatever movement he happened to be involved with at the time. Yet he always seemed a little too "religious" for his political associates and too "political" for his religious associates; too prone to mysticism for the taste of the practical minded and too prone to expedience for the taste of spiritual or political absolutists. To his admirers, he was a man of several parts; to skeptics, he seemed to be hedging his bets. Indifferent as he was to financial reward or any of the more conventional forms of success (his ill-fitting suits and frayed cuffs were part of radical lore), he was not without personal ambitions. His career in many ways paralleled that of Norman Thomas—both had been ministers, religious pacifists, and Socialists of one or another variety, and both were influenced by Gandhi as well as Marx—but Muste never enjoyed the same measure of popular favor bestowed upon Thomas. Part of the explanation for this difference is that over the years Muste remained more radical than Thomas—the Cold Warriors on the American Committee for Cultural Freedom would never have considered Muste a suitable candidate for membership as they did Thomas. And Thomas's frequent campaigns for the presidency added to both his visibility and credibility. Although both men turned seventy in the mid-1950s (Thomas was born in November 1884, Muste a month and a half later), Thomas seemed comfortable with his emeritus role, whereas Muste was in some ways still a man on the make. When asked in the 1950s why he didn't join the Socialists, Muste replied a little testily, "because they already have a leader."[4]

As Muste prepared to step down from active leadership in the Fellowship of Reconciliation in the early 1950s, he began to cast around for a new role. He was searching for ways to fuse his revolutionary commitments with his pacifist beliefs. Muste's pacifism was never based simply on opposition to war alone. It was meant to serve as the means to the revolutionary transformation of society. And to further his ends he was willing to take on allies who did not share his religious or pacifist convictions. When approached by Max Shachtman in the early 1950s to work together to build up a "third camp" antiwar movement, Muste was eager to cooperate. Shachtman did not hold Muste in high regard, but for a time he persuaded himself that Muste was in touch with some kind of broad national constituency—"Protestants," Dave McReynolds would later note, were a "somewhat mysterious category" to Shachtman—and that through Muste the Independent Socialist League could break out of its political isolation. After jointly organizing a few poorly attended "Third Camp conferences" with Muste, Shachtman realized his mistake and their collaboration waned.[5]

Shachtman and Muste came to similar conclusions in 1956 about the opportunities presented by the Communist party's rapid disintegration. For Shachtman, the logic of the moment dictated a return to the Socialist party. He had no problem with accepting Norman Thomas's leadership, in a nominal sense—he had, after all, done it before in the 1930s. Muste, who had broken with the Trotskyists in the 1930s when they decided to enter the Socialist party, sought another vehicle. In June 1956, at Muste's suggestion, the FOR sponsored a meeting on "America's Road to Democracy and World Peace" at Carnegie Hall: Roger Baldwin of the American Civil Liberties Union moderated, while Muste, Thomas, Eugene Dennis of the Communist party, and W. E. B. DuBois (not yet a Communist, but closely associated with various Party fronts) shared the platform. The speakers did not find much they could agree upon, because Thomas devoted most of his speech to denouncing the CP for its bad faith in the united front efforts of the 1930s. But the event attracted a turnout of 2,000 listeners, probably more than had shown up at any radical meeting, Stalinist or anti-Stalinist, since the fiasco of the Wallace presidential campaign. In October 1956, Muste spoke at a similar meeting in Chicago, this time with an audience of 700. Muste was always good at gauging crowds, and the relative success of the events encouraged him in the belief that the time was right for a bold move that would encourage continued discussion between former antagonists on the Left, with the ultimate goal of creating a unified radical movement.[6]

In December 1956, Muste sent out an invitation to eighty prominent radical leaders, academics, editors, and writers. "We are in a new age," he declared.

The problems of that age need to be stated, not to mention resolved. It seems elementary that this could not be done if each [radical] group continued to live to itself and regard itself as the True Church, possessed of the true and authentic revelation to which others needed only to adhere or be damned. It would be a healthy thing if discussion which transcended the traditional high and hard walls could be resumed.

The recipients were invited to a two-day meeting in New York City to discuss the future of the Left. Among those invited to participate were Max Shachtman, Dave McReynolds, Farrell Dobbs of the Socialist Workers party, Paul Sweezy, Irving Howe, Carey McWilliams, Bayard Rustin, C. Wright Mills, and I. F. Stone. No Communist party members were invited, but Joe Starobin, who had only recently resigned, received an invitation.[7]

Thirty-five people attended Muste's meeting. The minutes revealed a general agreement on the desirability of some form of regroupment but no consensus as to how that goal could be achieved. According to an "American Socialist group member" (names were not used in the minutes in order to protect the participants from official harassment):

We are at a dead end—all feel need of new vehicle for socialism: Thinks there is basis for some kind of conciliation of groups in U.S. and eventual emergence of socialist movement which must be wedded to democracy. Wants "big play for discussion" now.

While some of those present (presumably including Shachtman and McReynolds) argued for basing regroupment on the Socialist party, others were more skeptical. An "Independent Socialist," apparently a former CP member (possibly Starobin), commented:

There are over 10,000 convinced socialists around, majority of whom have been in CP. . . . The CP in US bad as it has been came closer than any one else to building a socialist movement. Majority of those who were in Stalinist ranks don't feel apologetic. If I went back, with my present knowledge, I'd do things differently. The CP as now constituted or as it might be reconstituted is washed up . . . but it is not a case of *they* were damn well wrong and *we* right. All of us are "compromised" by sectarianism and futility. I want evidence that SP-SDF merger is not another exercise in futility.[8]

Two days of discussion brought the participants no closer to final agreement, but at least it left them on speaking terms. At a meeting in March 1957 some of the veterans of the December discussion met again and established the American Forum for Socialist Education, with Muste as its chairman.[9]

As its name suggested, the Forum itself was not intended as a substitute for any of the older established radical groups. It was a place for radicals from those groups, as well as those who belonged to no group, to discuss issues of common interest. In the year that followed, the Forum held meetings in New York, Chicago, Los Angeles, Seattle, and elsewhere. The initial meetings lived up to the expectations of the organizers. The crowds were large and the discussion was animated. But before the year was out, the Forum already had begun to fade out of existence. It suffered, first of all, from the defect of its principal virtue. Attempting to be all inclusive, it could spark lively debates but provided little direction to those who wanted to know what they should do to help rebuild a radical movement. As one of its principal organizers, Sidney Lens, later explained: "There was a limit to how much you could discuss before the attention span and the allegiances of your discussants began to flag."[10]

The Forum also suffered from Muste's decision to invite Communists to the March 1957 meeting, and to allow two of them, Doxie Wilkerson and Al Blumberg, to become members of the Forum's national steering committee. Muste made no secret of his desire to attract those who had already left or were in the process of leaving the Communist party into his regroupment effort. When taken to task by some on the anti-Stalinist Left for his willingness to associate with Communists, Muste replied that he did so with the ultimate purpose of encouraging them to leave the Party (as both Wilkerson and Blumberg, as well as John Gates, a frequent speaker at Forum events, would soon do). The inclusion of Communists among the Forum's sponsors left it vulnerable to Red-baiting attacks: J. Edgar Hoover, Herbert Philbrick, Senator Eastland's Internal Security subcommittee, and the *Saturday Evening Post* soon joined forces to "expose" the Forum as the latest Soviet conspiracy. Attacks from the Right were expected and might have been survived. Muste's decision proved fatal because it prevented the participation or led to the disaffiliation of others on the Left who were sympathetic to the idea of regroupment, but who remained opposed to undertaking any common organizational endeavor with the Communist party. *Dissent* criticized the Forum, and even Muste's own *Liberation* ran an editorial disclaiming affiliation with the Forum because of the Communist issue. Rather than functioning as a source of unity, the Forum became just another bone of contention among radicals. John Dickinson, a supporter in Boston, wrote to Muste to lament that "in the Boston area, the willingness of the Communists and of previously 'Progressive Party' oriented people to consider participation, and the unwillingness of the *Dissent* people to do so, will underscore the labels which have already been put on the [Forum]."[11]

Max Shachtman withdrew from Muste's project after the initial meeting, regarding it as a competitor to his own strategy to engineer a regroupment centered on the Socialist party. With the SP spurning any connection with the Forum, continued Independent Socialist League involvement would only complicate Shachtman's efforts to get his group accepted by the already suspicious SP Old Guard. One of Shachtman's lieutenants wrote to him in March 1957:

There are no "right-wing SPers" listed [among the sponsors of the Forum], that is no real SPers only those who string along with [Muste's] schemes like McReynolds. . . . There are no *Dissent* people listed. . . . This leaves you as the sole representative of your type.[12]

Shortly afterward Shachtman denounced the Forum in an open letter to Muste in *Labor Action*: he could not, he declared, belong to a group that included "those who find it impossible to repudiate . . . totalitarian denial of full rights to the people in the name of socialism." Given Muste's past cooperation with the ISL, Shachtman might have chosen to sever ties with the Forum quietly—but personal considerations counted little with Shachtman when he had more pressing political concerns. James Cannon boasted that the Trotskyist movement had won a great victory when it helped destroy the Socialist party in the 1930s. Shachtman was more discreet than his one-time comrade, but he operated on a similar set of principles—as one of his victims recognized. Sid Lens wrote privately to Shachtman to complain about the tactic of the "open letter."

I don't feel as strongly about entering the SP as you do, but I can understand that given that orientation one ought not to jeopardize the goal by making side forays. But why was it necessary to try to discredit the efforts of third-camp socialists like Muste and myself in the process? . . . Why do you leave the impression that we are being dupes of the Communists? . . . I can see no other reason but the fact that you didn't want the Forum to come into existence at all, because it was an obstacle—you felt—in the path toward the socialist party.[13]

Shachtman's maneuvers were not the only factor in the Forum's rapid demise, but they certainly helped poison the political atmosphere in which it attempted to operate. By October an ISL internal document reported with satisfaction that "The only 'American Forumites,' if we can call them that, seem to be the Cannonites, the National Guardian Stalinoids (a type more Stalinist than the Gates people in the CP) and Muste and his immediate friends." The "new age" that Muste had announced the previous December, when groups on the Left would abandon their "True Church" attitudes, was effectively over in a matter of a few months.[14]

The Communist Issue and SANE

Although it played no deliberate or conscious role in the debate over regroupment, the Committee for a Sane Nuclear Policy served briefly in the late 1950s as a kind of surrogate party of the Left. But SANE's leaders were soon to take steps to extricate the organization from this unsought-after role. SANE leader Norman Cousins had come out of the United World Federalists and had not forgotten how they had been virtually Red-baited out of existence in the early 1950s. That was an ordeal he was determined not to have to endure again. SANE insisted that its criticism of nuclear testing applied equally to the Soviet Union and the United States. The group couched its arguments in terms of technical expertise rather than a radical critique of American foreign policy. Nathan Glazer wrote in *Commentary*, in 1961, that SANE had overcome "the tradition of wooly-mindedness it inherited from the world federalist and pacifist background of its founders." (It was a sign of the changing political climate that by the late 1950s both *Commentary* and Glazer had stepped away from the rigid Cold War attitudes they professed a few years earlier and were attempting a modest opening to the Left.) The reasoning of some of SANE's policy papers, Glazer added in what were intended as words of praise, was "not inferior—either in point of realism or hard-headedness—to that of Mr. [Henry] Kissinger and Mr. [Herman] Kahn."[15]

SANE found itself less well received in other quarters. The thaw in the Cold War had yet to penetrate the Luce publications. *Time* pilloried the organization in a 1958 article entitled: "How Sane the SANE?" linking SANE to the British Campaign for Nuclear Disarmament, and summarizing CND's philosophy as one that held that "nuclear disarmament will probably bring Communist domination, but that domination is preferable to prospect of nuclear war." SANE's concerns about nuclear fallout did not impress *Time*: "Folks who listened to the horror stories without listening to the evidence" of the relative harmlessness of fallout were lending aid and comfort to "the sworn enemies of religion, liberty and peace itself."[16]

Despite such attacks, SANE continued to prosper. Its supporters took heart when the United States and the Soviet Union both suspended nuclear weapons tests in 1958. In the spring of 1960, SANE planned a rally in New York City's Madison Square Garden to coincide with the start of the Paris summit conference between Eisenhower and Khrushchev and other world leaders. With the 1958 test moratorium presumably the prelude to a formal test-ban treaty, and with the marked improvement in Soviet-American relations symbolized by Khrushchev's visit to the United States in the fall of 1959, many critics of the Cold War now began to emerge from cover. SANE was the most convenient vehicle for pacifists, liberals, and radicals of varying persuasions to work together for the short-term goal of banning nuclear tests, while perhaps contributing to a longer-term rapprochement between the United States and the Soviet Union.

Hopes for the imminent demise of the Cold War were abruptly dashed in early May 1960 when the Soviets revealed that they had shot down an American U-2 spy plane over their territory. Khrushchev boycotted the summit, and the "spirit of Camp David" withered. Notwithstanding this turn of events, SANE's rally went on as scheduled on 19 May 1960. Seventeen thousand people paid admission for seats in Madison Square Garden to hear speakers ranging from Norman Thomas to Alf Landon. The rally went on until late in the evening, and afterward 5,000 joined Norman Thomas and Walter Reuther on an impromptu march to the United Nations, singing "Onward Christian Soldiers" and "Down by the Riverside." It was the greatest pacifist gathering since the 1930s, and in Nathan Glazer's assessment: "For a moment it looked as though SANE might grow into a really powerful force in American politics."[17]

But appearances were deceptive. SANE went into the 19 May rally a troubled organization, and its troubles soon hit the headlines. Two weeks before the rally, Senator Thomas Dodd, vice-chairman of the Senate subcommittee on Internal Security and a leading Senate opponent of continuing the informal nuclear test moratorium, had contacted SANE leaders. He charged that Henry Abrams, who had been a Progressive party activist in 1948, and who had been hired by SANE as its chief organizer for the 19 May rally, was a Communist infiltrator. (Abrams had recently been involved in another venture into regroupment—the "Independent Socialist" campaign for governor and other New York state offices in 1958, which brought the Trotskyists and veterans of the defunct American Labor party together in an unlikely and short-lived coalition.)[18]

Abrams was summoned before Dodd's committee, where he took the Fifth Amendment when questioned about his political beliefs and affiliations. Norman Cousins, a personal friend and neighbor of Dodd in Connecticut, managed to head off any public attack on SANE for the moment. Cousins confronted Abrams with Dodd's charges, and when Abrams refused to state whether or not he was a Communist, Cousins fired him. All of this was done quietly, and the rally itself was unaffected.

A week after the rally Dodd went public with his charges. In a speech on the Senate floor, he offered Cousins some unwanted praise as a man who had proved himself willing to cooperate with his committee's efforts to uncover Communist subversion in the peace movement. Cousins, Dodd announced, had even "offered to open the books of the organization" to Senate investigators, an assertion that Cousins would later deny. In an emergency meeting the following day, SANE's directors adopted a statement declaring that Communists were not welcome in SANE, though adding that they resented "the intrusion of a congressional committee" into SANE's internal affairs. Dodd continued to express goodwill toward SANE's leaders and goals—while also continuing to subpoena SANE supporters, an effective divide-and-conquer strategy. Hoping to limit the political damage from Dodd's speech, Norman Thomas and other representatives from SANE met with one of Dodd's aides. The aide, according to an internal SANE document, "tried to assure the SANE representatives that the Senator was a known liberal who was not motivated by a desire to destroy SANE or other groups working for peace." SANE's leaders were understandably skeptical of Dodd's pronouncements of goodwill, but throughout the crisis their main concern was controlling public relations damage. They decided to purge their ranks of members who might prove to be political liabilities. SANE adopted new rules requiring that all local chapters receive their charters directly from the national office, and that the charters include provisions to exclude "persons who are not free because of party discipline or political allegiance to criticize the actions of totalitarian nations."[19]

Coming as they did in the wake of the Senate investigation, the actions taken by SANE's leaders only seemed to sanction Dodd's charges of undue Communist influence in the peace movement. If SANE's leaders admitted the need for a dramatic "house-cleaning" of its own membership, how could they logically go on to criticize Dodd for drawing attention to the problem in the first place? The attitude of SANE's directors seemed like a throwback to a despised era of liberal acquiescence to witch-hunting. The Queens chapter of SANE wrote to the national board and argued that the organization was "strong enough now to stand up against the Dodd Committee." SANE shouldn't have to apologize for its policies, "rather it is the Dodd Committee that has much to answer for in reviving McCarthy-ite tactics." SANE's national board had lacked the courage to defy Dodd; instead it defied its own members. As a result, SANE's membership dropped drastically as twenty-five out of fifty local SANE groups in New York refused to take out charters with the new requirements. Many prominent radical pacifists resigned, including A. J. Muste, who saw the affair as a reprise of the recent destruction of the American Forum:

We are living in a new period, and many people are in the process of revising their thinking and their associations. A good many former Communists and sympathizers are essentially sound people; it should not be necessary at this hour to argue against the idea that they will be Stalinists at heart forever. . . . But if they find in a peace organization the same kind of dogmatism, suspicion, and obsession with orthodoxy that finally drove them out of the Communist Party or its fronts, they will stop working.[20]

Some of the SANE members subpoenaed by the Dodd committee undoubtedly were or had been Communists. Joe Clark, who had left the Party at the height of the deStalinization crisis, recognized and was recognized by some of his former comrades at the May rally. As he complained to Muste,

My wife and I attended and enjoyed that Madison Square Garden Rally. But we were appalled to see old died in the wool Stalinists . . . in charge of the collection in our section. . . . They weren't even going to accept our contributions for SANE because they were still sure that we were deserters and traitors for having left the Communist ranks.[21]

But the Communists played a less sinister role in the Garden rally than Dodd had charged. Nathan Glazer offered an astute analysis in *Commentary*.

Who were these people? . . . [They were] people who were no longer or who had never been actual Communists, but who were temperamentally and intellectually committed to a fellow-traveling interpretation of world affairs.[22]

As far as Glazer was concerned, people who believed that "the Russian or Chinese or Yugoslav or Cuban dictatorships were in some sense superior 'socialist' societies, worthy of a special loyalty from the progressive-minded" had no business being in SANE in the first place, but their presence had little to do with any concerted Communist effort to capture the organization. Between its founding in 1958 and the Garden rally in 1960 many radicals, including former Communists, joined SANE. There was no place else to go. Ralph Shapiro, one of those subpoenaed by Dodd, was a veteran of the Progressive party and a member of the National Lawyers Guild, affiliations that meant that he moved in political circles in which the opinions of the Communist party, at least until the mid-1950s, had counted for a great deal. But his own motivations in joining SANE, as he recalled some years later, had nothing to do with any stratagem of the Communist party.

1960 was a Presidential election year of less than inspiring quality. What would be more logical and natural for a political person, unable and unwilling to shed the habits of a life-time, than to work in an organization that was addressing issues of the gravest importance?[23]

For a brief period, SANE served as a sort of surrogate "party" for veterans of 1930s and 1940s radicalism. It was more successful in that role than Muste's American Forum had been, because instead of endless discussions on the role of the Left in the United States it offered practical activities and a minimum program around which liberals and radicals could unite. Without Dodd's attack, SANE might have continued to develop in the 1960s as the center of an "adult" peace movement—indirectly it might even have played a role in the reconstitution of an "adult" Left. But Norman Cousins had a very different set of priorities from A. J. Muste. He wasn't interested in regrouping the Left; he was interested in stopping nuclear testing, and he did his best to save SANE from the fate of the United World Federalists by sacrificing its more politically vulnerable members to the Dodd committee. Viewed from the perspective of the hard lessons in political reality Cousins and many others had learned in the 1950s, his decision could be defended on pragmatic grounds because he did succeed in deflecting Dodd's attack and won SANE the reputation as a "safe" organization. Viewed with the advantage of hindsight, his decision seems less defensible, even on pragmatic grounds, because it stripped SANE of some of its most committed members, turned younger activists against the organization, and considerably reduced its influence in the politics of the peace movement in the decade to come.[24]

The Young People's Socialist League

The one other formal attempt at regroupment, Shachtman's strategy for opening up the Socialist party, never got off the ground. Although a few Socialist party locals began showing more signs of life after the merger with the Independent Socialist League, there was little evidence that the organization as a whole was prepared to take advantage of the new opportunities presented by the 1960s. Apart from the initial influx of a few hundred Shachtmanites, the SP hardly grew at all. In February 1960, the SP had 1,620 members; one year later it had added a total of three additional members.[25]

The merger had a much more impressive impact on the fortunes of the Young People's Socialist League, at least in the short run. YPSL's membership of 300 in 1960 nearly doubled within a year and grew to over 800 in 1962. Compared to the number that could be mustered by any of the student groups of the 1950s that was an impressive figure, one that placed YPSL far ahead of potential competitors on the campus. The Communists had dissolved their Labor Youth League in the late 1950s and had yet to organize a new youth group on a national level. The Socialist Workers party had created its first youth group since the 1930s, the Young Socialist Alliance (YSA), but it had only 100 members or so. The newly renamed campus affiliate of the League for Industrial Democracy, Students for a Democratic Society (SDS), had under 500 dues-paying members at the time it adopted its founding statement of principles at Port Huron, Michigan, in 1962; and as a self-consciously nonideological group it was regarded by YPSL more as a potential recruiting pool than as a serious competitor for the leadership of the campus Left.[26]

YPSL enjoyed the benefit of the most experienced and sophisticated leadership of any radical youth group that had come along since the 1930s, and at the start of the 1960s it was well established in the political arena that would be the most important setting for the emergence of a New Left, the civil rights movement. Michael Harrington would himself move on to a broader field of action as he gained fame as the author of *The Other America*, although he continued to play a supervisory role in student politics as a member of the League for Industrial Democracy's Student Activities Committee. His place was taken by younger Shachtmanites, including two particularly bright and talented organizers named Tom Kahn and Rochelle Horowitz, who had joined the Young Socialist League out of Brooklyn College in the late 1950s. Debbie Meier, who had joined some years earlier, recalled that when Kahn and Horowitz and others joined, "we were euphorically happy to have young, lively, intelligent people coming in." They soon formed the same kind of close bond with Shachtman that had marked his relations with young members since the 1930s. One of the most striking characteristics Meier noted in the new recruits was that

they were ambitious. We saw that as a hopeful sign. They were competent. In the 1950s we had had the feeling that we could only attract "nudniks." Who would join an organization that isn't going anywhere? If we were attracting people with ambitions, they must see in us that we have a future.[27]

Kahn and Horowitz soon proved their competence by their close collaboration with Bayard Rustin in organizing the 1956 Madison Square Garden rally in support of the Montgomery bus boycott, and again by their efforts to help organize a series of marches on Washington, which included the 1957 Prayer Pilgrimage for Freedom and the 1958 and 1959 Youth Marches for Integrated Schools, the latter attracting some 25,000 demonstrators. These demonstrations were precursors of the huge demonstrations of the 1960s and gave many people who later would be active in the New Left their first experience in public protest. Other non-Shachtmanite radicals were involved in organizing these events: in New York, Steve Max, who chaired the meeting that dissolved the high school division of the Labor Youth League, worked with Kahn, Horowitz, and Rustin on many of the same committees. He saw the youth marches as the beginning of a new political era: "After years of piddling around with fifteen or twenty people here and there, you could see something that was clearly catching the imagination of thousands, tens of thousands of people."[28] Yet no one else on the Left was as well situated to take advantage of these events as the Shachtmanites. Martin Luther King had turned to Bayard Rustin for organizational expertise; Rustin turned to Kahn and Horowitz—with whom he formed personal as well as political ties—and an alliance was founded that would have a significant impact on the politics of the civil rights movement and the campus Left in the mid-1960s. Tom Kahn would enroll as a student at Howard University in 1960, where he would come in contact with and exercise considerable influence over a group of black students who would soon play leading roles in the Student Nonviolent Coordinating Committee. One of this group, Mike Thelwell, recalled:

It was clear that Tom was "working." He soon became quite influential in a very practical way. "Well," he'd say, "what would happen if students at Howard University were to do this, do that?" He taught a lot of people about politics, how to do certain things. Tom became the conduit for contacts with white radical students. He'd talk about a meeting taking place, or a lecture, and engineered our contacts with YPSL.[29]

Some of the same impulses that brought thousands of recruits into SDS and other New Left groups in the later 1960s worked to benefit YPSL at the start of the decade. Dorothy Tristman grew up in Queens in the late 1950s, spent her weekends listening to the folk-singers in Washington Square, and clipped Jules Feiffer cartoons from the *Village Voice*. She had never considered herself a socialist until she enrolled at Hunter College in the fall of 1959. There she met some yipsels who ran a campus group called the Anvil Club, and they invited her down to their loft one Friday night to hear Michael Harrington speak. After that she became a regular.

There was always a speaker downtown on Friday nights. That's what I did for years on Fridays, go to YPSL meetings. There were speakers, debates, SWPers would come to heckle, Dave Van Ronk would play benefits for us, Bob Dylan showed up one night when he hit New York looking for a place to stay, there were discussions afterwards, sometimes there'd be parties, or we'd just to go a restaurant and have coffee and pie.

The Young People's Socialist League offered her a sense of community, friendship, commitment, and purpose. "There were a lot of smart people, a lot of funny people, we'd sing a lot together when we put out mailings, it was really like a family to me."[30]

On the other side of the country, Betty Denitch arrived in Berkeley in the fall of 1959 to begin graduate school. She had already met Young Socialist Leaguers while an undergraduate at Antioch, and soon after she arrived at Berkeley she was recruited into the Young People's Socialist League. When she joined YPSL it seemed to her a sort of existential gesture: "I was reading Camus, and I thought, well, you can't hope much will come out of it, but still, what do you do with your life?" Much to her surprise, within two months she found herself immersed in a genuine mass movement. The decision of four black freshmen from North Carolina Agricultural and Technical College to sit down at a lunch counter in a Woolworth's store in Greensboro on 1 February 1960 and ask for a cup of coffee set off a spectacular political chain reaction. Within six weeks there were sit-ins or picket lines in most Southern states, with perhaps 50,000 people involved. From Hunter to Berkeley, northern students began picketing to support the demands of the southern sit-ins. In Berkeley alone thousands of students got their first taste of demonstrating that spring in front of Woolworth's.[31]

In May 1960, when the House Un-American Activities Committee (HUAC) came to San Francisco to hold hearings on alleged Communist activities in the Bay Area (including the Woolworth's picketing), Denitch began to understand why her more experienced YPSL comrades had been so excited by the Woolworth's picket lines. She went down to City Hall to demonstrate against HUAC and found that a thousand other demonstrators were already there, responding to a call from an ad hoc coalition of campus radicals called the "Berkeley Student Committee for Civil Liberties." It was the first time in its nearly three decades of existence that the committee had ever been met with such a mass public protest.

The fact that all these people had already been out picketing Woolworths [and] understood that kind of politics, meant that when the call goes out let's picket City Hall, then, bang, instead of getting a couple of dozen regulars out, you got thousands.

"Black Friday," 13 May 1960, the second day of anticommittee picketing, brought Denitch and others another educational experience. A smaller group of 200 students showed up to protest, and, as had been the case the day before, HUAC officials had kept all but a few of the protesters out of the hearing room through the device of issuing admission tickets exclusively to its own supporters. The anti-HUAC group milled around outside in the hallway of City Hall. Denitch was out on the street in front of the marble stairs leading up to the building.

It was around noon-time when all of a sudden the riot squad shows up, with helmets and billy clubs, and runs up the stairs, and the next thing you knew there was water pouring down the stairs [from the firehoses police turned on students] and the cops were dragging people down stairs. It wasn't like the late sixties when this became a familiar scene. Here were students being dragged by their hair, dragged by their arms and legs down the stairs so that their heads were bouncing off the stairs.

Five thousand angry students showed up the next day to picket. According to Denitch, "that was the start of the sixties for me. After Black Friday the Berkeley student Left was in a constant state of mobilization, to picket something, to march somewhere."[32]

The Young People's Socialist League had thrown its members into both the Woolworth's picketing and the anti-HUAC demonstration; other groups were involved but most lacked the organizational resources to take advantage of the newly militant mood of Berkeley students. The Berkeley YPSL, with about twenty members at the start of 1960, tripled its membership that spring, and counted many more supporters in its immediate periphery. The group sponsored weekly forums and played an important role in the local Congress of Racial Equality (CORE) chapter. Dale Johnson, a leader of the Fair Play for Cuba Committee and not a YPSL supporter, wrote in *Studies on the Left* in 1961:

Since the May anti-HUAC "riots," new organizations and spontaneous protest movements have grown up: the socialist groups of the [Bay] area have reported a high degree of interest in their programs (the Young People's Socialist League and the Socialist Party-Social Democratic Federation of Berkeley, blessed with highly skilled leadership, have been particularly successful of late).

For Denitch, the transformation in her personal expectations could not have been more dramatic. "December 1959 was still this black winter of existential despair; by the spring of 1960 the radical movement was in full bloom and Berkeley YPSL was in the center of it."[33]

In 1960 YPSL seemed poised for success. The group had been invigorated, just as Shachtman had promised, by the infusion of the YSL cadres. These were people with political skills, a sense of mission, and a willingness to devote long hours to the movement. They imbued new YPSL recruits with the theory, outlook, and temperament of their own political tradition. Betty Denitch recalled of her mentors in the Berkeley YPSL:

They really identified with the Bolshevik tradition. They knew that you could start with a very small group and when a critical moment of history came, if you had your act together, you could play a role entirely disproportionate to your size. We were always studying historical examples, beginning with the French revolution, and working our way up. What happens when a group is on hand ready to take decisive action? Look at the Bolshevik Revolution of 1917. What happens when a group fails to take decisive action? Look at the German revolution of 1923. There was this whole background of looking at things in terms of historical opportunities. It was a very special kind of training.

It was also a tradition that promoted among YPSL leaders, as it had among so many of their predecessors, an inward-looking self-preoccupation and inflated sense of self-importance. "History" could be relied upon to deliver its "opportunities." The real question was the subjective preparation of the revolutionary élite: "Will someone be there to take advantage?" That, Denitch remembered, was "what obsessed these men, and they were mostly men. Were they going to be ready at the right moment? Were they going to have the right line?" Dorothy Tristman went through a similar disenchantment with YPSL in time, wearying of the "hard, masculine" style of YPSL's internal debates and the obsession with "types" (a characteristic verbal tic of the Shachtmanites all during the 1950s and into the 1960s was the habit of defining everyone they encountered according to type: there were "*Monthly Review* types," and "Muste types," and "Stalinoids," among others). Tristman remembered that

The worst thing was to be considered "soft," which could mean being insufficiently anti-Communist, or just too speculative. Liberals were "mush." I think it was a neurosis, honestly, this fear of softness.

Mike Thelwell and the other black Howard students who were being courted by Tom Kahn eventually tired of the "disputation of talmudic texts" that seemed to characterize every Young People's Socialist League meeting.

There was a splitting of hairs, and a love of language and rhetoric to it. The love of language ain't alien to the black community. But that kind of scholasticism was. That kind of sectarianism was. And the difference in practical political terms between a Trotskyite and a Shachtmanite was not very impressive to us. The intellectual violence with which these issues were engaged struck us as being "white folks' business."[34]

As long as the Young People's Socialist League's animus was directed outward against the "types" that were to be found in competing groups on the Left, it could survive. Once turned inward with one YPSL "type" pitted against another, the organization began a rapid descent into an all-absorbing and self-consuming factionalism that ended only in the splintering of the organization.

Shachtman's continued political odyssey rightward triggered the internal YPSL warfare. Within the SP, Shachtman's followers soon became known as the "realignment" faction, so named for their insistence on bending all efforts to promote a political realignment within the Democratic party. From the New Deal on through the mid-1950s, Shachtman and his followers had derided the Democrats as "tweedle-dee" to the Republican "tweedle-dum." But in the late 1950s, the Shachtmanites began to change their minds. They saw in the rise of the civil rights movement not only the opportunity for American blacks to gain equality but also the chance to break the control that a coalition of southern Democrats and conservative Republicans had wielded in Congress since the late 1930s. With a one-party system prevailing in the South, and with the black portion of the southern electorate effectively disenfranchised, southern Democrats were the chief beneficiaries of seniority rules in the House and Senate that awarded them disproportionate power over key congressional committees and indirectly within the deliberations of the Democratic party. If southern blacks gained the vote and helped unseat those conservative Democrats, then it was possible that the whole political complexion of national politics would shift significantly toward the Left. Hence, it was in the interest of Socialists and all progressives to do everything they could to hasten the process of "realignment" within the Democratic party, linking liberals and labor to the civil rights movement and encouraging them to defy the power of the Dixiecrats.[35]

At first, Shachtman hoped that the coalition of Northern liberals, labor, and blacks, once "realigned," would pull out of the Democratic party. But by the early 1960s Shachtman had adopted a significantly revised version of a realignment strategy. If a new liberal-labor-black coalition was about to take shape within the Democratic party, why go to the trouble and risk of splitting off to form a third party? Why not just leave the coalition where it was once it had taken form, and let it rule the existing party? If anyone had to leave, let it be the Dixiecrats, to go their own way or join the Republicans if they wanted to. Freed of the influence of its southern conservative wing, the Democratic party would then become, in essence, the American equivalent of the British Labour party.[36]

In Shachtman's mind, all this was consistent with his life-long political goals of gaining power for the working class: he simply was changing his idea of the medium through which that power best could be expressed. His assumptions were still "Marxist" in the sense that they assumed the centrality of the working class to any meaningful process of social transformation. In the past, Shachtman had identified working-class interests with whatever the party he was involved with at the time said they were. Abandoning that delusion, he now went to another extreme and defined those interests solely in terms of what the official leadership of AFL-CIO said they were—a tendency that was reinforced when some of his young associates, like Horowitz and Kahn, found jobs working under Al Shanker on the staff of the United Federation of Teachers (Shanker was himself a veteran of the 1950s Left, having been a member of the Student League for Industrial Democracy at Columbia in 1953). Increasingly, Shachtman measured the worth of all causes and movements by the willingness of top labor leaders to support them. Step by step, Shachtman and his followers moved away from their initial conception of winning the labor movement's support for the new protest movements to one of disciplining those movements to fall in line with the AFL-CIO's political outlook. And when, in the later 1960s, the Vietnam War and racial disorders had exacerbated the political situation to the point that it was no longer possible to straddle the two camps, Shachtman had no hesitation indicating where his loyalties lay. He would not desert the "working class"—meaning George Meany and Hubert Humphrey—to support the protest movements led by Martin Luther King and Eugene McCarthy.[37]

This choice of domestic allies complemented his increasing preoccupation with the Russian Question, which he had temporarily downplayed while wooing the Gatesites in the late 1950s. In April 1961, Shachtman came to Berkeley to give two talks, one sponsored in the evening by the Socialist party and the other scheduled for the following day on the Berkeley campus. Coincidentally Shachtman arrived on April 18, the day after the abortive CIA-organized Bay of Pigs invasion of Cuba began. Berkeley yipsels decided to use Shachtman's already scheduled speech as the centerpiece of an antiintervention rally. But that evening, when Shachtman gave his first speech under the auspices of the Socialist party, he astonished many in his audience by offering the invaders a qualified endorsement, since, he noted, they included in their ranks some good Cuban trade unionists. Berkeley yipsels met in emergency session late that night to decide how to respond. As Betty Denitch remembered:

I was too young to appreciate the seriousness of the situation for people from the old movement, people for whom Max represented the movement, Max represented Trotsky. There was a continuity there that went back to Marx, you just didn't mess with something like that. . . . All I knew was the invasion of Cuba was an atrocity. We had already put up signs saying we were going to have a rally to protest the invasion. How could we then have our major speaker come and take an equivocal position?[38]

After a furious debate, YPSL voted to withdraw Shachtman as the speaker and replace him with Hal Draper, a veteran Shachtmanite who was becoming an influential figure on the Berkeley Left. Draper, who had been harboring suspicions about Shachtman's political reliability since the Korean War, decided that Shachtman had finally slipped over the boundary from anti-Stalinism to "Stalinophobia." Shachtman was furious and never again spoke at Berkeley, even when his own supporters regained control of the YPSL chapter there.[39]

Within YPSL an intense factional battle broke out between those who espoused a version of Shachtman's politics circa 1949 (prolabor party and third camp) and those who preferred Shachtman in his most recent guise (pro-Democratic party and moving into the Cold War camp). Already by 1962 the situation had grown so bad that Norman Thomas was discouraging young people he encountered from joining YPSL, telling them to go into SDS instead. The battle led, finally, to the collapse of the Young People's Socialist League in 1964, with most of the "labor party" adherents leaving for new allegiances (some of them joining Hal Draper's new Independent Socialist Club, which went on in various forms to play a role in Bay Area radical politics for the remainder of the decade). When the YPSL was reconstituted in the later 1960s, it was securely attached to the Shachtman wing of the Socialist party. On the few campuses on which it had any adherents, YPSL opposed the New Left with a ferocity matched only by the right-wing Young Americans for Freedom.[40]

Despite its initial promise, YPSL proved to be the vanguard of the new radicalism in one respect only: through it a portion of the new generation of campus radicals made its first acquaintance with the intensely preoccupying inner life of sectarianism. Many more would follow in the path blazed by the Young People's Socialist League before the decade came to an end.

The Student Peace Union

John F. Kennedy's election in 1960 had a mixed impact on the fortunes of the radical movement. Kennedy campaigned as a Cold War partisan, charging that the Republicans had allowed the United States to fall behind in military preparedness, as evidenced by the alleged "missile gap." Kennedy, in his inaugural address, promised to "pay any price, bear any burden, meet any hardship" in a "long twilight struggle" with unnamed enemies whose identities were not hard to guess. In the first two years of his administration, Kennedy's inclinations were generally hawkish, and the United States and the Soviet Union drifted closer to war than they had at any time since the death of Stalin. Administration doves were pushed out or learned to hold their tongues. Only in 1963, with the signing of the Test Ban Treaty and with his American University speech calling for a reassessment of Cold War beliefs did Kennedy begin steering a more pacific course in foreign policy. But the impact of his administration even from 1961 to 1962 was more than the sum of his policies. His youthful glamour, his wit, his vigor, his promises to "get America moving," his call for a "peace race," and his sponsorship of such initiatives as the Peace Corps, all contributed to the perception of Kennedy as a voice for change. At the very least, to speak of peace as a positive goal no longer automatically branded one as a friend of the Kremlin. Kennedy's first years in office thus raised both the fears and the hopes of pacifists and had a particularly dramatic impact on the peace movement on the nation's campuses.[41]

The first steps in the reemergence of a significant campus antiwar movement were taken before Kennedy's election. Ken Calkins, whose fractured pelvis in the Cheyenne protest had been a source of debate within the Committee for Non-Violent Action, returned to Chicago to take over Brad Lyttle's job in the local American Friends Service Committee office. Among Calkins's new responsibilities was running peace seminars in local high schools, which enabled him to develop contacts with students throughout the Chicago area. In the spring of 1959 he pulled together his contacts and organized them into the Student Peace Union (SPU). At the end of the school year the group had over 100 members.

From such modest beginnings, the Student Peace Union grew steadily. In 1960 it broke out of its midwestern isolation by merging with the College Peace Union, which had been organized on campuses in the Northeast by the Fellowship of Reconciliation. By December 1961, the SPU had 1,500 dues-paying members in dozens of chapters in the Midwest and Northeast; its membership doubled the following year, and the organization began to make its first inroads on the West Coast and in the South. For several years the Student Peace Union would remain the largest and most influential group of the New Left.[42]

The Student Peace Union enjoyed a number of lucky breaks in its first years. Not only did it happen onto the scene at a moment just before the civil rights movement and Kennedy's election lent legitimacy to its efforts, it also benefited from the internal difficulties of its only potential rival, Student SANE. Both groups focused on the issue of nuclear disarmament, but Student SANE had the misfortune of being caught in the aftershocks of the Dodd affair, when SANE had purged its own membership in order to avoid congressional harassment. Student SANE drew a large proportion of its members from New York City schools (or from colleges where large numbers of New Yorkers enrolled, such as Cornell, Wisconsin, and Rochester), and as one unfriendly observer noted at its 1960 national conference, many were "the children of 1930s radicals . . . searching for a political vehicle."[43]

The SPU was not exactly ideologically innocent itself, although it maintained useful ties with religious pacifists and developed an appeal on some midwestern campuses such as Shimer, Knox, North Central, and Lake Forest colleges, which had not been known for radical activism in the past. SPU's most popular slogan was "No Tests, East or West," and its statement of principles, adopted in 1962, declared:

Because both East and West have pursued foreign policies which are not in the interests of their own people or the people of the world . . . the Student Peace Union believes that the peace movement must act independently of both East and West, [and] must apply the same standard of criticism to both.[44]

It was not accidental that this had a distinct "third camp" ring to it, because from very early on the Young People's Socialist League had poured its members into the Student Peace Union. Mike Parker, a YPSL member and student at the University of Chicago, joined the SPU in 1959, and became its national secretary the following year. The SPU outspokenly condemned both Soviet and American foreign policy and ridiculed Student SANE for its tendency to push the slogan of "peaceful coexistence" as a solution to all international tensions.[45] They were also at some pains to distinguish their own views from the "mush" of Kennedy-style liberalism. SPU leader Gail Paradise complained in 1963 that many students

believe that Kennedy is a liberal—they see that he uses liberal, if not revolutionary rhetoric (as in the Alliance for Progress) and makes small moves toward peace (like the Arms Control and Disarmament Agency).[46]

As much as they might complain about Kennedy, SPU leaders were not unaware of the advantages they gained from Kennedy's image as someone sympathetic to their cause. When SPU members fasted and vigiled in front of the White House in November 1961 to protest the United States decision to resume nuclear testing, the *New York Times* ran a surprisingly favorable story, calling their actions an "earnest symbol of a small but active ferment on college campuses across the land." The *Times* also noted that

President Kennedy is listening at least. When he heard of the picketing, he invited leaders of the pickets to confer with his disarmament advisers. And he has received petitions signed by students at several colleges protesting the resumption of nuclear testing.[47]

Despite their cynicism about the value of Kennedy's "listening," Student Peace Union leaders reprinted the article and sent it out to supporters. When members of the group returned to Washington in February 1962 for their most ambitious project to date, two days of demonstrations and lobbying, called Washington Action, they carried signs with the critical but respectful message, "President Kennedy: We Support Your Words, Give Us a Chance to Support Your Actions." To the surprise of everyone, including its organizers, Washington Action turned out to be the largest student demonstration in Washington since the days when Eleanor Roosevelt was on a first-name basis with the leaders of the American Youth Congress. More than 5,000 students responded to Student Peace Union's call, with busloads of students coming from campuses as far away as St. Louis.

The idea for Washington Action originated with a group at Harvard loosely affiliated with SPU, called TOCSIN. In an organization whose general style was a mixture of midwestern Protestant pacifism and third-camp socialism, TOCSIN was definitely an anomaly, with its Harvard-bred taste for discussion groups, research papers, and high-level contacts with academic and government disarmament specialists. Todd Gitlin, chairman of TOCSIN in 1962, later described the organization as one that "straddled, in a complicated way, radical pacifism and technocratic arms-controllism." Gitlin initially came up with the idea for Washington Action in the fall of 1961 but had a hard time selling it to national SPU leaders. They felt it was a typical Harvard élitist approach that would only encourage further illusions about Kennedy's liberalism. Dave McReynolds, who was playing the role of adult mentor to SPU, smoothed over the differences between TOCSIN and the SPU leadership. After lengthy negotiations, the plans for Washington Action emerged as a combination of TOCSIN-style lobbying effort, with a decidedly Old Left-flavored march and rally, the latter featuring Emil Mazey of the United Auto Workers and Norman Thomas as principal speakers.[48]

Student Peace Union organizers would have been happy with a turnout of 1,000 students, and were delighted when more than 5,000 showed up. The demonstrations against nuclear testing and Civil Defense planning were spirited but orderly (Kennedy, with a deft touch, won headlines if not the hearts of SPU leaders by sending out an urn of coffee to several hundred students who were picketing the White House in a snowstorm on the first day of the event). Despite the presence of counterpicketers from the Young Americans for Freedom, who carried signs demanding "Ban the Beatnik," press coverage was generally sympathetic and stressed the clean-cut appearance and political moderation of the demonstrators. One Harvard senior was quoted in the *New York Times* account: "We're the right wing among the disarmament groups. We're not pacifists. We're not for selling out to the Russians." A secretary to Maryland Republican Senator John Marshall Butler was overheard whispering to a colleague as SPU lobbyists entered the office: "They couldn't be with that peace march. They look like such nice kids. They look so respectable." To the probable relief of more radical SPU leaders, close contact with Congress, State Department, and administration officials had a disillusioning impact on participants in the weekend's events. State Department officials patronizingly lectured the students, and according to the SPU *Bulletin*, students complained of "being talked down to like children."[49]

Though Student SANE, and Students for a Democratic Society had cosponsored the event, the Student Peace Union got most of the credit in the press and on college campuses. Student SANE dissolved within a few months, and Students for a Democratic Society still had only about one-tenth of SPU's membership. SPU remained active that spring, sponsoring a large demonstration in New York against nuclear testing that was attacked by police in the first violent street confrontation of the decade between police and antiwar protesters. In the fall, SPU chapters sponsored protest demonstrations on campuses across the country during the Cuban missile crisis. Two thousand students showed up in Washington for a march protesting Kennedy's blockade of Cuba, on only a few days notice. The organization continued to gain chapters and members through the end of 1962, peaking at around 3,500 members. And yet by the end of 1963, Student Peace Union was close to collapse.[50]

SPU was, in part, the victim of the very "peaceful coexistence" slogan its leaders had sneered at. The Cuban missile crisis had a paradoxical impact on both international relations and domestic politics. On the one hand, the world had been brought close to a nuclear apocalypse (at Harvard, TOCSIN went into virtually nonstop emergency session, though no one really had any idea what to do; as Gitlin recalled, "people thought they were going to die"). On the other hand, leaders of both nations were as scared by the experience as their populations: they had learned something from the experience, and had drawn back. Conflicts between the superpowers now would be managed so that they were containable and neither side would feel pushed to the wall; hence "detente" was able to flourish through the bloodiest years of the Vietnam War. And because a lessening of international tensions followed this brush with catastrophe, the whole issue of arms control seemed less rather than more pressing. With the signing of the Nuclear Test Ban Treaty, single-issue groups like the Student Peace Union were suddenly at a disadvantage in the world of radical student politics. With fears of war—or at least of nuclear holocaust—declining, the country as a whole seemed more amenable to appeals for domestic reforms. Without the Russians to worry about constantly, perhaps it was time for the United States to give more attention to long-neglected problems like domestic poverty and racism. Student Peace Union just couldn't shift gears to become a civil rights or antipoverty group: too much of its identity, and even its name, was bound up with another issue. Students for a Democratic Society did not have this problem.[51]

SPU had other woes. From the start, it had to contend with all the normal problems besetting student organizations. Ken Calkins wrote to Dave McReynolds in March 1960 complaining that the group's student members were continually running into "papers, tests, vacations, etc." That meant that the few paid staff members in the group's Chicago headquarters carried an excessive burden.

We have become too successful too quickly. We barely have time to answer our mail within a week of the day when it arrives. I keep getting things going at new campuses, but have no time to follow up adequately. . . . Only at four or five schools in the midwest have we found the leadership necessary to keep things going without outside help—and even these people tend to lose their energy if we do not write to them from time to time.

SPU's national staff lived a hand-to-mouth existence, sleeping in the squalid back rooms of its Chicago headquarters, an old house on the border of a black ghetto. The demands on personal time of "movement" existence were never ending and the burnout rate accordingly high. "Our apartment is a constant madhouse," Calkins complained to McReynolds:

We have perhaps two or three evenings a month when there are not between 2 and a dozen visitors working, talking, and just generally getting into my hair. This is a necessary evil of an organizational life, but it makes creative thought well nigh impossible.[52]

Calkins would soon resign as SPU's national secretary.

SPU had another cross to bear. It was increasingly turning into a YPSL front group. YPSL strategists took care to see to it that their own members remained a minority of the delegates at SPU conventions, and that liberal Protestants continued to occupy prominent positions, but they also made sure that no ideologically suspect "types" were able to move into power. As early as 1960, Dave McReynolds worried over the potential effect of YPSL influence on SPU's ability to attract recruits. He wrote to Ken Calkins in July 1960 outlining the special problems that SPU would run into when it tried to gain members in New York.

Any youth group here must be able to deal with the procommunist student element which is very strong. This city not only had a "communist element," it had a "communist culture." . . . The more political students grew up in this atmosphere. Almost every young Jew in New York City has a parent or a close relative who was or still is in the CP. We must win these kids to the pacifist position.[53]

McReynolds warned that the yipsels in SPU, with their preoccupation with containing the "Stalinists" and "Stalinoids," would only hold SPU back in this effort.

YPSL members in SPU also alienated other important constituencies. Todd Gitlin scarcely knew what YPSL stood for when he began to work with SPU's national leaders in December 1961 to plan Washington Action. His relations with them quickly soured.

They thought we were soft on Russia. I thought they were dull, dull and cramped, there was something cramped about their tone . . . small-minded, provincial, losers.[54]

Increasingly, the debates within SPU became a kind of shadow play of the factional struggle within YPSL. Thanks to Mike Parker's influence, SPU had developed into a stronghold of the "labor party tendency" of YPSL. (Since there was no "labor party" for them to get involved with, adherents of this line gravitated to organizations like the SPU which were not primarily concerned with electoral action.) As SPU increased in importance after 1960, "realignment tendency" yipsels, those who remained closest to Max Shachtman in his rightward trajectory, sought a means of undermining their opponents' control of SPU. They thought they found their weapon when SANE approached the SPU to see if it would consider merging with Student SANE. SPU leaders momentarily were tempted by the offer of the financial subsidy SANE could provide, but they finally declined, both because they valued SPU's independence and because they were just as glad to have the "Stalinists" confined to Student SANE. (Student SANE, which had lost members steadily since 1960, was finally disowned by SANE in the spring of 1962 and dissolved.) SANE's proposal found a more sympathetic hearing from those YPSL leaders who were not directly involved in the SPU. In the fall of 1961, Rochelle Horowitz submitted a proposal to the YPSL leadership calling for unity between SPU and Student SANE on the basis of the slogan "No Tests, East or West." If successful, such a merger would have diluted the influence of "labor party" factional leaders in the merged organization and placed it under the control of SANE's liberal leaders. Given the choice between a genuinely radical SPU under the leadership of factional opponents and a tamer SPU under the control of Norman Cousins, the Shachtmanites much preferred the latter. When Mike Parker learned of the proposal he dispatched an angry letter to Horowitz, complaining that she misunderstood the relationship between YPSL and SPU.

Most of the SPU members who are YPSL members started in SPU and were then recruited to YPSL. As such we have a basic commitment to SPU and will not manipulate it at the will of the [YPSL leaders].

Parker rejected any talk of merger with Student SANE because of its Stalinist leadership and because he believed adult SANE would not countenance the use of civil disobedience tactics by its student affiliate.

It would be too bad if SPU lost the committed types who enter the peace movement by jumping on submarines because we would have nothing to say to them. But more important no civil disobedience would isolate us from the peace activity that more kids are engaged in in New York than in any other activity—Civil Defense protest.[55]

Parker was able to preserve SPU's independence, but the spillover of YPSL factionalism continued to eat away at SPU's vitals. While most local chapters continued their activities oblivious to the existence or meaning of the struggle at the top, SPU leaders divided among themselves over when, if ever, to support peace candidates for elected office, and over far more esoteric questions, such as whether SPU should have supported India in its border dispute with China, and whether Juan Bosch should have armed the workers of the Dominican Republic. Those with longer memories, like McReynolds, found it all dismally reminiscent of the pointless political in-fighting of the early 1950s. He wrote a despairing letter early in 1964 to Phil Altbach, one of the Student Peace Union's original founders.

The real problem [in SPU] is the sectarianism which I think YPSL is responsible for. We are so desperately tired around here—and this means all of us in the pacifist wing of things—with the term "Stalinoid" and "soft" etc.[56]

The Student Peace Union went into fatal decline just at the moment when foreign policy issues again began to seem relevant to many college students. The group's leaders had been slow to concern themselves with protests against the war in Vietnam (a struggle that did not lend itself readily to a third-camp analysis), and the group finally dissolved in the spring of 1964. Students for a Democratic Society, which had prospered in the meantime through its focus on domestic issues, now had the leadership of the campus antiwar movement left to it by default.[57]

Students for a Democratic Society

By the end of 1962, Students for a Democratic Society had emerged as the most important of the new campus radical groups; soon it would be regarded as virtually synonymous with the "New Left." Its growth over the next few years was spectacular: in 1961 SDS had roughly 300 dues-paying *members*; by 1968 it had roughly that many *chapters*. Owing to the chaotic state of the organization's bookkeeping and the fact that so many activists in local chapters did not bother to send dues into the national office, Students for a Democratic Society's actual membership in the late 1960s is impossible to determine, but estimates at the time ranged from 30,000 upward to 100,000. This was an immense group by the standards of the 1950s, or for that matter, the 1930s: at its height SDS had perhaps three to four times as many members as the American Student Union claimed thirty years earlier.[58]

It was by no means apparent at the start of the decade that SDS was going to emerge as the winner in the competition for preeminence in New Left politics. People in various sections of the Old Left kept a watchful eye on the potential of such groups. YPSL, for example, was careful to keep a foot in the door with SDS, but at the start of the decade devoted far more attention to the Student Peace Union—with the result that the SPU became the battleground upon which competing YPSL factions refought the issues of the 1950s one last time. SDS was smaller and slower to draw attention to itself than the SPU and thus gained crucial breathing space during which it could develop its own distinctive brand of politics. One veteran of Old Left politics who did guess the correct winner in the campus radicalism sweepstakes was Steve Max, who had been involved with several abortive attempts at creating a new radical youth group in the late 1950s. In 1961 he encountered the SDS leaders for the first time and decided they represented the wave of the future.

What appealed to me about SDS, what made it look like it was really going to happen was three things. First of all, it wasn't a New York-centered group as most of the others were, where the constant problem was how do you break out? Secondly, it wasn't a Left group in the traditional sense: it wasn't held back by people having a peculiar language or odd issues or fights from the thirties. It was a clean slate. (The LID [League for Industrial Democracy] was something else, but the SDS people weren't like that.) Finally, it was multi-issue, and had a good balance between wanting to do educational work and wanting to do activism. All of those things made it just about right for that time.[59]

A few years earlier no knowledgeable observer would have said that Students for a Democratic Society's predecessor, the Student League for Industrial Democracy, was "right for its time." SLID was the direct descendant of the Intercollegiate Socialist Society, founded in 1905 by Upton Sinclair, and it had known good years and bad in the decades since. The 1930s had been good years, up until the moment when SLID merged with a Communist student group to form the ASU. The SLID was reconstituted after World War II, enjoyed a brief and minor revival, and then went on to the worst decade of its history. In the 1950s it managed to beat off Bogdan Denitch's and Michael Harrington's attempts to capture the group for the "third camp," which saved it from the near-certain fate of having the League for Industrial Democracy subsidy cut off, but that was its single achievement of the decade. By every other indicator— membership, the number of functioning chapters, the number of delegates attending its annual convention—the organization should have dried up and disappeared long before the end of the decade.

In the late 1950s the Student League for Industrial Democracy had no more than a hundred or so "active" members and three barely functioning chapters. The number of delegates at its convention dropped from thirty-nine in 1957 to a mere thirteen the following year. Andre Schiffrin, the group's most dynamic leader in the 1950s, who was responsible for creating one of the more active chapters at Yale before moving on to the SLID presidency, later referred to the group as a "training ground for marginality." In 1958 a SLID officer reported to the LID executive board on the results of a midwestern campus organizing tour in which he visited seven campuses. The results could not have been less inspiring.

Several years have literally elapsed since any of these colleges have been visited by us. As a result I had very little to work with. . . . At the University of Michigan we had three members who have now increased to eight; at Madison, of course, is our lone Midwestern chapter. At each of the other institutions [Oberlin, Ohio State, Indiana, Purdue, and Minnesota] we had one member. And these meagre contacts were our sole relationship to the student body of these colleges, for outside of a surprising large number of faculty persons and adults in general, SLID is almost completely unknown.[60]

SLID did gain one valuable political resource in the late 1950s, and that was a young visionary by the name of Robert (Al) Haber, son of a former LID member and University of Michigan professor. As an undergraduate at Michigan, Al Haber was active in the Political Issues Club, out of which would develop VOICE, a radical campus political party that was the local equivalent of Berkeley's SLATE. Haber's political involvement led to his election as SLID vice-president in 1959, his appointment to its one full-time, paid position as field secretary in 1960, and his election to the presidency the same year. One of the more symbolic changes that Haber and some other members pushed for at the end of the decade was a more meaningful name. Various possibilities were discussed, but at Schiffrin's suggestion the one finally decided upon was Students for a Democratic Society, officially adopted on 1 January 1960.[61]

Students for a Democratic Society made its first public appearance later that spring as sponsor of a conference entitled "Human Rights in the North," held at the University of Michigan, bringing veterans of the southern sit-ins to meet with northern campus sympathizers, along with such familiar fixtures at such events as Bayard Rustin and Michael Harrington. The activist slant that Haber intended to give SDS did not go down well with the yipsels then sitting on the LID's students activities committee. They didn't want SDS to become another "protest group"—perhaps fearing it would trespass on what YPSL considered its own turf in the civil rights movement. The dispute grew so heated between Haber and his LID opponents that in March 1961 he was fired from his position as field secretary, and he sent in his resignation from SDS. The differences were finally smoothed over—for one thing, Haber frightened LID with the specter of his going on to organize a new and competing campus group; and for another, YPSL seemed to have decided in the meantime that it could use an expanding SDS for its own purposes. And so, Haber was rehired and given relatively free rein over the next year to build up SDS as he thought best.[62]

Among those attending that first Students for a Democratic Society conference was the student editor of the *Michigan Daily*, Tom Hayden. At the end of the 1960 school year Hayden took an eventful trip to California, where he spent some time absorbing the radical atmosphere in Berkeley in the aftermath of the House Un-American Activities Committee confrontation and then went down to Los Angeles to cover the Democratic convention for the *Michigan Daily*. There he met Michael Harrington, who was helping organize a civil rights vigil and protest march outside the Democratic convention. Hayden was impressed with Harrington, who came from a midwestern Catholic background similar to his own, and who managed to combine the roles of writer and activist in a way that Hayden sought to emulate. In an article published the following year in *Mademoiselle*, entitled, "Who are the Student Boat-rockers?" Hayden listed Harrington as one of three radical leaders who had "won [the] respect" of the new activists (the other two were C. Wright Mills and Norman Thomas).[63]

Back in Ann Arbor, Hayden was approached by Haber to join SDS. He was skeptical of the group's ties with the League for Industrial Democracy, but Haber persuaded him that working within the framework provided by the LID was easier than starting a new organization from scratch. After graduating from Michigan in 1961, Hayden went South to do what he could in SDS's name to support the Student Nonviolent Coordinating Committee's (SNCC) organizing efforts. Haber and Hayden had complementary styles that worked to the benefit of the young group. Haber devoted himself selflessly to office work, tending the SDS membership list as if it were a rare and valuable species of orchid. Hayden was self-assured and charismatic, an effective writer and speaker who was not afraid to "put his body on the line," as he proved that first fall in the South when he was beaten on one occasion and jailed on another in civil rights activities. Together Haber and Hayden were able to give SDS both stability and visibility. The two of them began drawing together a network of talented student activists—newspaper editors, student government leaders, veterans of National Student Association conventions, from Michigan, Swarthmore, Oberlin, and similar élite colleges. Haber's strategy was to link SDS through conferences and common activities with other student groups like SNCC, SPU, and Campus ADA, portraying SDS as a place where all the disparate strands of student activism could be woven together. Students for a Democratic Society was to serve as the "think tank" for the movement, and as an activist organization in its own right.[64]

The Old Left was not without influence in SDS's formative years—as shown, for example, by Steve Max's election to its national executive committee in December 1961. Even before Max joined SDS, "red diaper babies," the offspring of Communist families, had been well represented among its founders. In the early 1960s, Ann Arbor, Michigan, was not only home to Hayden and Haber but also to a number of radical New Yorkers looking for a politically congenial place to attend college. Bob Ross was one of them—a Michigan undergraduate when he got involved in SLID, he was Haber's steadiest ally in the first battle with the LID over SDS's new direction. Dick Flacks, a veteran of the LYL and a graduate student at Michigan, got involved in SDS early on, and in his mid-twenties he served as a "father figure" to his slightly younger comrades.

SDS found a direct link to the world that Ross and Flacks had come out of when the group that Steve Max led in New York, the FDR/Four Freedoms Club, affiliated as an official SDS chapter. Max represented the "right wing" that emerged from the Communist party youth milieu—his father, a *Daily Worker* editor, had been a leading Gatesite during the 1956 crisis. Max and his allies retained a rhetoric ("FDR/Four Freedoms") and political habits reflective of their background, but they were disenchanted with the Soviet Union and Leninist models of organization. In essence, they spoke for a kind of loose Popular Front politics—but without a Party working behind the scenes. (From that same CP youth milieu emerged another grouping of young radicals who retained their Leninist outlook, and found the People's Republic of China an attractive alternative to the Soviet Union as the center of world revolution. In the early 1960s they would form the Progressive Labor Party [PLP], a group destined for a fateful encounter with SDS later in the decade.)[65]

For Max, a product of New York's Upper West Side who claimed that it was many years before he learned "that people in other places actually lived in houses," SDS was the vehicle through which the FDR/Four Freedoms Club could break out of its cosmopolitan provincialism. Hayden and Haber, whom Max met at the Students for a Democratic Society office in New York in 1961, impressed him because they "were clearly more native, less New York." They offered "a window on the rest of the world." They, in turn, were interested in what Max and his group had to offer—a number of bodies, plus a certain sophistication about the intricacies of left-wing politics and theory. What their alliance represented was a merging of traditions and resources rather than simply a break with the past.[66]

Todd Gitlin had a reaction similar to Max's when he first encountered a graduate student at Harvard named Robb Burlage, who worked with Gitlin on H. Stuart Hughes's senatorial campaign in 1962 and who subsequently recruited him into SDS. Unlike Steve Max, Gitlin was not a red diaper baby, but having grown up in New York the child of liberal Jewish parents, he had a certain sense of cultural and political estrangement from the dominant mores of the 1950s. Harvard only partially alleviated that sense of alienation. "It dawned on me much later how much of TOCSIN's membership had been Jewish," Gitlin would remember. "TOCSIN was a little enclave within which I could stand and be proud of my difference from the preppies rather than feel cowed by them." Burlage stood out as a new kind of radical in Gitlin's eyes.

He was like Hayden, a political person who's real, has his feet on the ground, he's from America. That was another issue for me, coming from New York. Hayden coming from Michigan, Burlage coming from Texas, seemed more "American." . . . At the SDS national council meeting in New York in December 1963 I remember going around the room and counting who was Jewish and who was not, and being struck by the fact that very few people were, only four or five out of seventeen on the national executive committee.[67]

SDS was operating on a political terrain where the terms of conflict had long been defined by the Old Left, and they could not start anew without first considering how to contend with the potential appeal of surviving Old Left groups to student activists. In an internal memorandum written in May 1961, Haber argued that it was important to appeal to "Stalinoids" on the campus, those students who because of the influence of "family background, early influences, inadvertent organizational ties or whatever" tended to adopt a defensive attitude when they heard criticisms of the Soviet Union but who nonetheless "are basically with us ideologically and in terms of positive goals and program." If SDS wasn't able to appeal to them, then other groups would. At present "Communist agents" had virtually no influence on campus: "Hoover is wrong; Huac is wrong." Students, even those from Old Left backgrounds, were suspicious of ideology and "don't want to be tied down to a political formula." That of course was why there was now room for a group like SDS to develop. But, Haber insisted, the suspicion of ideology could prove a double-edged sword as far as the democratic Left was concerned.

In effect . . . the suppression of questions of ideology or of an integrating framework of values, gives respectability to anti-democratic formulations. . . . It is a kind of an intellectualized popular front to which pro-soviet kids are beginning to gravitate. It seems to be the official preference of the CP and is generally promoted in party oriented publications. Potentially, it is the most dangerous development on the student scene. It allows the entry of an anti-American orientation of an anti-democratic position and it puts a muzzle on any counter-force of democratic argument.[68]

It wasn't enough that SDS simply seek to work with radical students on issues of common concern. If students were going to resist the blandishments of the Communists, they had to be given a positive faith, "an integrating framework of values" upon which they could base their political involvements. This was, in embryo, the impulse that over the next year led to SDS's adoption of the Port Huron statement. Haber, of course, wrote his memo with one eye on the reaction of the LID board, and there was nothing more likely to please them than to think that their campus affiliate was intent on doing battle against the revival of Stalinism. But Hayden, less concerned with diplomatic niceties vis-à-vis LID, offered a very similar argument in his "Letter to the New (Young) Left," published in *The Activist* early in 1961. Probably bearing YPSL in mind, Hayden criticized those on the Left who made habitual and "paranoiac" use of terms like "stalinoid" and "stalinist." Nevertheless, he added, "red-baiting is no more or less dogmatic . . . than its current opposite, 'anti-anti-communism' or 'issues orientation,' which tends to seal off critical, freewheeling discussion in the worthless name of 'group unity.' " What was needed was a "radical program" embodying a set of values capable of sustaining a "slow and exhaustingly complex [struggle] lasting at the very least for our lifetimes."[69]

The decision to adopt a statement outlining SDS's political philosophy was taken at the December 1961 national executive committee meeting, and Hayden was assigned the task of composing the initial draft. Ironically, the process of writing and adopting this statement—designed in part to counter the potential appeal of communism on the campus—would lead the LID elders to decide that SDS was dangerously "soft" on communism. The ensuing battle between the generations would do much to start SDS on a political trajectory leading first toward the "anti-anti-communism" that Hayden had so recently condemned, and then onward toward an identification with Third World Communist movements and governments, a path that took SDS steadily further away from the very radical democratic values it initially sought to champion.

The draft of the statement that Hayden brought to the founding convention of SDS in mid-June 1962 (held at a United Auto Workers educational camp in Port Huron, Michigan) openly challenged some of the beliefs of older radicals.

Consider the old slogans: Capitalism Cannot Reform Itself, United Front Against Fascism, General Strike, All Out on May Day. Or, more recently, No Cooperation with Commies and Fellow Travellers, Ideologies are Exhausted, Bipartisanship, No Utopias. These are incomplete.

Hayden wanted to make a fresh start, and he deliberately addressed the statement to his peers: "We are people of this generation," the statement began, "bred in at least modest comfort, housed in the universities, looking uncomfortably to the world we inherit." In ways that Hayden was probably unaware of at the time he wrote it, the Port Huron statement echoed a series of personal declarations reaching back to the immediate aftermath of the Second World War, declarations in which adherents of the Old Left had announced their renunciation of the dogmas to which they had once pledged allegiance. "What is really important?" the Port Huron statement asked, sounding much like Dwight Macdonald in "The Root is Man": "Can we live in a different and better way? if we wanted to change society, how would we do it?" And, sounding much like Lewis Coser in

"What Shall We Do?" Hayden contrasted the sham, unrepresentative, image-fixated character of conventional politics with the alternative, a "participatory democracy," in which individuals shared "those social decisions determining the quality and direction of his life." Hayden drew consciously on sources like C. Wright Mills and Albert Camus, but he owed as much or more to ideas that were just "in the air" in radical circles in the 1940s and 1950s.[70]

Hayden's emphasis upon "making values explicit," and only then considering political strategies and realities was new only in one important sense. Dwight Macdonald and Lewis Coser had spoken for and to only a few thousand people who had gone through a similar process of disillusionment. The Port Huron statement, distributed in tens of thousands of mimeographed copies over the next few years, spoke for a generation of activists determined to begin their political involvement without the illusions that had destroyed the Old Left. It proved to be one thing to take the high ground of a transcendent morality and use it as a vantage point from which to criticize the inadequacies of the failed movements of the past; it would prove to be something quite different to use that same morality as the foundation upon which an entirely new movement was to be created.

Despite Hayden's mocking of certain political assumptions dear to the League for Industrial Democracy ("No Cooperation with Commies and Fellow Travellers"), the Port Huron statement was not intended to trigger any fights with the adult organization. There was much in the final document that LID could live with comfortably. Thanks to both Michael Harrington and Steve Max's insistence, the statement endorsed the strategy of political realignment: "An imperative task for these publicly disinherited groups [i.e., civil rights and peace groups as well as the labor movement] . . . is to demand a Democratic Party responsible to their interests." Other sections in the statement, like its criticism of AFL-CIO leaders for their failure to organize the unorganized or to come to the aid of the civil rights movement, were probably less to LID's liking, but were balanced by the admonition that "middle-class students . . . have yet to overcome their ignorance, and even vague hostility, for what they see as 'middle class labor' bureaucrats."[71]

LID's subsequent condemnation of the Port Huron statement astounded its young framers. The "values" section of the statement, to which Hayden had devoted most of his work, didn't interest LID leaders one way or the other. What they focused on instead were: first, the sections of the statement dealing with foreign policy, which to their suspicious eyes seemed to reveal a pro-Soviet bias; and second—what LID regarded as a related failing—the decision taken by the delegates at Port Huron to allow a member of the Communist party's youth group to be seated as an observer.

Michael Harrington had attended the convention as LID's representative. Shortly before the convention he had written in *Dissent* that the older generation on the Left was going to have to handle certain questions delicately, like the popularity that Fidel Castro was currently enjoying among adherents of the New Left.

These attitudes must be faced and changed. But they cannot be done by regaling the newly radical students with the facts of the past. It cannot be done from a lecture platform, from a distance. Rather, the persuasion must come from someone who is actually involved in changing the status quo here, and from someone who has a sympathy for the genuine and good emotions which are just behind the bad theories.[72]

If anyone appeared well suited for that task, it was Harrington himself, who enjoyed good relations with the Michigan SDSers and was clearly someone "involved in changing the status quo." But at Port Huron old habits from the 1950s seemed to reassert themselves. Harrington harangued the students about what he regarded as the manifold shortcomings of the document, as well as the decision to admit a Communist observer. Changes were made in the statement to placate him, and he left apparently satisfied. The final draft of the document, however, had not been decided on (in part because of delays resulting from Harrington's attacks), and its completion was left in the hands of a committee of SDS leaders meeting after the convention. Back in New York a few days later, Harrington received a phone call from one of the YPSL observers at the convention—he later could not recall just who exactly—telling him that all the agreed upon changes had been thrown out. What followed is an oft-told tale: Harrington went to LID leaders to alert them to the apostasy at Port Huron. The LID executive committee met secretly without informing Haber, Hayden, or other SDS leaders (though Haber was officially a member of the executive committee). They then summoned the SDS leaders for a dressing down, fired Haber, and changed the locks on the SDS office. Eventually tempers cooled, Harrington and other LID leaders got around to reading the final text of the document and discovered it wasn't as bad as they had been led to believe, SDS mobilized some of its own adult supporters (including a major LID financial backer), and a compromise was worked out allowing SDS back into its office. It was a story of misunderstandings, hasty decisions, and generational paranoia. But it was also a story with a political context that has not been fully explored.[73]

A year earlier, an internal SDS memorandum probably written by Al Haber took up a variety of organizational problems then facing the group. It included one section entitled "Relationship with YPSL." According to the document, several Socialist party leaders, including Harrington, had recently suggested that "SDS take under its wing a number of autonomous 'political clubs' in which YPSLs are active." These were groups like the Politics Club at the University of Chicago that the Shachtmanites had maintained in one form or another since the late 1940s. SDS was not adverse to taking in new members in large chunks when it could, as it did with the FDR/ Four Freedoms Club. But Haber feared this offer as a Trojan Horse.

YPSL seems to be actively pushing . . . both the affiliation of clubs, and individual YPSLs joining the SDS. Whatever the relation we want ultimately to establish on this score, it does not bode well for them to make policy relative to the SDS . . . without prior consultation with us. . . . Our policy should be that we don't want YPSLs to assume the leadership in the formation of new chapters. . . . It is another issue whether we want them joining existing chapters, and here the thing we want to preserve is the issue rather than ideology orientation of the chapter.[74]

SDS didn't go for the plan. Its leaders may have been still relatively new to the world of radical politics, but they knew enough to want to keep out of YPSL's embrace. If they had any doubts on the matter, all they had to do was look over to the Student Peace Union to see the consequences of a too close relationship with the Shachtmanites. The Young People's Socialist League, or at least that section of its leadership that remained closest to Max Shachtman, was not to be denied that easily. As SDS began to make a name for itself from 1960 to 1962, it became an increasingly desirable political property—not to mention the fact that it had a paid staff position that could be put at the disposal of whoever controlled the organization. Yipsels involved themselves, formally and openly, in SDS's leadership. Dick Roman, Harrington's successor as YPSL chairman, sat on the SDS national executive committee, and Tom Kahn was elected to the committee at Port Huron. But Roman and Kahn carried little weight in the deliberations of the organization, and the adoption of the Port Huron statement signaled SDS's continued progress away from YPSL-style politics. If something didn't change soon, the SDS leadership would consolidate a new political identity and a membership base that would prove invulnerable to YPSL ambitions. The deliberations of YPSL leaders are unavailable to the historian— they met frequently and informally with Shachtman at his house to discuss strategy—so what follows is purely speculation. It is possible that the tense, ambiguous outcome of the Port Huron convention may have suggested to some YPSL leaders their last, best chance for a coup within SDS. A deliberately incendiary telephone call, even if it was meant to deceive one of their own, would not have been the worst thing the Shachtmanites had ever done. Whether or not the exact scenario as described actually took place, there is no question that YPSL's factional maneuvers from 1961 to 1962 left SDS leaders feeling aggrieved and suspicious. There were two ironic aspects involved in this sequence of events: first, that the initial effort by a disciplined cadre organization to capture Students for a Democratic Society was launched not by the "Maoist" Progressive Labor Party (which would begin its own infiltration of SDS only in 1966) but rather by the "democratic socialist" Young People's Socialist League; and second, that the chief political lesson SDSers drew in the aftermath of the Port Huron imbroglio, that "liberals" could not be trusted, was based on a complete misapprehension of what had transpired. Whatever else YPSL represented in 1962—Bolshevism-in-senility or Neoconservatism-in-embryo seem equally valid approximations—it was not "liberalism."[75]

Port Huron was both an ending and a beginning. It was an ending because it represented the culmination of a period of disillusionment, rethinking, and rebuilding that began just after World War II. What did American radicals dream of in the 1950s as they stood amid the shambles of the old parties and ideologies, if it was not something very much like the early Students for a Democratic Society—an authentically native, nondogmatic, open, hopeful movement of young radicals? "The kids are fed up," the poet Kenneth Rexroth, a veteran of the John Reed Clubs, wrote in *Nation* in the summer of 1960:

During the past couple of years, without caring about the consequences, making up their techniques as they went along, organizing spontaneously in the midst of action, young people all over the world have intervened in history.[76]

Their radical elders tended to regard the early New Left with a touch of parental pride, as bold, brash, and innovative, and the young radicals saw no reason to disagree with such flattering assessments. Jack Newfield, a veteran of the FDR/Four Freedoms Club, contrasted the New Left with the Communist, Trotskyist, and Socialist youth groups derived from "the organizations and dogmas of the 1930s" in a 1965 *Nation* article.

The enthusiasts of SNCC and SDS do not engage in sterile, neurotic debates over Kronstadt or the pinpoints of Marxist doctrine. They are thoroughly indigenous radicals: tough, democratic, independent, creative, activist, unsentimental.[77]

The New Left represented the kind of generational rebellion that in its early stages was capable of satisfying young and old alike: the "kids," after all, were rejecting dogmas that most of the parents had themselves already discarded. The revolt of the New Left thus validated the agony of the Old Left. In this sense, Port Huron was as much a part of the history of the Old as of the New Left.

But Port Huron also represented the beginning of something new. And here is where it becomes apparent how little the League for Industrial Democracy understood the document that Hayden had brought to Port Huron. There *were* political dangers lurking in its pages, but they had nothing to do with the shadings of pro- or anti-communism to be found there. Todd Gitlin's memory of his first encounter with the document is telling:

I had read a draft of what was to be the Port Huron statement. I remember being absolutely enraptured by it, thinking "My God, this is what I feel." I wouldn't even say "think" because my thoughts were too inchoate. And yet there's this disjuncture, since it seemed to call for a transformation of life, and yet ends up calling for party realignment. Not that I had any principled opposition to the idea of realignment, but it just didn't seem commensurate.[78]

Old Leftists discarded dogmas they once passionately believed in, and what remained to them was a commitment to a cautious, pragmatic reformism and the hope that in the distant future all those reforms would incrementally add up to some sort of democratic socialism. New Leftists repudiated dogmas they had never shared and then turned with the passionate intensity of the newly converted to building a movement based on what was left to them: personal morality, ethics, and sincerity. What did "party realignment" have to do with the Port Huron statement's promise that "politics" could bring people "out of isolation and into the community . . . a necessary, though not sufficient, means of finding meaning in personal life?" The substance of realignment politics, compromise and coalition, was irrelevant and even antithetical to the vision of a transforming politics that triumphed at Port Huron. Compromise couldn't build community, and coalition couldn't provide meaning in personal life.[79]

The LID reaction to Port Huron sowed the seeds of distrust of liberalism within SDS, and the events of the next few years nurtured and brought them to full bloom: the Justice Department's laconic response to racial terrorism in the South and the willingness of liberals at the 1964 Democratic convention to compromise away the challenge presented by the Mississippi Freedom Democratic party proved to most SDSers that liberals at best could be unreliable allies when it came to promoting domestic reform; the Cuban missile crisis in 1962, and the intervention in Santo Domingo and the escalation of the war in Vietnam in 1965, proved that liberals at worst could be the enemy when it came to the shaping of foreign policy. Steve Max represented an increasingly lonely voice for the realignment perspective within SDS's leadership; his "Political Education Project" was grudgingly funded by SDS in 1964 (chiefly remembered for the buttons it issued during the election campaign, "Part of the Way with LBJ") and dropped the following year. The very size of the Johnson victory in 1964 undercut the realignment argument. The fears of a far Right revival, so prevalent in the mid-Kennedy years, now faded into obscurity. Unlike radicals who could remember back to the 1950s and who viewed the present political climate as a recent and fragile development, radicals who became active in the early 1960s tended to take it for granted that liberal Democrats would remain in power forever—the only important issue was how far and how fast the balance of political power in the nation could be shifted toward the Left.[80]

The young radicals found confirmation that they were destined to succeed where their elders had failed everywhere they looked—and in everything they listened to. Mary Travers, a Red Diaper baby who had studied guitar with Pete Seeger in the 1950s, teamed up with two other young folksingers to form a group called Peter, Paul, and Mary. They took the Old Left anthem "If I Had a Hammer," first performed by Seeger's group, the Weavers, at Communist rallies in 1949, and recorded a version that went to the top of the hit parade in 1962. Another young Seeger protégé, Bob Dylan, came out of a little town in the Midwest and soon took the folk-music scene in New York by storm. He had his first hit with a song promising that social change was "blowin' in the wind." Folk music expressed something of the tremendous sense of excitement of the moment, a sense of intoxicating potential, an affirmation of all that seemed hopeful and uncorrupted in America. Paul Cowan, a member of TOCSIN at Harvard in the early 1960s, and later a volunteer for the Freedom Summer project, recalled, "Whenever I attended one of Seeger's concerts I felt a belief, nearly religious, that there was a generation of people like myself preparing to help America break free." While the folk music of the early 1960s celebrated the redemptive mission of the young, its attitude toward the old tended toward the dismissive, or at best an impatient tolerance. "Come mothers and fathers throughout the land," Dylan implored in his nasal twang in "The Times They Are A-changing" in 1963, "and don't criticize what you can't understand." The times *were* "a-changing," and Dylan soon left his acoustic guitar and his tone of gentle chiding behind. "Something is happening, and you don't know what it is," he sneered in "Ballad for a Thin Man" in 1965, "do you . . . Mister Jones?"[81]

Sincerity, commitment, audacity, and self-sacrifice, the virtues of the young, would carry all before them. Students for a Democratic Society had as little use for those who questioned that perspective as Bob Dylan had for the well-meaning but befuddled "Mr. Jones." "Too many traditional radicals," Hayden complained in 1965, "are still engulfed by the Communist–anti-Communist debate; adhere to overly bureaucratic conceptions of organizing, or are limited fundamentally by their job and family situations, to be considered mainstays of a new movement." When SDS leaders met with *Dissent* editors, they found little to agree upon. Years later Todd Gitlin recalled being approached by Joseph Buttinger at the end of the evening:

I remember Buttinger giving me a copy of his memoir, *In the Twilight of Socialism* (which is an extraordinary book). I remember Tom [Hayden] and I looking at each other knowingly, as if to say, "well, for these guys it's twilight, but we know better."[82]

Perhaps the most breathtaking example of SDS's heedless self-confidence was its decision to establish a series of community organizing projects, collectively known as the Educational Research and

Action Project (ERAP). Most of the group's founding generation of leaders joined the projects (Haber and Max were among the hold-outs) and thus removed themselves from close involvement with the very campus-based movement they had done so much to bring into existence. In 1962, the framers of the Port Huron statement had placed the university at the center of their design for remaking America, the potential home of a student Left "with real intellectual skills," a "community of controversy," a "base for [the] assault upon the loci of power." In the 1964 to 1965 academic year, with the appearance of the Berkeley Free Speech Movement and the teach-in movement, the predictions of the Port Huron statement became a living reality on dozens of campuses. Seldom in history has a group of political visionaries been so swiftly rewarded by the appearance of a movement that so neatly fit their original vision; perhaps never before has anyone so blessed then proceeded to abandon that movement just as it began to realize its potential in favor of other pursuits. It was as if John L. Lewis, having formed the Congress of Industrial Organizations, decided in mid-1936 that what he really wanted to do with his life was resign the CIO presidency and join Dorothy Day in handing out old clothing in one of the Catholic Worker's "Houses of Hospitality"—a worthwhile pursuit, to be sure, but not one that would have made the best use at that particular moment of Lewis's particular talents. But nothing in the experience of the SDS leaders inclined them to think in terms of protecting what they had already assembled. They were tired of being on campus; they were drawn to the heroic example set by SNCC workers in the southern voter registration projects; they, too, wanted to go someplace where they could work with "real people" and not have to have any further dealings with perfidious liberals. They proceeded to go off into the ERAP projects in full confidence that it would all turn out for the best, for themselves and for SDS. They would move to the slums of Newark and Chicago and build "an interracial coalition of the poor," while new leaders would take their places in SDS and generate future community organizers from the ranks of campus radicals; and in the end, the movement would have more of everything it needed: more leaders, more followers, more projects, and an ever-expanding power base in both the slums and on the campuses.[83]

And, for a moment, it seemed to work. Steve Max remembered that by the mid-1960s:

The progression in SDS was to be more and more movement and less and less organization. It was a situation of a movement looking for a place to happen. SDS was the organization that had the budget, and the staff, and the communications lines, to feed the movement, and yet was open to everything and the movement could just pour into it. The more you did to shape it differently, the more the movement would have had to have happened somewhere else.[84]

Things came too easily for SDS. The history of the 1960s was one long series of timely shots-in-the-arm for the New Left, right up to the end. Members poured in regardless of what responsible decisions SDS leaders took, or failed to take, to build the organization. "This last year . . ." Hayden wrote in his 1961 article on the "student boat-rockers" (with a solemnity that would not have appeared out of place in *Dissent* in the mid-1950s), "has seen a lot of dropouts among students who were in the liberal movement just for thrills. 'There will never be another spring 1960,' says an integrationist in Atlanta. 'There is less glory now, and more and more daily plugging.' "[85] Contrary to Hayden's expectations, the thrills and glory would soon be back; the spring of 1960 would be followed by the spring of 1965 and the spring of 1968. After 1961, Hayden never looked back. Students for a Democratic Society expanded with an effortless abandon that was the envy of those in the radical movement with longer memories. "As you know," president Paul Potter commented in an April 1965 mailing to key members, "SDS is growing at an incredible rate. Chapters seem to come in the mail, almost mystically on occasion, coming as often as not from campuses where there has been virtually no direct contact with SDS."[86]

Whenever SDS's growth slowed, another massive new stimulus came along, leading to still another exponential increase in SDS membership. The Cuban missile crisis, Birmingham, Neshoba County, Berkeley, Selma, Watts, the bombing of North Vietnam, Detroit, Newark, the Tet offensive, the May 1968 uprising in Paris, King's assassination—all fed a sense of outrage, a sense of moving with the tide of history, armed with the hammer of justice and the bell of freedom, but gave no occasion for introspection, no suggestion that a careful husbanding of political resources might ever be in order, no premonition that someday the favorable external stimuli might disappear.

The lessons that the New Left learned from the collapse of the Old Left were valuable ones: a distaste for ideological hairsplitting and rigidly centralized organizations gave SDS a flexible and open style that made it particularly well suited to take advantage of the opportunities presented both by the idealism generated by the civil rights movement and the disenchantment generated by the Vietnam War. The lessons that the New Left failed to learn from the experience of the Old Left might have proven of equal or greater value: the need for a patient, long-term approach to building movements; an emphasis upon the value of winning small victories as part of a strategy preparing the way for larger ones; a willingness to work with others with differing viewpoints around limited goals; a commitment to internal political education; an understanding of the need for a representative organizational structure that holds leaders responsible to their own constituents rather than to the priorities established by the media; an appreciation of the value and fragility of civil liberties; and a sense of historical irony that would allow its adherents to keep both victories and defeats in perspective. As its inheritance from the Old Left, the New Left took to heart those lessons that in the short run allowed it to grow spectacularly, but not the lessons that in the long run might have allowed it to survive fruitfully.[87]

NOTES

Preface

1. Maurice Isserman, *Which Side Were You On? The American Communist Party During the Second World War* (Middletown, Conn.: Wesleyan University Press, 1982), pp. 255–256.

2. Lillian Hellman, *Scoundrel Time* (New York: Bantam, 1977); I. F. Stone, *The Haunted Fifties* (New York: Vintage, 1969); Fred J. Cook, *The Nightmare Decade: The Life and Times of Senator Joe McCarthy* (New York: Random House, 1971); Stefan Kanfer, *A Journal of the Plague Years* (New York: Atheneum, 1973); Dalton Trumbo, *The Time of the Toad: A Study of Inquisition in America* (New York: Harper & Row, 1972); David Caute, *The Great Fear: The Anti-Communist Purge Under Truman and Eisenhower* (New York: Simon & Schuster, 1978); Cedric Belfrage, *The American Inquisition: 1945–1960* (Indianapolis: Bobbs-Merrill, 1973); Stanley I. Kutler, *The American Inquisition: Justice and Injustice in the Cold War* (New York: Hill and Wang, 1982).

3. Isserman, *Which Side Were You On?* p. 256.

4. *Time*, 15 August 1977, p. 68.

5. For a recent interpretation of the history of the New Left written in a confessional mode that brings to mind some unpleasant parallels with the 1950s, see the 1985 *Encounter* article "Who Killed the Spirit of '68" by Peter Collier and David Horowitz. "Casting our ballots for Ronald Reagan [in 1984]," they wrote, "was . . . a way of finally saying goodbye to all that— to the self-aggrandising romance with corrupt Third Worldism: to the casual indulgence of Soviet totalitarianism; to the hypocritical and self-dramatising anti-Americanism which is the New Left's bequest to mainstream politics." (*Encounter* editor Melvin Lasky prefaced their article with an endorsement of it as a "notable confession and recantation.") *Encounter* 65 (October 1985):69. See also Jeffrey Herf, "The New Left and its Fading Aura," *Partisan Review* 53:2 (1986):242–252. Anthony Ashbolt offers a perceptive critique of the Collier/Horowitz piece in "Requiem for the Sixties? David Horowitz and the Politics of Forgetting," *Radical America* 19:6 (1985):65–73.

6. Stanley Rothman and S. Robert Lichter, *Roots of Radicalism: Jews, Christians, and the New Left* (New York: Oxford University Press, 1982).

7. For examples of psychological interpretations of the history of American communism, see Morris L. Ernst and David Loth, *Report on the American Communist* (New York: Holt, 1952); and Gabriel A. Almond, *The Appeals of American Communism* (Princeton: Princeton University Press, 1954). Nathan Glazer, whose credentials as a critic of communism should require no elaboration, took issue with such psychological interpretations in his book *The Social Basis of American Communism*: "For certain social groups, for certain milieux, *it was neither eccentric nor exceptional to become a Communist.* The 'normal' Communists, the Communists who joined the party in the course of a relatively common psychological development, far, far outnumber those who had exceptional and rare psychological reasons for joining." Nathan Glazer, *The Social Basis of American Communism* (New York: Harcourt, Brace & World, 1961), p. 6.

8. Rothman and Lichter, *Roots of Radicalism*, p. 13.

9. The citation for Kahn's talk in *Roots of Radicalism* (the designation "keynote speech" is of Rothman and Lichter's own invention, and serves to further inflate its significance) is to Mitchell Cohen and Dennis Hale's anthology *The New Student Left*. A note that appears after Kahn's speech in the Cohen/Hale anthology clearly identifies him as a past leader of the Young People's Socialist League, and current director of the League for Industrial Democracy. Rothman and Lichter, *Roots of Radicalism*, p. 13, p. 414n; Mitchell Cohen and Dennis Hale, *The New Student Left* (Boston: Beacon Press, 1966), p. 68. The main point of Kahn's speech, incidentally, as opposed to the inflammatory portion that Rothman and Lichter lifted out of

context, is an argument in favor of the "realignment strategy" described in the last chapter of this book, a strategy that would have radicals work within the Democratic party for social change.

10. Dan Georgakas, "Young Detroit Radicals, 1955–1965," in *C. L. R. James, His Life and Work*, ed. Paul Buhle (London: Alison & Busby, 1986), pp. 89–94.

11. The concept of "political language" is discussed in Gareth Stedman Jones's introduction to *Languages of Class: Studies in English Working Class History, 1832–1982* (Cambridge, England: Cambridge University Press, 1983), especially pp. 19–24.

12. *Daily Worker*, 10 July 1956.

Chapter 1

1. Sources on the attack on the Communists in these years include David Caute, *The Great Fear: The Anti-Communist Purge Under Truman and Eisenhower* (New York: Simon & Schuster, 1978); Robert Goldstein, *Political Repression in Modern America: 1870 to the Present* (Cambridge: Schenkman, 1978), pp. 285–396; Peter L. Steinberg, *The Great "Red Menace": United States Prosecution of American Communists, 1947–1952* (Westport, Conn.: Greenwood Press, 1984); Michael R. Belknap, *Cold War Political Justice: The Smith Act, the Communist Party, and American Civil Liberties* (Westport, Conn.: Greenwood Press, 1978); and Stanley I. Kutler, *The American Inquisition: Justice and Injustice in the Cold War* (New York: Hill and Wang, 1982). For a personal account, see Steve Nelson's *The Thirteenth Juror: The Inside Story of My Trial* (New York: Masses and Mainstream, 1955) and Steve Nelson, James R. Barrett, and Rob Ruck, *Steve Nelson, American Radical* (Pittsburgh: University of Pittsburgh Press, 1981), pp. 298–379.

2. "National Board Minutes," 8 February 1944, TS. From the collection of Philip Jaffe.

3. These events are described in greater detail in Joseph Starobin, *American Communism in Crisis, 1943–1957* (Berkeley: University of California Press, 1972), pp. 3–120; and Maurice Isserman, *Which Side Were You On? The American Communist Party During the Second World War* (Middletown, Conn.: Wesleyan University Press, 1982).

4. For Foster's exercise in self-criticism, see *Political Affairs* 35 (October 1956):15–45.

5. Starobin, *American Communism in Crisis*, pp. 155–194; David Shannon, *The Decline of American Communism* (New York: Harcourt, Brace & World, 1959), pp. 104–106; Nelson, Barrett, Ruck, *Steve Nelson*, pp. 287–289.

6. Al Richmond, *A Long View from the Left: Memoirs of an American Revolutionist* (New York: Delta, 1972), pp. 312–314, 362–363; George Charney, *A Long Journey* (Chicago: Quadrangle, 1968), pp. 215, 224–227; Steinberg, *The Red Menace*, pp. 77–78, 148–150, 192–193, 262–263; Nelson, Barrett, Ruck, *Steve Nelson*, p. 318; John Gates, *On Guard Against Browderism, Titoism, Trotskyism* (New York: New Century, 1951).

7. On the thaw in the Cold War, see Adam Ulam, *Expansion and Coexistence: Soviet Foreign Policy 1917–1973* (New York: Praeger, 1974), pp. 560–571. On the waning of the apocalyptic mood in the CP, see Steinberg, *The Red Menace*, pp. 263–266; *Daily Worker*, 5 December 1955. For one Communist leader's decision to "surface," see Gil Green, *Cold War Fugitive: A Personal Story of the McCarthy Years* (New York: International Publishers, 1984), pp. 138–158.

8. Joseph Starobin, *From Paris to Peking* (New York: Cameron Associates, 1955); idem, "1956: A Memoir," *Problems of Communism* 15 (November-December, 1966):65; John Gates, *The Story of an American Communist* (New York: Thomas Nelson, 1958), p. 160. The influence of Starobin's book was cited by some CP dissenters during the deStalinization crisis in explaining the evolution of their own thinking. See for examples, *Daily Worker*, 13, 24 April 1956.

9. *Daily Worker*, 15, 16, 17, 21 February 1956. See also Alec Nove, *Stalinism and After* (London: George Allen & Unwin, 1975), pp. 127–134.

10. This argument is presented in more detail in Isserman, *Which Side Were You On?*, pp. 3–14; and Isserman, "The 1956 Generation: An Alternative Approach to the History of American Communism," *Radical America* (March-April 1980):42–51. A different interpretation of the period can be found in Harvey Klehr, *The Heyday of American Communism: The Depression Decade* (New York: Basic Books, 1984); and in Theodore Draper, "American Communism Revisited," *New York Review of Books*, 9 May 1985 and "The Popular Front Revisited," *New York Review of Books*, 30 May 1985. Draper's articles were reprinted as an epilogue to a new edition of his *American Communism and Soviet Russia* (New York: Vintage, 1986), pp. 445–482. For an overview of the debate over the proper interpretation of CP history see Isserman, "Three Generations: Historians View American Communism," *Labor History* 26 (Fall 1985): 517–545.

11. Frank Meyer to Earl Browder, 29 November 1943. Earl Browder Papers, II-157. Irving Howe offered an interesting reappraisal of the Popular Front in his recent collection of essays on American socialism: "The most interesting group of party members consisted of people with some standing and experience who, almost against their will and perhaps to their own surprise, came to value the Popular Front as both a shrewd maneuver and more than that— indeed, may even have come to believe that, for America at least, this was the way radicals should go. . . . We may doubt that many of them went so far as to recognize that the Popular Front really signified a break from classical Leninism and even, perhaps, the start of an adaptation to the special circumstances of American life. But most changes of thought occur hesitantly, and language always lags behind impulse and feeling." Irving Howe, *Socialism and America* (New York: Harcourt Brace Jovanovich, 1985), p. 101.

12. Joseph Clark, *The Real Russia* (New York: International Publishers, 1954), pp. 19–20.

13. *Daily Worker*, 12 March 1956.

14. *Daily Worker*, 13 March 1956.

15. *Daily Worker*, 16, 28 March 1956.

16. *Daily Worker*, 22 March 1956.

17. *Daily Worker*, 9 April 1956.

18. *Daily Worker*, 29 March 1956.

19. *Daily Worker*, 30 March, 2, 11, 12, 13, 16 April 1956. See also *Jewish Life* 10 (May 1956): 37, 40; (June 1956):3, 30; and Morris Schappes, "The Martyred Soviet Yiddish Writers," *Jewish Currents* 34 (May 1980):12–16.

20. *Daily Worker*, 11 April 1956.

21. Irving Howe and Lewis Coser, *The American Communist Party: A Critical History, 1919–1957* (Boston: Beacon Press, 1957), p. 491.

22. In fact some dissenting Communists made use of the same analogy to explain the crisis in 1956. See, for example, Abner Berry's column, "Stalin Wasn't God—And We Weren't Angels," *Daily Worker*, 14 June 1956.

23. See Foster's column in mid-April in which he conceded Stalin was responsible for many policies of a "reactionary character," but defended Stalin's "good intentions." *Daily Worker*, 19 April 1956.

24. George Charney offered this revealing description of Dennis: "He was cast into the role of chief public spokesman and yet had an irrational fear of public confrontations, of freewheeling clashes of opinion. Perhaps this fear was simply motivated by an obsession with formulations in which each thought had to be carefully processed, laundered, dry-cleaned, chastened to the point of absolute purity." Charney, *Long Journey*, p. 266. Steve Nelson said of Dennis that he "seemed to have an unlimited capacity for vacillation." Nelson, Barrett, Ruck, *Steve Nelson*, p. 385. For a very different interpretation of Dennis's role from the one presented here see Peggy Dennis, *The Autobiography of an American Communist: A Personal View of a Political Life, 1925-1975* (Westport, Conn.: Lawrence Hill, 1977), pp. 226–227; Dennis, letter to the Editors, *Socialist Review* 12 (September-October 1982):140–143; idem, "A Half-View of History" (privately circulated manuscript, 1982); and James Wigren, "Eugene

223

Dennis and the 'Americanization' of the Communist Party, USA" (MA thesis, George Washington University, 1985).

25. *Daily Worker,* 27 June 1956.

26. *Daily Worker,* 3 May 1956.

27. *Daily Worker,* 4 July 1956.

28. Jessica Mitford, *A Fine Old Conflict* (New York: Knopf, 1977), p. 326.

29. *Daily Worker,* 29 June 1956.

30. *Daily Worker,* 29 May 1956.

31. *Daily Worker,* 13, 17 April, 3, 4, 17 May 1956.

32. Chick Mason, "Sources of Our Dilemma," mimeo, July 1956, p. 5. In the Tamiment Institute Collection at New York University, hereafter Tamiment Collection, OF: CPUSA, 1956. See also *Daily Worker,* 17 April 1956. See also *Daily Worker,* 13 April, 14 June, 12 September 1956, 28 February, 2 March 1957.

33. Mason, "Sources," p. 19.

34. *Daily Worker,* 10 July 1956. See also *Daily Worker,* 20, 27 August 1956, 24 January 1957.

35. *Daily Worker,* 26 March 1956.

36. *Daily Worker,* 5 June 1956.

37. *The Anti-Stalin Campaign and International Communism* (New York: Columbia University Press, 1956), p. 23. The complete text of the speech is on pp. 1–89.

38. Interview with Dorothy Healey, 30 May 1984.

39. The quotation from Dorothy Healey is from Julia Reichert and Jim Klein's 1984 documentary film, *Seeing Red: Stories of American Communists.* See also Charney, *Long Journey,* p. 270; Nelson, Barrett, Ruck, *Steve Nelson,* pp. 386–387; Dorothy Healey, "Tradition's Chains Have Bound Us," vol. 1 (Los Angeles: University of California, 1982), pp. 439–446. "Tradition's Chains" is the transcript of a series of interviews conducted by Joel Gardner with Dorothy Healey in the early 1970s, under the auspices of the UCLA Oral History Program.

40. Eugene Dennis, *The Communists Take a New Look* (New York: New Century, 1956).

41. Gates, *Story,* pp. 164–169; Charney, *Long Journey,* p. 280; *Daily Worker,* 15, 20 June, 19 September, 24 October 1956; *Party Voice* (September 1956).

42. Charney, *Long Journey,* pp. 280–284; Shannon, *Decline,* pp. 319–320. Doxie Wilkerson and Abner Berry were prominent black Communists who sided with the reform forces in 1956.

43. Max Gordon to the author, 10 October 1980.

44. *New York Times,* 3 August 1956, 27 January 1957.

45. Max Gordon to the author, 10 October 1980.

46. Alvah Bessie, *Men in Battle, A Story of Americans in Spain* (New York: Scribners, 1939), p. 194.

47. *Daily Worker,* 6 November 1956. See also Nelson, Barrett, Ruck, *Steve Nelson,* p. 393.

48. Interview with Dorothy Healey, 30 May 1984. See also articles by Max Weiss, *Daily Worker,* 5, 6 April 1956, and by Max Gordon, *Daily Worker,* 24 April 1956.

49. *Political Affairs* 35 (November 1956):55–56.

50. *Party Voice* (January 1957):12.

51. Healey, "Tradition's Chains," vol. 1, pp. 437–438, 459, 462, 464.

52. *Proceedings (Abridged) of the 16th National Convention of the CPUSA* (New York: Communist Party, 1957), p. 59.

53. Ulam, *Expansion and Coexistence,* pp. 581–582. See also the editorial on "The Poznan Tragedy," *Daily Worker,* 2 July 1956.

54. *Daily Worker,* 5 November 1956.

55. *Daily Worker,* 12 November 1956.

56. Minutes of debate on Hungary question, MS, in Dorothy Healey's personal collection; *Daily Worker,* 20 November 1956; *Political Affairs* 35 (December 1956):1–5; Healey, "Tradition's Chains," vol. 1, pp. 468–470; Nelson, Barrett, Ruck, *Steve Nelson,* pp. 390–391.

57. *Daily Worker,* 2 November 1956.

58. *Daily Worker,* 14 November 1956.

59. *Proceedings,* pp. 237–238. See also Shannon, *Decline,* pp. 324–332.

60. Healey, "Tradition's Chains," vol. 2, p. 519; interview with Dorothy Healey, 30 May 1984.

61. Healey, "Tradition's Chains," vol. 2, p. 496; *New York Times,* 11 May 1957; *Daily Worker,* 7 June 1957.

62. *Daily Worker,* 10 September 1957.

63. *New York Times,* 27 December 1957; Gates, *Story,* pp. 189–191.

64. *Daily Worker,* 13 July 1956.

65. Charney, *Long Journey,* pp. 308, 310. Saul Wellman made the interesting point that the 500 to 600 full-time cadre who left the Party during the deStalinization crisis were less likely to remain politically active than less well-known ex-Communists who had not depended on the Party for their paycheck. Wellman himself became an apprentice in the printing trade at the age of forty-five after years of Party work. Interview with Saul Wellman, 8 November 1984. Steve Nelson details his own difficult struggle to make a living after resigning from the Party in *Steve Nelson,* pp. 403–408.

66. Irving Howe, "New Styles in 'Leftism,' " *Dissent* 12 (Summer 1965):300–301.

67. Ibid., p. 301.

68. For attempts to discredit the civil rights and peace movements by calling attention to the presence of former or alleged Communists in their ranks, see David Garrow, *Bearing the Cross: Martin Luther King, Jr., and the Southern Christian Leadership Conference* (New York: William Morrow, 1986), pp. 235, 304; and U.S. Senate, Committee on the Judiciary, *The Anti-Vietnam Agitation and the Teach-In Movement, The Problem of Communist Infiltration and Exploitation,* 89th Cong., 1st sess., 1965, pp. 45–90.

Chapter 2

1. "The Reminiscences of Max Shachtman," vol. 1, pp. 1–6. Cited with permission. Shachtman was interviewed in 1963 for the Columbia University Oral History Research History Office collection. Hereafter listed as "Reminiscences." See also Albert Glotzer, "Max Shachtman—A Political-Biographical Essay," *Bulletin of the Tamiment Institute* 50 (April 1983):3–8.

2. Shachtman, "Reminiscences," vol. 1, pp. 10–13; Theodore Draper, *The Roots of American Communism* (New York: Viking Press, 1957), pp. 333–343.

3. Shachtman, "Reminiscences," vol. 1, pp. 15–19; interview with Albert Glotzer, 4 October 1984.

4. Shachtman, "Reminiscences," vol. 1, p. 70, vol. 2, pp. 148–154, 161–170; interview with Albert Glotzer, 4 October 1984; Theodore Draper, *American Communism and Soviet Russia: The Formative Period* (New York: Viking Press, 1960), pp. 362–376; Constance Ashton Myers, *The Prophet's Army: Trotskyists in America, 1928–1941* (Westport, Conn.: Greenwood Press, 1977), pp. 27–32.

5. Irving Howe, *A Margin of Hope: An Intellectual Biography* (New York: Harcourt Brace Jovanovich, 1982), p. 40.

6. Shachtman, "Reminiscences," vol. 3, pp. 356–380; Myers, *Prophet's Army,* pp. 134–135, 201.

7. For Cannon's attitude toward intellectuals, see *James P. Cannon As We Knew Him,* ed. Jack Barnes (New York: Pathfinder Press, 1976), pp. 28–29. For the special appeal of Trotskyism to intellectuals in the 1930s, see Dwight Macdonald, *Memoirs of a Revolutionist* (New York: Farrar, Strauss & Cudahy, 1957), p. 13; Max Shachtman, "Radicalism: The Trotskyist View," *As We Saw the Thirties,* ed. Rita James Simon (Urbana: University of Illinois Press, 1967), pp.

41–43; James Gilbert, *Writers and Partisans: A History of Literary Radicalism in America* (New York: Wiley, 1968), pp. 188–221; Irving Kristol, "Memoirs of a Trotskyist," *New York Times Magazine*, 23 January 1977; and Alan Wald, "The Menorah Group Moves Left," *Jewish Social Studies* 38 (Summer-Fall 1976):289–320. Cannon told a sly anecdote, after he and Shachtman split, to illustrate what he regarded as Shachtman's ineptitude in the class struggle. During the 1934 general strike in Minneapolis, Shachtman and Cannon were on hand to direct the efforts of the Trotskyist faction within the Teamsters Union. The city had been placed under martial law, and the Trotskyist leaders rarely left their hiding place. One night they ventured downtown to see a movie and were spotted by city detectives. As Cannon told the story: "Shachtman was wearing a great big ten-gallon cowboy hat—where he got it, or why in God's name he wore it, I never knew—and that made him conspicuous." The two were promptly arrested. No one in the Trotskyist movement, with the possible exception of Leon Trotsky, would have looked more out of place in a cowboy hat than Shachtman. James Cannon, *The History of American Trotskyism* (New York: Pathfinder Press, 1944), p. 162.

8. Interview with Phyllis Jacobson, 21 April 1984; Howe, *Margin of Hope*, p. 50; interview with Julius Jacobson, 21 April 1984; Julius Jacobson, "The Two Deaths of Max Shachtman," *New Politics* 10 (Winter 1973):96. See also Lionel Abel, *The Intellectual Follies: A Memoir of the Literary Venture in New York and Paris* (New York: Norton, 1984), pp. 56–57.

9. Interview with Gordon Haskell, 15 July 1983. My portrayal of Shachtman's personality draws upon conversations I have had with Haskell, Hal Draper, Julius and Phyllis Jacobson, Irving Howe, Michael Harrington, Albert Glotzer, Bogdan Denitch, Debbie Meier, Manny Geltman, and David McReynolds, not all of whom would agree with my conclusions.

10. Cannon, *American Trotskyism*, pp. 251–252.

11. Interview with Hal Draper, 29 December 1983. Standard accounts of the SP-Trotskyist imbroglio include Daniel Bell, "The Background and Development of Marxian Socialism in the United States," *Socialism and American Life*, vol. 1, ed. Donald Drew Egbert and Stow Persons (Princeton: Princeton University Press, 1952), pp. 384–388; David A. Shannon, *The Socialist Party of America* (New York: Macmillan, 1955), pp. 251–254; W. A. Swanberg, *Norman Thomas, The Last Idealist* (New York: Scribner, 1976), pp. 217–219; and Myers, *Prophet's Army*, pp. 123–142. See also Patti McGill Peterson, "The Young Socialist Movement in America from 1905 to 1940: A Study of the Young People's Socialist League" (Ph.D. diss., University of Wisconsin, 1974). For Trotskyist strategy in the 1930s, see Cannon, *American Trotskyism*; Shachtman, "25 Years of American Trotskyism," *New International* 20 (January–February 1954); and Isaac Deutscher, *The Prophet Outcast, Trotsky: 1929–1940*, vol. 3 (New York: Vintage, 1963).

12. Ernest Erber to author, 3 July 1984.

13. On the debate over "bureaucratic collectivism" see Leon Trotsky, "The USSR in the War," *New International* 5 (November 1939):325–332; James P. Cannon, "Speech on the Russian Question," *New International* 6 (February 1940):8–13; Trotsky, "Again and Once More on the Nature of the USSR," ibid.:13–17, and "Resolution on Russia," ibid.:17–24; Trotsky, "A Petty Bourgeois Opposition in the Socialist Workers Party," *New International* 6 (March 1940):35–42, and "From a Scratch—to the Danger of Gangrene," ibid.:51–64; Shachtman, "The Crisis in the American Party, An Open Letter in Reply to Comrade Leon Trotsky," ibid.: 43–51; Shachtman, "The Soviet Union and the World War," *New International* 6 (April 1940): 68–71. See also Shachtman, "Reminiscences," vol. 3, pp. 307–315, and his collected essays in *The Bureaucratic Revolution: The Rise of the Stalinist State* (New York: Donald Press, 1962); Deutscher, *The Prophet Outcast*, pp. 459–477; and John Diggins, *Up from Communism: Conservative Odysseys in American Intellectual History* (New York: Harper & Row, 1975), pp. 181–189; Hannah Arendt, *The Origins of Totalitarianism* (New York: Harcourt Brace Jovanovich, 1973).

14. Workers Party, *Information Bulletin* no. 24 (10 October 1940) in Shachtman Collection, Reel 3361.

15. Interview with Gordon Haskell, 15 July 1983. See also comments by Albert Glotzer in the transcript of the "Workers Party Standing Fast Conference," held at the Tamiment Institute, New York University, 6–7 May 1983, celebrating the opening of the Shachtman Collection, hereafter, Standing Fast transcript.

16. Stan Weir offers a firsthand account of the war years by a WP union activist in "American Labor on the Defensive: A 1940s Odyssey," *Radical America* 9 (July-August 1975):163–185. Jon Bloom has kindly shown me his graduate seminar paper, "Wartime Revolutionaries: The Workers Party and World War II." On the CIO's internal politics and the controversy over the no-strike pledge, see Nelson Lichtenstein, *Labor's War at Home: The CIO in World War Two* (New York: Cambridge University Press, 1982). See also Harvey Swados's novel, *Standing Fast* (Garden City, New York: Doubleday, 1970). Swados was a leader in the Buffalo WP branch and a United Auto Worker activist during the war years.

17. Ernest Lund [Ernest Erber], "The Turn to a Mass Party," n.d. [1943], mimeo, OF: WP (3) Tamiment Collection; Ernest Erber to author, 18 June 1984, 26 October 1984; Erber, "My Political Biography," unpublished TS in author's possession; interview with Gordon Haskell, 15 July 1983; interview with Albert Glotzer, 4 October 1984.

18. Blake Lear [C.K. Stewart], "The objective basis of our failure to recruit" (19 September 1943), mimeo, OF: WP (3) Tamiment Collection; Ernest Erber to author, 18 June 1984.

19. Daniel Bell, "Marxian Socialism in the United States," p. 222n. See also Lewis Coser, "Sects and Sectarians," *Dissent* 1 (Autumn 1954):360–369. For descriptive accounts of left-wing sectarianism in the United States, see Robert J. Alexander, "Splinter Groups in American Radical Politics," *Social Research* 20 (Fall 1953):297–303; and Alexander, "Schisms and Unifications in the American Old Left, 1953–1970," *Labor History* 14 (Fall 1973):536–561. "Never before," Irving Howe would write of this period in his memoirs, "and surely never since, have I lived at so high, so intense a pitch, or been so absorbed in ideas beyond the smallness of self. It began to seem as if the very shape of reality could be molded by our will, as if those really attuned to the inner rhythms of History might bend it to submission." Howe, *Margin of Hope*, p. 42.

20. There *were* occasional discouraging moments when WPers caught a glimpse of the final destination of some of those papers. Gordon Haskell worked as a locomotive fireman during the war and proved an effective rank-and-file union activist. But he was unable to interest many of his fellow workers in the WP. Like many other party members with wartime jobs, he kept *Labor Action* informed of his own activities and of important developments in his industry and union: "I wrote a series of articles on the situation with the railroads, which I thought was right down to earth. When it came out I saw to it that bundles were put out at all the round-houses and wash up places where railroad workers gathered. I remember one time watching a man in the change room looking at a copy of *Labor Action* very carefully. He had spread out the paper and was leafing through it very thoughtfully. And I thought, 'Boy, you know, I've really got to mark this guy down.' And then he took his dirty overalls, put them on the paper, wrapped them up, and put them in his bag." Interview with Gordon Haskell, 15 July 1983.

21. Comments by Julius Jacobson, Standing Fast transcript, p. 2; *Labor Action*, 2 August 1943.

22. Shachtman, "An Epigone of Trotsky," *New International* 10 (August 1944):266.

23. *Labor Action*, 8 March 1948.

24. E. R. McKinney to Max Shachtman, 10 March 1948, Reel 3380, Shachtman Collection; *Labor Action*, 17 May 1948. On McKinney, see his obituary, *New York Times*, 1 February 1984. Shachtman's response displayed his commitment to maintaining the right to dissent within the Workers party. While agreeing with McKinney's sentiments, he also reiterated Howe's right to express his opinions, however misguided: "I am quite prepared and even anxious to have people begin thinking out their thoughts to the end . . . instead of mumbling to themselves in a disjointed and incoherent way . . . so that we may thereupon be able to take the questions before the party . . . and establish which point of view really corresponds to the

interests of the party and the working class." See Max Shachtman to E. R. McKinney, 5 May 1948, Reel 3380, Shachtman Collection.

25. Michael Harrington encountered many former WPers while visiting Detroit as a Shachtmanite youth organizer in the mid-1950s: "By that point there was a joke going around the UAW staff that the best way to become a union bureaucrat was to join the Shachtmanites. Reuther made a point of coopting his opposition as fast as he possibly could, so with a couple of articles to your credit in *Labor Action* you were a likely candidate to be appointed to UAW staff." Interview with Michael Harrington, 19 November 1982.

26. Gordon Haskell to Political Committee, November 1948, OF: WP (3), Tamiment Collection.

27. "Membership Figures, November 23, 1946 and October 1, 1947," mimeo, Reel 3363, Shachtman Collection.

28. "Keeping some of the old language," Irving Howe would later write, "we twisted it to new ideas. Isn't that how most people change their ideas, insisting that they are still faithful to old verities and merely introducing a few adjustments?" Howe, *Margin of Hope*, p. 80.

29. Ernest Erber to Ed Findley, 8 October 1948, in author's possession. Emphasis in original. The contents of this letter are discussed on pp. 53–55.

30. Irving Howe and Stanley Plastrik to Political Committee, 12 October 1952, TS, Reel 3370, Shachtman Collection. See also Erber, "Statement of Resignation," *Bulletin of the Workers Party* 4, Part 1 [1949]; Erber, "My Political Biography"; Erber to author, 26 August 1984; Shachtman, "Under the Banner of Marxism," *Bulletin of the Workers Party* 4, Part 2 [1949]; *Labor Action*, 25 October 1948.

31. Howe and Plastrik to Political Committee, 12 October 1952, TS, Reel 3370, Shachtman Collection; interview with Gordon Haskell, 15 July 1983; interview with Hal Draper, 29 December 1983.

32. *Labor Action*, 25 April 1949; interview with Hal Draper, 29 December 1983.

33. Shachtman, "Aspects of the British Labour Government," *New International* 17 (January-February 1951):12; *Labor Action*, 23 July 1951. See also Theodore Rosenof, "The American Democratic Left Looks at the British Labour Government, 1945–1951," *Historian* 38 (1975):98–119.

34. Howe, *Margin of Hope*, pp. 106–107; *Labor Action*, 10 April 1950. The complete text of the Shachtman-Browder debate was published in *New International* 16 (May-June 1950):145–176. Michael Harrington said of the conclusion of the debate, "That story was told and retold; it practically became a folk song." Interview with Michael Harrington, 19 November 1982.

35. *Labor Action*, 27 February 1954, 15 March 1954; interview with Hal Draper, 29 December 1983; interview with Julius Jacobson, 21 April 1984.

36. *Labor Action*, 29 April 1946; interview with Julius Jacobson, 21 April 1984.

37. Julius Falk [Julius Jacobson], "American Student Movement: A Survey," *New International* 15 (March 1949):84–91; William R. McIntyre, "Student Movements," *Editorial Research Reports* 2 (11 December 1957):926; Kirkpatrick Sale, *SDS* (New York: Vintage Books, 1974), pp. 684–687; James P. O'Brien, "The Development of a New Left in the United States, 1960–1965" (Ph.D. diss., University of Wisconsin, 1971), pp. 55–56; Curtiss D. MacDougall, *Gideon's Army* (New York: Marzani and Munsell, 1965), vol. 1, p. 159, vol. 3, pp. 588–591. Robert L. Tyler, "The American Veterans Committee: Out of a Hot War into the Cold," *American Quarterly* 18 (Fall 1966):419–436. Eileen M. Eagan has kindly shown me her unpublished paper "Student Political Activism in the Post World War II Period."

38. Philip G. Altbach, *Student Politics in America: A Historical Analysis* (New York: McGraw-Hill, 1974), p. 114; interview with Ronald Radosh, 10 July 1984; interview with Andre Schiffrin, 19 June 1983.

39. On the CP's influence over the folk revival of the 1940s, see Richard A. Reuss, "American Folklore and Left-Wing Politics: 1927–1957" (Ph.D. diss., Indiana University, 1971). And

on the Trotskyist response, see R. Serge Denisoff and Richard Reuss, "The Protest Songs and Skits of American Trotskyists," *Journal of Popular Culture* 6 (Fall 1972):407–424.

40. *Labor Action,* 11 April 1949, 20 June 1949; interview with Michael Harrington, 19 November 1982; Michael Harrington, *Fragments of the Century* (New York: Simon & Schuster, 1973), pp. 33–49; interview with George Rawick, 17 August 1984; Allen Ginsburg, *Howl* (San Francisco: City Lights, 1956), p. 15.

41. George Rawick, "The American Student: A Profile," *Dissent* 2 (Autumn 1954):393–398; Jack Newfield, *A Prophetic Minority* (New York: New American Library, 1970), pp. 28–29.

42. Interview with Betty Denitch, 6 August 1984.

43. My portrayal of Michael Harrington draws upon conversations with Betty Denitch, Bogdan Denitch, Debbie Meier, Dorothy Tristman, and Irving Howe, as well as my own impressions. See also Harrington, *Fragments,* pp. 64–93.

44. Interview with Bogdan Denitch, 7 December 1984; "Statement of James Farmer Before YPSL Convention, December 20, 1951," SDS Papers, Box 3, Tamiment Collection; Bogdan Denitch to James Farmer, 4 April 1952, SDS Papers, Box 3, Tamiment Collection; Arthur Mitzman, "The Campus Radical in 1960," *Dissent* 7 (Spring 1960):143–144; *Hammer and Tongs,* Spring 1958 (Socialist party internal discussion bulletin), p. 25.

45. Harrington, *Fragments,* p. 71. See also Michael Harrington to "Paula," 30 April 1956, Reel 3379, Shachtman Collection.

46. Interview with Michael Harrington, 19 November 1982; Peterson, "The Young Socialist Movement in America"; Altbach, *Student Politics in America,* pp. 57–108.

47. *Young Socialist Challenge,* 17 May 1954.

48. Interview with Dave McReynolds, 19 July 1984.

49. *Young Socialist Review* 1, 22 May 1954, 15 August 1954; Harrington, *Fragments,* p. 61.

50. Interview with Michael Harrington, 19 November 1982; *Young Socialist Challenge,* 21 June 1954. "Must Our Youth Die in Indochina?" asked a headline in *Young Socialist Challenge* on 26 April 1954, a question that probably would have seemed bizarre to most Americans in 1954, but which turned out in the long run to have been fairly prescient.

51. Harrington, *Fragments,* p. 62.

52. *Labor Action,* 26 March 1956.

53. *Labor Action,* 26 April 1956.

54. Interview with Dave McReynolds, 19 July 1984; *Hammer and Tongs,* May 1956; Alexander, "Schisms and Unifications," pp. 540–541.

55. Interview with Dave McReynolds, 19 July 1984; *Labor Action,* 25 June 1956.

56. Max Shachtman to Barney Cohen, 22 February 1958, Reel 3377, Shachtman Collection. Emphasis in original.

57. *New International* 21 (Fall 1956):139–178.

58. Hugh Cleland to Max Shachtman [n.d., 1957], Shachtman Collection.

59. Max Shachtman to Barney Cohen, 28 February 1958, Reel 3377, Shachtman Collection.

60. *Labor Action,* 8 July 1957; *Young Socialist Review* 3 (4 March 1957); Tim Wohlforth, "What Makes Shachtman Run? The Life and Death of a Tendency," mimeo (August 1957), Box 40, Shachtman Collection; interview with Tim Wohlforth, 29 August 1976 in Oral History of the American Left series, Tamiment Collection; Alexander, "Schisms and Unifications," p. 556.

61. Norman Thomas to Max Shachtman, 20 September 1957, OF: ISL, Tamiment Collection; interview with Dave McReynolds, 19 July 1984.

62. Max Shachtman to Norman Thomas, 1 October 1957, OF: ISL, Tamiment Collection.

63. Max Shachtman to Norman Thomas, 1 October 1957, OF: ISL, Tamiment Collection; interview with Michael Harrington, 19 November 1982; interview with Bogdan Denitch, 7 December 1984; *Hammer and Tongs,* Spring 1958, p. 5. Other SPers pointed to the presence of a number of experienced UAW activists in ISL ranks as a reason to support the merger. See

letter from Al Nash and Bernie Rifkin to Socialist party-Social Democratic Federation National Committee, 24 February 1958, Reel 3370, Shachtman Collection.

64. Letter from Robin Myers to Socialist party members, 16 June 1958, Reel 3370, Shachtman Collection.

65. Interview with Dave McReynolds, 19 July 1984. McReynolds's memories of this meeting are substantiated by a letter he sent to Shachtman, 24 July 1958, Reel 3380, Shachtman Collection.

66. *Labor Action*, 22 September 1958; *New International* 24 (Spring-Summer 1958):72–75, 148.

67. Interview with Hal Draper, 29 December 1983; interview with Julius Jacobson, 21 April 1984; interview with Debbie Meier, 19 April 1986.

Chapter 3

1. Ignazio Silone, *Bread and Wine* (New York: New American Library, 1963), p. 216.
2. *Dissent* 3 (Winter 1956):74.
3. James Gilbert, *Writers and Partisans: A History of Literary Radicalism in America* (New York: Wiley, 1968), p. viii. See also Lionel Trilling, *The Liberal Imagination* (New York: Viking, 1951), pp. 93–103; Terry A. Cooney, *The Rise of the New York Intellectuals: Partisan Review and its Circle, 1934–1945* (Madison: University of Wisconsin Press, 1987); Lewis Coser, *Men of Ideas, A Sociologist's View* (New York: Free Press, 1970), pp. 121–132.
4. Irving Kristol, "Memoirs of a Trotskyist," *New York Times Sunday Magazine*, 23 January 1977, p. 57. Irving Howe described his initial encounter with *Partisan Review* in *Creators and Disturbers: Reminiscences by Jewish Intellectuals of New York*, ed. Bernard Rosenberg and Ernest Goldstein (New York: Columbia University Press, 1982), p. 281.
5. Irving Howe, *A Margin of Hope: An Intellectual Biography* (New York: Harcourt Brace Jovanovich, 1982), p. 85.
6. Ibid., pp. 2–3.
7. Irving Howe, "The New York Intellectuals, A Chronicle and A Critique," *Commentary* 46 (October 1968):30.
8. Kristol, "Memoirs," p. 55. For biographical details see Howe, *A Margin of Hope*, and Estelle Gilson, "The Shaping of a Free Man, Irving Howe Profiled," *Present Tense* 6 (Spring 1979): 26.
9. Interview with Lewis Coser, 3 May 1985.
10. Interview with Hal Draper, 29 December 1983.
11. *New International* 8 (February 1942):20–24; 8 (April 1942):90–93.
12. *Partisan Review* 21 (March-April 1954):235. Howe dismissed the anecdote in his response as "tittle-tattle," but in his memoirs acknowledged that Warshow had scored a legitimate point. See Howe, *A Margin of Hope*, p. 124.
13. Richard H. Pells, *The Liberal Mind in a Conservative Age: American Intellectuals in the 1940s and 1950s* (New York: Harper & Row, 1985), pp. 23–24; Stephen J. Whitfield, "Dwight Macdonald's 'Politics' Magazine, 1944–1949," *Journalism History* 3 (Autumn 1976):86; Casey Blake, "A Radical's Unorthodoxy," *Nation* 240 (12 January 1985):21–24.
14. *Politics* 3 (December 1946):397.
15. Dwight Macdonald, "The Root is Man: Part Two," *Politics* 3 (July 1946):209–210. Richard Pells offers a good summary of the general shift away from radical political involvement among intellectuals in the aftermath of the war: "Where the search for community had captured the imagination of the Left in the 1930s, the search for identity inspired the writers and artists of the 1950s. Where social critics had once insisted on the need for collective action,

they now urged the individual to resist the pressures of conformity." Pells, *The Liberal Mind*, p. 187.

16. *Politics* 3 (October 1946):326–327, 329, 333. See also Howe, *A Margin of Hope*, pp. 116–117.

17. Howe, *A Margin of Hope*, p. 111. For Coser's political ties in this period see Bernard Rosenberg, "An Interview with Lewis Coser," *Conflict and Consensus: A Festschrift in Honor of Lewis A. Coser*, ed. Walter W. Powell and Richard Robbins (New York: Free Press, 1983), p. 39.

18. R. Fahan (Irving Howe) and H. Judd (Stanley Plastrik), "The New Labor Action," *Forum* (March 1951):19.

19. Irving Howe to author, 19 August 1984. Howe and Plastrik's letter of resignation, dated 12 October 1952, was printed in the ISL *Forum* (January 1953). Howe's resignation was not accepted with good grace by the ISL. In the same issue of the *Forum* ISL functionary Al Glotzer described Howe's appearance at a meeting in New York that fall to explain his reasons for resignation as "undignified in its utterly subjective character, ungraceful in the material used, ungrateful in the failure of appreciation of what our movement has given him. . . . Only an unwarranted snobbery could have produced this speech."

20. Howe, *A Margin of Hope*, p. 183; interview with Bernard Rosenberg, 16 October 1983; interview with Lewis Coser, 3 May 1985; interview with Michael Walzer, 20 March 1986. In his memoirs Abram Sachar offered a slightly befuddled account of the inexperienced thirty-three-year-old professor's arrival at Brandeis: "A major coup was achieved in 1953 with the arrival of Irving Howe, the literary critic and editor of *Dissent* who, though scarcely in his forties, already had three or four teaching posts behind him." Sachar, *A Host at Last* (Boston: Little, Brown, 1976), p. 124.

21. Interview with Bernard Rosenberg, 16 October 1983; interview with Manny Geltman, 19 March 1985.

22. Interview with Michael Walzer, 20 March 1986; Howe, *A Margin of Hope*, pp. 185–189.

23. Irving Howe, ed., *25 Years of Dissent, An American Tradition* (New York: Methuen, 1979), p. xv.

24. Rosenberg, "An Interview with Lewis Coser," pp. 41–42; Irving Howe, "Forming *Dissent*," in Powell and Robbins, eds., *Conflict and Consensus*, pp. 62–63; interview with Manny Geltman, 19 March 1985; interview with Lewis Coser, 3 May 1985.

25. *Dissent* 1 (Winter 1954):3.

26. Interview with Michael Walzer, 20 March 1986.

27. Ibid.

28. Ibid.

29. *Commentary* 17 (February 1954):204. *Dissent*'s editors were both pleased at the attention Glazer's attack brought the new journal and outraged by what he had to say. A decade later Howe still fumed at the memory: "What was troubling [about the Glazer review] was the fact than an intellectual socialist journal, such as would simply have been taken for granted in any free European country, occasioned such venom and rage, as if somehow a deviation from the standard Cold War sentiments were a scandal, even a kind of treason." *Dissent* 10 (Spring 1963):111. According to Manny Geltman, Glazer's initial attack was even stronger—so much so that it bordered on libel, and on the advice of *Commentary*'s lawyer was toned down after that issue had already started its press run. Interview with Manny Geltman, 19 March 1985.

30. Irving Howe, "This Age of Conformity," reprinted in *A World More Attractive: A View of Modern Literature and Politics* (New York: Horizon Press, 1963), p. 261.

31. *Commentary* 17 (April 1954):404.

32. *Dissent* 2 (Winter 1955):17–18.

33. *Dissent* 3 (Winter 1956):71.

34. See also Howe's comments on Turgenev, Martov, and the "politics of hesitation" in *Politics and the Novel* (New York: Fawcett, 1967), pp. 140–141.

35. Daniel Bell, *The End of Ideology* (Glencoe, Ill.: Free Press, 1960), p. 297. See also Alexander Bloom, *Prodigal Sons: The New York Intellectuals and Their World* (New York: Oxford University Press, 1986), pp. 288–289.

36. Interview with Irving Howe, 24 January 1982.

37. *Dissent* 1 (Spring 1954):138.

38. "Who cannot remember the sense of elation we felt at the stunning defeat *our* party administered to Winston Churchill?" Stanley Plastrik wrote in *Dissent* 7 (Winter 1960):17 (emphasis in the original).

39. *Dissent* 7 (Winter 1960):31–32.

40. *Dissent* 3 (Fall 1956):374–375. On Rosenberg's role in the radical intellectual world of the 1950s see Howe, *A Margin of Hope*, pp. 134–135; Casey Blake, "The Defense of Good Ideas," *Nation* 242 (12 April 1986):526–529; J. Hoberman, "Harold Rosenberg's Radical Cheek," *Village Voice Literary Supplement* (May 1986):10–13.

41. Irving Howe, "Intellectual Freedom and Stalinists," *New International* 15 (December 1949):231–236; Victor Navasky, *Naming Names* (New York: Viking, 1980), pp. 43–44; Gilbert, *Writers and Partisans*, pp. 284, 290. See also comments by Hook and Howe in "Liberal Anti-Communism Revisited," *Commentary* 44 (September 1967):44–52.

42. Howe, *A Margin of Hope*, pp. 217–219; Bloom, *Prodigal Sons*, pp. 259–273; Mary Sperling McAuliffe, *Crisis on the Left: Cold War Politics and American Liberals, 1947–1954* (Amherst, Mass.: University of Massachusetts Press, 1978), pp. 115–129; William L. O'Neill, *A Better World, The Great Schism: Stalinism and the American Intellectuals* (New York: Simon & Schuster, 1982), pp. 298–308. Michael Harrington offered a perceptive contemporary analysis of the prevailing mood within ACCF circles: "A good number of [the ACCF] leaders are people who have had bitter and scarring experiences with Stalinism, whether through party membership, front association, denunciations as Trotskyists real or assumed, etc. Some of them are people with a feeling that *only they* appreciate the urgency of combatting Stalinism.... This feeling is rather similar, though it is not quite the same, as that which has been described by Hannah Arendt as the 'ex-Communist' syndrome—*only they* can know the cunning and power of the enemy. It is not a feeling likely to make for either a supple politics or a firm defense of cultural freedom." *Dissent* 2 (Spring 1955):121.

43. *Dissent* 1 (Summer 1954):249–254.

44. Leslie Fiedler, *An End to Innocence* (Boston: Beacon Press, 1955), pp. 23, 70.

45. *Dissent* 2 (Autumn 1955):317–328.

46. *Dissent* 1 (Autumn 1954):309.

47. *Dissent* 2 (Winter 1955):91.

48. On the origins of the mass culture debate, see Gilbert, *Writers and Partisans*, pp. 221–224, 232; Martin Jay, *The Dialectical Imagination: A History of the Frankfurt School and the Institute of Social Research, 1923–1950* (Boston: Little, Brown, 1973), pp. 212–218; Bernard Rosenberg and David White, eds., *Mass Culture* (Glencoe, Ill.: Free Press, 1957); Leon Bramson, *The Political Context of Sociology* (Princeton: Princeton University Press, 1961), pp. 121–139; Richard H. Pells, *Radical Visions and American Dreams: Culture and Social Thought in the Depression Years* (New York: Harper & Row, 1973), pp. 334–346.

49. *Politics* 1 (February 1944):22; James Gilbert, "Dwight Macdonald," *In These Times* (2–8 February 1983), p. 12.

50. Irving Howe, "Notes on Mass Culture," *Politics* 5 (Spring 1948):120–123.

51. *Dissent* 1 (Spring 1954):141.

52. *Dissent* 3 (Fall 1956):392–393.

53. *Dissent* 3 (Winter 1956):27–28.

54. Edward Shils, "Daydreams and Nightmares: Reflections on the Criticism of Mass Culture," *Sewanee Review* 65 (Fall 1957):588–590. See also Lewis Coser's response in *Dissent* 5 (Summer 1958):268–273.

55. Howe, "The New York Intellectuals," p. 36.

56. *Dissent* 3 (Summer 1956):331–332; 5 (Winter 1958):14–19. Pachter, who often contributed to *Dissent* under the pen name of Henri Rabassiere, described his own background in Rosenberg and Goldstein, eds., *Creators and Disturbers*, pp. 113–134. See also *Socialism in History, Political Essays of Henry Pachter*, ed. Stephen Eric Bronner (New York: Columbia University Press, 1984).

57. *Dissent* 6 (Winter 1959):7.

58. *Dissent* 5 (Autumn 1958):318.

59. *Dissent* 6 (Autumn 1959):371. See also Harvey Swados, "The Myth of the Happy Worker," *Nation* 185 (17 August 1957):65–68.

60. Irving Howe, B. J. Widick, *The UAW and Walter Reuther* (New York: Random House, 1949).

61. Interview with Bernard Rosenberg, 16 October 1983.

62. *Dissent* 4 (Summer 1957):219–233.

63. Ibid., p. 229. See also Marquart's autobiography, *An Auto Worker's Journal: The UAW from Crusade to One-Party Union* (University Park, Pa.: Pennsylvania State University Press, 1975).

64. Studs Terkel, *Working* (New York: Avon, 1975); Department of Health, Education and Welfare, *Work in America* (Cambridge: MIT Press, 1973); *Dissent* 3 (Spring 1956):191. Another prescient article in *Dissent* on the future of work was Daniel Bell's "The Meaning of Work," *Dissent* 6 (Summer 1959):242–249.

65. *Dissent* 6 (Autumn 1959):416.

66. Interview with Manny Geltman, 19 March 1985; interview with Michael Harrington, 19 November 1982. See also letter from Henry Judd (Stanley Plastrik) objecting to the official Workers party line on the Marshall Plan in *New International* 14 (September 1948):223. Dwight Macdonald's declaration of allegiance in the Cold War came in a debate with Norman Mailer at Mount Holyoke College in 1952. See "I Choose the West," reprinted in Dwight Macdonald, *Politics Past* (New York: Viking, 1970), pp. 197–201.

67. *Dissent* 1 (Summer 1954):218–219.

68. *Dissent* 1 (Autumn 1954):334.

69. For an example of articles in which writers attempted to identify suitably anti-Stalinist Third World revolutionaries, see *Dissent* 3 (Spring 1956):143–145, 202; 6 (Spring 1959):129–133.

70. On Buttinger's background and role at *Dissent* see Howe, *A Margin of Hope*, p. 235; "Forming *Dissent*," p. 63; and Muriel Gardiner, *Code Name "Mary*," pp. 67–70, 169–171.

71. Joseph Buttinger, *The Smaller Dragon: A Political History of Vietnam* (New York: Praeger, 1958).

72. Eugene Burdick and William Lederer, *The Ugly American* (New York: Norton, 1958).

73. *Dissent* 6 (Summer 1959):318, 339; interview with Irving Howe, 24 January 1982. See also Gardiner, *Code Name "Mary*," pp. 169–170. Buttinger's ties with Diem are described in James Aronson, *The Press and the Cold War* (Boston: Beacon Press, 1973), p. 184. Buttinger would subsequently sharply revise his views and become a critic of American involvement in Vietnam. See for example his review of the "Pentagon Papers" in *Dissent* 19 (Spring 1972):407–441.

74. *Dissent* 1 (Summer 1954):218–219. See also Burdick's response to Buttinger's review in *Dissent* 7 (Winter 1960):82.

75. *Dissent* 1 (Winter 1954):9.

76. *Dissent* 2 (Summer 1955):196. Stanley Plastrik played an important role in coordinating *Dissent*'s foreign coverage, drawing upon a wide range of personal contacts in Europe and Asia. He put together several special issues of *Dissent* in the 1950s focusing on different regions and offering viewpoints and a depth of coverage otherwise unavailable in all but the most specialized American publications. See, for example, the Summer 1956 issue devoted to Africa. It included an article by George Houser of the American Committee on Africa predicting

that a combination of internal resistance and condemnation would eventually bring an end to the apartheid system in South Africa. *Dissent* 3 (Summer 1956):294. One country conspicuous by its absence from *Dissent*'s scrutiny in the 1950s was the new state of Israel. Sentiment toward Israel on the largely Jewish editorial board ranged from indifference to Pachter's pronounced anti-Zionism. In a rare passing reference to Israel in an article devoted to the Suez crisis, Stanley Diamond wrote: "Israel tends to consider itself a beacon of civilization in a benighted area in much the same way that early American settlers viewed the Indians. . . . There is an undercurrent of expansionism in Israel which is part of the very dynamic of state formation." *Dissent* 4 (Winter 1957):8–11. Bernard Rosenberg and Michael Walzer both harbored Labor Zionist sympathies, and slowly helped convert most of their fellow editors to a change of heart on the issue. Interview with Bernard Rosenberg, 16 October 1983; Howe, *A Margin of Hope*, pp. 276–277.

77. *Dissent* 1 (Autumn 1954):398.

78. *Dissent* 1 (Winter 1954):32–49.

79. *Dissent* 4 (Winter 1957):5.

80. *Dissent* 3 (Spring 1956):107, 117, 121.

81. *Dissent* 5 (Autumn 1958):360–374; 6 (Spring 1958):149–153; 6 (Summer 1959):223–236.

82. *Dissent* 7 (Spring 1960):118–119; (Autumn 1960):373.

83. Interview with Michael Walzer, 20 March 1986. Another response to the emergence of the civil rights movement came from *Dissent*'s most idiosyncratic editor, Norman Mailer, who predicted after the Montgomery events that "A time of violence, new hysteria, confusion and rebellion will . . . replace the time of conformity." *Dissent* 4 (Summer 1957):284, 291. Howe would come to regret publishing Mailer's "The White Negro" because it included a line that seemed to celebrate the "courage" it took for "two strong eighteen year old hoodlums . . . to beat in the brains of a candy-store keeper." As he later explained the decision to go ahead and publish the Mailer piece as submitted: "After you've edited 25 pieces by sociologists who can't write English and you get in a piece like 'The White Negro' which is full of bounce and brilliance—and I was probably the first person to read it—this sensational piece which he contributes for nothing, for which he could have gotten thousands of bucks even then, and it helps liven and sell the magazine and get it around, it would have taken a lot of strength of character to get fussy with him. I probably was afraid he'd say, 'well, screw you, I'll sell it to Esquire' or something." Interview with Irving Howe, 24 January 1982. For Mailer's relationship with his fellow-editors at *Dissent* see Peter Manso, *Mailer, His Life and Times* (New York: Simon & Schuster, 1985), pp. 135–136, 286; and Norman Mailer, *The Armies of the Night* (New York: Signet, 1968), p. 35.

84. *Dissent* 3 (Spring 1956):156–163.

85. *Dissent* 7 (Winter 1960):37.

86. *Dissent* 3 (Winter 1956):6.

87. *Dissent* 6 (Winter 1959):7–8. But see dissenting opinions of some of the other editors, pp. 8–12.

88. *New Yorker* 38 (19 January 1963), pp. 82–132.

89. *Dissent* 10 (Spring 1963):110–114.

90. *Dissent* 7 (Spring 1960):142–148.

91. *Dissent* 9 (Spring 1962):179–182.

92. *Dissent* 9 (Spring 1962):129.

93. Interview with Michael Walzer, 20 March 1986; interview with Todd Gitlin, 29 December 1983.

94. Interview with Michael Walzer, 20 March 1986.

95. Howe, *A Margin of Hope*, p. 315.

96. Irving Howe, *Steady Work: Essays in the Politics of Democratic Radicalism, 1953–1966* (New York: Harcourt Brace and World, 1966), p. 247.

97. Howe, *Steady Work*, p. 247; *A Margin of Hope*, pp. 243–245.

98. *Dissent* 6 (Spring 1959):191–196; C. Wright Mills, *The Causes of World War III* (New York: Simon & Schuster, 1958).

99. *Dissent* 6 (Summer 1959):295–301.

100. Wallace Markfield, *To an Early Grave* (New York: Simon & Schuster, 1964), p. 188.

101. *Dissent* 8 (Autumn 1961):496–498.

102. *Dissent* 9 (Winter 1962):88–92.

103. Howe, *A Margin of Hope*, pp. 291–293; interview with Todd Gitlin, 29 December 1983.

104. Interview with Michael Walzer, 20 March 1986.

105. Howe and Walzer debated the Vietnam question in *Dissent* 12 (Spring 1965):151–156. Lewis Coser also opposed the "immediate withdrawal" demand, on the pragmatic grounds that it lacked sufficient political appeal. *Dissent* 12 (Autumn 1965):403–404. For Howe's change of mind on the issue see *Dissent* 15 (March-April 1968):99.

106. Howe, *A Margin of Hope*, p. 309. "There are different ways of feeling beleaguered. In the 50s we were proud, happy, pleased about it. We felt beleaguered, but we felt good. In the late 60s I felt beleaguered, but I didn't feel good." Interview with Irving Howe, 24 January 1982.

107. Irving Howe to "Tom" (Kahn), 10 June 1969, Reel 3380, Shachtman Collection. In the mid-1960s Jack Newfield referred to Howe in an article in the *Nation* as part of a group of "revisionist liberals" who had responded to the New Left with "scorn and skepticism." *Nation* 200 (10 May 1965), p. 494. Howe wrote an indignant reply, rejecting both the label of "revisionist liberal" and the charge that he was an enemy of the New Left: "My sympathies are strongly with the students and not with such of their critics as [Sidney] Hook, [Max] Lerner, and [Nathan] Glazer." *Nation* 200 (24 May 1965), letters page.

108. Interview with Michael Walzer, 20 March 1986; *Dissent* 19 (Spring 1972):309. On the change in *Dissent*'s publishing schedule Howe would remember: "It was undertaken because we felt life was getting exciting, we wanted to get into the act, but it didn't work. A bimonthly has neither the advantages of a quarterly or a monthly. You can't really stay on top of topical events in a bimonthly, but you're more tempted to than in a quarterly. To go to a monthly would have meant a tremendous change, to have a full-time staff, and we could have never afforded it." Interview with Irving Howe, 21 October 1982.

109. *Dissent* 9 (Spring 1962):159; 12 (Summer 1965):295–323; Irving Howe, "The Welfare State" in *The Revival of American Socialism: Selected Papers of the Socialist Scholars Conference*, ed. George Fischer (New York: Oxford University Press, 1971), pp. 68–70.

110. The quotation from Murray Hausknecht is from *Dissent* 15 (September-October 1968): 391; the quotation from Michael Harrington is from *Dissent* 13 (November-December 1966): 628.

Chapter 4

1. Albert Bigelow, "Why I am Sailing into the Pacific Bomb-Test Area," *Liberation* 2 (February 1958):4–6.

2. *Life* 44 (16 June 1958):38.

3. *Dissent* 5 (Summer 1958):279–281.

4. Charles DeBenedetti, *The Peace Reform in American History* (Bloomington: Indiana University Press, 1980), pp. 39–56.

5. John Haynes Holmes, *My Gandhi* (New York: Harper & Brothers, 1954), p. 26. See also Krishnalal Shridharani, *War Without Violence: A Study of Gandhi's Method and its Accomplishments* (New York: Harcourt, Brace, 1939), p. 71; and George Hendrick, "The Influence of Thoreau's 'Civil Disobedience' on Gandhi's *Satyagraha*," *New England Quarterly* 29 (December 1956):462–471.

6. *World Tomorrow* 15 (14 September 1932):253.

7. Jo Ann Ooiman Robinson, *Abraham Went Out: A Biography of A.J. Muste* (Philadelphia: Temple University Press, 1981), pp. 54–66.

8. Interview with Dave Dellinger, 24 January 1985; interview with Ralph DiGia, 7 December 1984; James Peck, *Upperdogs vs. Underdogs* (New York: AMP & R Publisher, 1980), pp. 14–33; Patti McGill Peterson, "Student Organizations and the Antiwar Movement in America, 1900–1960," *American Studies* 13 (Spring 1972):139–140; Philip G. Altbach, *Student Politics in America: A Historical Analysis* (New York: McGraw-Hill, 1974), pp. 57–108; Hal Draper, "The Student Movement of the Thirties," in *As We Saw the Thirties*, ed. Rita James Simon (Urbana: University of Illinois Press, 1967), pp. 170–179.

9. Lawrence S. Wittner, *Rebels Against War: The American Peace Movement, 1933–1983* (Philadelphia: Temple University Press, 1984), pp. 19–22.

10. James Wechsler, "Politics on the Campus," *Nation* 149 (30 December 1939):732–733; Maurice Isserman, *Which Side Were You On? The American Communist Party During the Second World War* (Middletown, Conn.: Wesleyan University Press, 1982), pp. 58–67; DeBenedetti, *Peace Reform*, p. 133.

11. Richard Gregg, *The Power of Non-violence* (Philadelphia: Lippincott, 1934); ibid., *Pacifist Program in Time of War, Threatened War or Fascism* (Pendle Hill, Pa: 1939), p. 43; Robinson, *Abraham Went Out*, p. 78; Wittner, *Rebels Against War*, pp. 71–72; DeBenedetti, *Peace Reform*, pp. 133–134.

12. Peck, *Underdogs*, p. 95; Peck, "A Note on Direct Action," *Politics* 3 (January 1946):21–22; Wittner, *Rebels Against War*, pp. 87–89; Roy Finch, "The New Peace Movement," *Dissent* 10 (Winter 1963):91.

13. Interview with Ralph DiGia, 7 December 1984.

14. Finch, *New Peace Movement*, p. 92.

15. *Politics* 2 (November 1945):343. See also *Against the Tide: Pacifist Resistance in the Second World War, An Oral History* (New York: The 1984 War Resisters League Calendar). Penina Glazer has written the most perceptive study of the impact of the World War II conscientious objector experience on the American pacifist movement. She concluded: "The informal groupings which developed out of these activities became formal organizations after the war. . . . The war . . . transformed the doctrines and techniques of a relatively sectarian group into a major program for dissenters." Glazer, "From the Old Left to the New: Radical Criticism in the 1940s," *American Quarterly* 24 (December 1972):597.

16. Interview with Ralph DiGia, 7 December 1984; Peck, *Underdogs*, p. 86.

17. David R. Newman, "The Macedonia Community," *Politics* 5 (Winter 1948):27–30; "A Specific Experiment," *Alternative* 1 (March-April 1949):1; Staughton Lynd, "The Individual was Made for Community," *Liberation* 1 (January 1957):15–18.

18. Interview with Dave Dellinger, 15 January 1984; Robinson, *Abraham Went Out*, pp. 82–84.

19. Penina Glazer, "A Decade of Transition: Marxists and the Non Violent Left in the 1940s" (Ph.D. diss., Rutgers University, 1970), p. 118. Glazer commented on the Committee for Non-Violent Revolution and other radical pacifist groups in the late 1940s: "No longer did pacifists . . . define war as a breakdown, an unfortunate occasional accident. . . . For the first time they organized continual protest against an increasingly militarized society." Ibid., pp. 155–156. See also *Politics* 3 (April 1946):118–119.

20. Quoted in *Politics* 3 (July 1946):208.

21. Quoted in Neil H. Katz, "Radical Pacifism and the Contemporary American Peace Movement: The Committee for Nonviolent Action, 1957–1967" (Ph.D. diss., University of Maryland, 1974), pp. 10–11.

22. Interview with Dave Dellinger, 15 January 1985; Glazer, "A Decade of Transition," pp. 73–76.

23. John Mueller, *War, Presidents and Public Opinion* (New York: Wiley, 1972), pp. 43–52.

24. *Daily Worker* (2 July 1951):1, 3; Joseph Starobin, *American Communism in Crisis, 1943–1957* (Berkeley: University of California, 1972), p. 211.

25. Joseph E. Slater, "Voices in the Wind: American Opposition to the Korean War" (Senior thesis, Oberlin College, 1983), pp. 54–60; Michael Harrington, *Fragments of the Century* (New York: Simon & Schuster, 1973), pp. 68–69.

26. Peck, *Underdogs*, p. 106. See also Mark Solomon, "Black Critics of Colonialism and the Cold War," in *Cold War Critics: Alternatives to American Foreign Policy in the Truman Years*, ed. Thomas G. Patterson (Chicago: Quadrangle Books, 1971), pp. 205–239; and Norman Kaner, "I.F. Stone and the Korean War," ibid., pp. 240–265.

27. "Minutes of Peacemakers Executive Committee," 22 February 1952, 28 February 1958, CNVA Papers, Swarthmore College Peace Collection (hereafter SCPC).

28. *Liberation* 1 (March 1956):3–6; 3 (May 1958):3, 18.

29. William Spinrad, "The Political Atmosphere," *Dissent* 6 (Spring 1959):182–184; Adam Ulam, *Expansion and Coexistence: Soviet Foreign Policy 1917–1973* (New York: Praeger, 1974), pp. 539–571.

30. Frank Earle Myers, "British Peace Politics: The Campaign for Nuclear Disarmament and the Committee of 100, 1957–1962" (Ph.D. diss., Columbia University, 1965), pp. 45–74; Doris Lessing, *The Four-Gated City* (New York: New American Library, 1976), pp. 348–350.

31. August Meier and Elliott Rudwick, *CORE: A Study in the Civil Rights Movement, 1942–1968* (New York: Oxford University Press, 1973), pp. 4–5, 33–71; James Farmer, *Lay Bare the Heart: An Autobiography of the Civil Rights Movement* (New York: Arbor House, 1985), pp. 72–116, 176; Glazer, "Decade of Transition," pp. 161–166.

32. Stephen B. Oates, *Let the Trumpet Sound: The Life of Martin Luther King, Jr.* (New York: New American Library, 1982), pp. 30–33, 39–40; David Garrow, *Bearing the Cross*, pp. 66–70.

33. Bayard Rustin, *Down the Line: The Collected Writings of Bayard Rustin* (Chicago: Quadrangle Books, 1971), pp. 13–49; *Liberation* 1 (April 1956):7–10; Aldon D. Morris, *The Origins of the Civil Rights Movement: Black Communities Organizing for Change* (New York: Free Press, 1985), pp. 57, 83–84, 115, 157–159; Eugene Pierce Walker, "A History of the Southern Christian Leadership Conference, 1955–1965: The Evolution of a Southern Strategy for Social Change" (Ph.D. diss., Duke University, 1978), pp. 31–40, 84; Robinson, *Abraham Went Out*, 117; Farmer, *Lay Bare the Heart*, pp. 186–187.

34. *Liberation* 1 (April 1956):3–6; Garrow, *Bearing the Cross*, p. 73.

35. "Suggestions for Action on the Montgomery Boycott," 14 March 1956, McReynolds Papers, SCPC.

36. *New York Times*, 15 June 1955, p. 1; 16 June 1955, p. 1, 19.

37. *New York Times*, 16 June 1955, p. 19; Mel Piehl, *Breaking Bread: The Catholic Worker and the Origin of Catholic Radicalism in America* (Philadelphia: Temple University Press, 1982), p. 214; Robinson, *Abraham Went Out*, pp. 162–163; Wittner, *Rebels Against War*, p. 265.

38. *Village Voice*, 11 May 1960, p. 1; *Peacemaker* 13 (28 May 1960):1; Piehl, *Breaking Bread*, p. 215.

39. *Village Voice*, 4 May 1960, p. 1.

40. *New York Post*, 4 May 1960 (clipping in Muste Papers, microfilm reel 89.10, SCPC).

41. Kempton quoted in Nancy Lee Roberts, "Dorothy Day and the Catholic Worker, 1933–1982" (Ph.D. diss., University of Minnesota, 1982), p. 175. See also *Peacemaker* 13 (28 May 1960):1; and "Civil Defense Protest Day" leaflet, CNVA Papers, SCPC.

42. Jules Feiffer, *Jules Feiffer's America: From Eisenhower to Reagan* (New York: Knopf, 1982), pp. 26–30.

43. *Liberation* 2 (May 1957):14–15; 3 (April 1958):12–14; Neil Katz, "Radical Pacifism," pp. 31–32. See also Robert A. Divine, *Blowing on the Wind: The Nuclear Test Ban Debate, 1954–1960* (New York: Oxford University Press, 1978), pp. 3–35, 161–163; Paul Boyer, "From Activism to Apathy: The American People and Nuclear Weapons, 1963–1980," *Journal of American History* 70 (March 1984):823–824.

44. Milton S. Katz and Neil H. Katz, "Pragmatists and Visionaries in the Post-World War II American Peace Movement: SANE and CNVA" in *Doves and Diplomats,* ed. Solomon Wank (Westport, Conn.: Greenwood Press, 1978), pp. 267–268.

45. Milton S. Katz, "Peace Liberals and Vietnam: SANE and the Politics of 'Responsible' Protest," *Peace and Change* 9 (Summer 1983):21; ibid., "Peace, Politics, and Protest: SANE and the American Peace Movement, 1957–1972" (Ph.D. diss., St. Louis University, 1973), pp. 69–88; "Seven Years for a SANE Nuclear Policy," *SANEWORLD* 3 (15 April 1964):1.

46. Peck, *Underdogs,* pp. 108–111; *New York Times,* 6 August 1957, p. 2; 7 August 1957, p. 6; 8 August 1957, p. 8; Neil Katz, "Radical Pacifism," pp. 36–46. Brief biographies of the participants were provided in a press release from NVAANW, 4 August 1957, CNVA Papers, SCPC.

47. *Liberation* 2 (September 1957):3–4, 19.

48. Interview with Albert Bigelow, 15 December 1984; Albert Bigelow, *The Voyage of the Golden Rule* (Garden City, N.Y.: Doubleday, 1959), pp. 44–46.

49. NVAANW Executive Committee Meeting Minutes, 12 November 1957, 18 December 1957, CNVA Papers, SCPC.

50. *New York Times,* 26 March 1958, p. 33, 12 April 1958, p. 1; NVAANW Executive Committee Meeting Minutes, 25 April 1958, CNVA Papers, SCPC; Bigelow, *Voyage of the Golden Rule,* pp. 51–115.

51. *New York Times,* 2 May 1958, p. 1; Bigelow, *Voyage of the Golden Rule,* pp. 116–156.

52. *Newsweek* 51 (10 February 1958):74–75; *National Guardian,* 24 February 1958; *New York Times,* 5 May 1958, p. 21, 11 May 1958, p. 45, 2 June 1958, p. 14; Bigelow, *Voyage of the Golden Rule,* pp. 159–160; Wittner, *Rebels Against War,* p. 249.

53. Press clippings, CNVA Papers, Box 3, SCPC; Bigelow, *Voyage of the Golden Rule,* pp. 163–164.

54. *New York Times,* 5 June 1958, p. 38; Bigelow, *Voyage of the Golden Rule,* pp. 181–202; Peck, *Underdogs,* pp. 111–118; *Liberation* 3 (June 1958):4–8, 13; Neil Katz, "Radical Pacifism," pp. 59–62.

55. *Redbook,* July 1959, pp. 52–53, 86–90; Earle Reynolds, "Forbidden Voyage," *Nation* 187 (15 November 1958):358–360, 368.

56. Larry Scott, Memo, 28 July 1958, CNVA Papers, SCPC.

57. Neil Katz, "Radical Pacifism," pp. 72–73.

58. "Six Reasons Why We Ask You to Stop Work on Missile Site Construction," leaflet signed by Kenneth Calkins, Ellanor Calkins, and Ted Olson, in Muste Papers, microfilm reel 89.7, SCPC; *Denver Post,* 29 August 1958, newspaper clipping in Muste Papers, microfilm reel, 89.7, SCPC; Wittner, *Rebels Against War,* pp. 252–253; Katz, "Radical Pacifism," pp. 74–75; Robinson, *Abraham Went Out,* p. 164.

59. Larry Scott to George Willoughby, A. J. Muste, Bayard Rustin, and Bob Pickus, 28 August 1958, Muste Papers, microfilm reel 89.7, SCPC.

60. Emphasis in original, *Liberation* 3 (November 1958):10–11. See also Katz, "Radical Pacifism," pp. 77–78.

61. A. J. Muste to Brad Lyttle, 3 November 1958, Muste Papers, microfilm reel 89.7, SCPC; interview with Dave Dellinger, 15 January 1985.

62. Interview with Dave Dellinger, 15 January 1985.

63. Barbara Deming, "The Peacemakers," *Nation* 191 (17 December 1960):474; Ted Olson, memo (n.d., July 1961?), CNVA Papers, SCPC.

64. Ted Olson, memo (n.d., July 1961?), CNVA Papers, SCPC.

65. Quoted in Neil Katz, "Radical Pacifism," p. 71.

66. *Liberation* 4 (Summer 1959):3–4; Katz, "Radical Pacifism," pp. 79–84; Wittner, *Rebels Against War,* p. 262; Robinson, *Abraham Went Out,* pp. 165–166.

67. Steven Fine, "Peace Coalition Politics: The Liberal Experiment, 1954–1965" (Senior thesis, Oberlin College, 1982), p. 75.

68. *New London Day,* 1 June 1960, p. 1, 4 June 1960, p. 3, 18 June 1960, p. 2, 13 August 1960, p. 2.

69. *New London Day,* 25 August 1960, p. 1, 26 August 1960, p. 1, 19 November 1960, p. 9, 22 November 1960, p. 1; *New York Times,* 26 August 1960, p. 7, 27 August 1960, p. 2, 30 August 1960, p. 21, 21 October 1960, p. 1, 23 November 1960, p. 1; *Peacemaker* 13 (3 September 1960):1, 11 March 1961, p. 1; *Newsweek* 56 (5 December 1960):31–32.

70. *New London Day,* 20 June 1960, p. 8, 19 August 1960, p. 8; *Nation* 191 (17 December 1960):472–473.

71. Robin Prising to Dave McReynolds, 30 July 1960, McReynolds Papers, SCPC; *New London Day,* 25 August 1960, p. 1.

72. *Politics* 3 (August 1946):245–246.

73. Albert Bigelow to Brad Lyttle, 27 May 1960, and Albert Bigelow to CNVA, 15 June 1960, Muste Papers, microfilm reel 89.7, SCPC; Fine, "Peace Coalition Politics," p. 105.

74. A. J. Muste to Albert Bigelow, 4 July 1960, Muste Papers, microfilm reel 89.7, SCPC.

75. Ted Olson, memo (n.d., July 1961), CNVA Papers, SCPC. Olson would resign from CNVA in 1963. Fine, "Peace Coalition Politics," p. 142.

76. Fine, "Peace Coalition Politics," pp. 141–142, 164, 167.

77. Jack Newfield, "Revolt Without Dogma: The Student Left," *Nation* 200 (10 May 1965):494; Nancy Zaroulis and Gerald Sullivan, *Who Spoke Up? American Protest Against the War in Vietnam* (Garden City, N.Y.: Doubleday, 1984).

78. Bill Ayers, "A Strategy to Win," p. 188 in *Weatherman,* ed. Harold Jacobs (San Francisco: Ramparts Press, 1970).

79. Brad Lyttle to Lyle Tatum, 17 October 1958, Muste Papers, microfilm reel 89.7, SCPC.

Chapter 5

1. "The new Left: What should it look like?" *National Guardian,* 29 October 1956, p. 8.

2. Michael Harrington, "The New Left," mimeo (New York: YPSL, 1959), OF: YPSL, Tamiment Collection. See also "Dalton Trumbo at Guardian Anniversary, the new American Left," *National Guardian,* 26 November 1956, p. 10.

3. Two somewhat neglected histories have considered the links between Old and New Left in the late 1950s and early 1960s, and provided a useful starting point for my own exploration of this period: Philip G. Altbach, *Student Politics in America: A Historical Analysis* (New York: McGraw-Hill, 1974); and George R. Vickers, *The Formation of the New Left: The Early Years* (Lexington, Mass.: Lexington Books, 1975).

4. Nat Hentoff, *Peace Agitator: The Story of A. J. Muste* (New York: Macmillan, 1963); Jo Ann Ooiman Robinson, *Abraham Went Out: A Biography of A. J. Muste* (Philadelphia: Temple University Press, 1981); interview with Bernard Rosenberg, 16 October 1983; interview with Dave Dellinger, 24 January 1985; interview with Wally and Juanita Nelson, 10 July 1985.

5. Interview with Dave McReynolds, 19 July 1984; for Muste and Shachtman's collaboration in the early 1950s see *Labor Action,* 22 September 1952, 26 October 1953, 7 December 1953, 14 December 1953, 15 November 1954.

6. *Labor Action,* 4 June 1956, 22 October 1956.

7. A. J. Muste to select list, 4 December 1956, and "Private Invitation to a Discussion" (n.d., Fall 1956?), Box 35, Shachtman Collection.

8. "Paraphrase of Discussion in New York, December 8–9, 1956," Box 35, Shachtman Collection.

9. "Report on American Forum Meeting to Discuss Organization, March 23, 1957," Box 35, Shachtman Collection.

10. Robinson, *Abraham Went Out*, pp. 101–102; Sidney Lens, *Unrepentant Radical: An American Activist's Account of Five Turbulent Decades* (Boston: Beacon Press, 1980), p. 234.

11. Interview with Dave McReynolds, 19 July 1984; Sidney Lens to author, 26 August 1984; *Dissent* 4 (Summer 1957):332–333; *Liberation* 2 (June 1957):13–16; John Dickinson, memo on "Boston Area Forum Planning Meeting, March 8, 1958, March 13, 1958," Muste Papers, Reel 89.7, Swarthmore College Peace Collection (hereafter called SCPC).

12. Herman Benson to Max Shachtman, 14 March 1957, Reel 3377, Shachtman Collection. The contemptuous attitude displayed toward McReynolds, then Shachtman's closest ally within the Socialist party, is typical of the way Shachtman and other Independent Socialist Leaguers dealt with people outside their own ranks.

13. *Labor Action*, 27 May 1957; Sidney Lens to Max Shachtman, 22 August 1957, Reel 3380, Shachtman Collection.

14. Sam Bottone to "Comrades," 3 October 1957, Reel 3370, Shachtman Collection.

15. Nathan Glazer, "The Peace Movement in America—1961," *Commentary* 31 (April 1961):294. For the fate of the World Federalists see Jon A. Yoder, "The United World Federalists, Liberals for Law and Order," *American Studies* 8 (Spring 1972):120–122.

16. "How Sane the SANE?," *Time* (21 April 1958):13–14.

17. *New York Times*, 20 May 1960, p. 1; *Commentary* 31 (April 1961):290; Milton Katz, "Peace, Politics and Protest," pp. 113–114.

18. *National Guardian*, 2 June 1958.

19. "Special Board Meeting," 26 May 1960, SANE Papers, SCPC; "Board of Directors" meeting minutes, 9 September 1960, SANE Papers, SCPC; Milton Katz, "Peace, Politics and Protest," pp. 115–136; Barbara Deming, "The Ordeal of SANE," *Nation* (11 March 1961):201.

20. Milton Katz, "Peace, Politics and Protest," pp. 143–151; Glazer, "The Peace Movement in America," p. 293; Deming, "The Ordeal of SANE," pp. 202–203.

21. Joe Clark to A. J. Muste, 25 February 1961, Muste Papers, microfilm reel 89.7, SCPC.

22. Glazer, "The Peace Movement in America," p. 292.

23. Ralph Shapiro to the author, 23 November 1984.

24. A year later Women Strike for Peace, another peace group accused of harboring Communists, was able to defuse a congressional investigation with a strategy of gracious and gently mocking resistance, marking the beginning of the end for the House Un-American Activities Committee. See Amy Swerdlow, "Ladies Day at the Capitol: Women Strike for Peace Versus HUAC," *Feminist Studies* 8 (Fall 1982):493–520.

25. Irwin Suall to Max Shachtman, 11 April 1961, Reel 3383, Shachtman Collection.

26. Young People's Socialist League membership figures are from Irwin Suall to Max Shachtman, 11 April 1961, Reel 3383, Shachtman Collection, and interview with Michael Harrington, 19 November 1982. The estimate of SDS membership is from Kirkpatrick Sale, *SDS* (New York: Vintage, 1974), p. 46. For an insider's account of the formation and early history of the Young Socialist Alliance, see the interview with Tim Wohlforth, 29 August 1976 in the Oral History of the American Left collection, Tamiment Institute. Already in the mid-1960s YPSL's role in the early days of the revival of campus radicalism had been forgotten: see, for example, the offhand way in which the organization was dismissed in Paul Jacobs and Saul Landau, *The New Radicals: A Report with Documents* (New York: Vintage, 1966), p. 55; and Jack Newfield, *A Prophetic Minority* (New York: New American Library, 1967), p. 137.

27. Interview with Debbie Meier, 19 April 1986.

28. Interview with Steve Max, 14 May 1986.

29. Interview with Mike Thelwell, 10 July 1986. For Tom Kahn's early influence on future Student Nonviolent Coordinating Committee leaders like Stokeley Carmichael, see Clayborne Carson, *In Struggle: SNCC and the Black Awakening of the 1960s* (Cambridge: Harvard University Press, 1981), p. 163. Michael Harrington referred to the behind-the-scenes operation in the youth marches as the "Bayard Rustin Marching and Chowder Society, which meant Bayard, Tom and Rochelle doing the office stuff, and me running around doing a lot of the

outside work." Many of the demonstrators were drawn from CP-influenced Left circles in New York. As Harrington recalled, "We'd get on the buses [to Washington] and discover that when we started singing 'Solidarity Forever' people knew all the verses, and we'd work our way on up to the 'Internationale' and they'd still know all the verses." Interview with Michael Harrington, 19 November 1982. For accounts of the late 1950s civil rights marches see *National Guardian*, 27 May 1957, 3 November 1958, 27 April 1959.

30. Interview with Dorothy Tristman, 4 July 1984.

31. Interview with Betty Denitch, 6 August 1984; Carson, *In Struggle*, p. 11.

32. Interview with Betty Denitch, 6 August 1984; Walter Goodman, *The Committee: The Extraordinary Career of the House Committee on Un-American Activities* (New York: Farrar, Straus & Giroux, 1968), pp. 445–456; *National Guardian*, 23 May 1960; Milton Mayer, "The Found Generation," *The Progressive* 25 (March 1961):9–12.

33. Dale Johnson, "On the Ideology of the Campus Revolution," reprinted in Jacobs and Landau, *The New Radicals*, p. 97; interview with Betty Denitch, 6 August 1984.

34. Interview with Betty Denitch, 6 August 1984; interview with Dorothy Tristman, 4 July 1984; interview with Mike Thelwell, 7 July 1986.

35. The genesis of the realignment thesis can be found in two articles in the Shachtmanite press: Gordon Haskell, "Labor Movement Too is Put on the Spot by the Historic Negro Fight in the South," *Labor Action*, 5 March 1956; and Herman Benson, "The Communist Party at the Crossroads," *New International* 22 (Fall 1956).

36. For a transitional moment in the evolution of the realignment thesis, when it's not entirely clear whether the labor-liberal-black coalition will reside within or outside of the Democratic party, see Michael Harrington, "The New Left," mimeo (New York: YPSL, 1959), pp. 6–7, OF: YPSL, Tamiment Collection.

37. Julius Jacobson, "The Two Deaths of Max Shachtman," *New Politics* 10 (Winter 1973): 99; David McReynolds, "Thunder on the Old Left," *The Activist* (Spring 1969):23–25.

38. Interview with Betty Denitch, 6 August 1984.

39. Hal Draper printed a taped transcript of Shachtman's remarks on the Bay of Pigs invasion along with his own commentary: Draper, "Two Views of the Cuban Invasion" (Oakland, privately printed, May 1961). For Shachtman's reaction to Draper's pamphlet see Barney Cohen to Max Shachtman, 9 May 1961, and Shachtman's response, 7 June 1961, Reel 3377, Shachtman Collection.

40. The history of YPSL's mid-1960s collapse can be pieced together from the YPSL files in the Tamiment Collection. For one YPSL member's response to the SDS strike at Harvard in 1969, see Steve Kelman, *Push Comes to Shove: The Escalation of Student Protest* (Boston: Houghton Mifflin, 1970).

41. Bernard A. Weisberger, *Cold War, Cold Peace: The United States and Russia Since 1945* (New York: American Heritage, 1984), pp. 200–229.

42. Howard Metzenberg, "Student Peace Union, Five Years Before the New Left" (Senior honors thesis, Oberlin College, 1978), pp. 16–26; SPU *Bulletin* (November 1959):1; George R. Vickers, *The Formation of the New Left: The Early Years* (Lexington, Mass.: D. C. Heath, 1975), pp. 51–52; Altbach, *Student Politics in America*, pp. 186–187; James P. O'Brien, "The Development of a New Left in the United States, 1960–1965" (Ph.D. diss., University of Wisconsin, 1971), pp. 169–170. Metzenberg's precocious senior thesis is the best account I've found on the Student Peace Union.

43. Mike Parker to Tom Barton, 9 December 1960, OF: YPSL 1951–1961, Tamiment Collection; interview with Barbara Epstein, 24 April 1984.

44. Student Peace Union "Statement of Purpose," in Massimo Teodori, *The New Left: A Documentary History* (Indianapolis: Bobbs-Merrill, 1969), pp. 125–126; Metzenberg, "Student Peace Union," pp. 27–28; Vickers, *Formation of the New Left*, p. 54.

45. Student SANE's softer line was probably less a product of Communist-inspired subterfuge than a genuine distaste for ideological hairsplitting. As Arthur Mitzman reported of a

conversation he had with a Student SANE member from a CP family background, "when asked why she put in so much time for SANE [she replied] that she didn't want to feel responsible if she heard of someone dying of leukemia. No slogans, no programs; just a direct emotional response." *Dissent* 7 (Spring 1960):146–147.

46. Metzenberg, "Student Peace Union," p. 101.

47. *New York Times*, 24 November 1961, reprint in Student Peace Union Papers, SCPC.

48. Interview with Todd Gitlin, 29 December 1983; Dave McReynolds to the author, 1 May 1985; SPU *Bulletin* (February-March 1962):3–5; Metzenberg, "Student Peace Union," pp. 71–75.

49. *New York Times*, 17 February 1962, p. 1, 18 February 1962, p. 3; Steven V. Robert, " 'Something Had to Be Done' . . . ," *Nation* 194 (3 March 1962):187–190; SPU *Bulletin*, (February-March 1962):3–5.

50. SPU *Bulletin* (February-March 1962):1–2, 5; (November 1962):1–2, 15–16; Metzenberg, "Student Peace Union," pp. 78, 88–90.

51. Interview with Todd Gitlin, 29 December 1983.

52. Ken Calkins to Dave McReynolds, 5 March 1960, McReynolds Papers, SCPC; Metzenberg, "Student Peace Union," pp. 31, 67–69.

53. Dave McReynolds to Ken Calkins, 11 July 1960, McReynolds Papers, SCPC.

54. Interview with Todd Gitlin, 29 December 1983.

55. Mike Parker to Rochelle (Horowitz), 19 November 1961, OF: YPSL 1962, Tamiment Collection.

56. Quoted in Metzenberg, "Student Peace Union," p. 95. See also Dave McReynolds to Gail Paradise, 15 September 1964, SPU Papers, SCPC; "Resolution on Electoral Action," SPU Papers, SCPC.

57. The Student Peace Union was formally dissolved in the spring of 1964. A new SPU was reconstituted that fall by some of the younger members, with the aid of Dave McReynolds. Though never very visible on a national level, the new group maintained chapters through the mid-1960s at many schools not known for New Left activism, including Shippenburg State College in Pennsylvania, St. Peters College in New Jersey, Idaho State University, and Rocky Mountain College in Montana. In February 1967 the group merged with Campus Americans for Democratic Action to form a group called the Independent Student Union. See "SPU Chapter List," 6 December 1966, SPU Papers, SCPC.

58. Sale, *SDS*, p. 529.

59. Interview with Steve Max, 14 May 1986.

60. Student Report to League for Industrial Democracy Board, 15 May 1958, Reel 1, SDS Papers; interview with Andre Schiffrin, 19 June 1983; Andre Schiffrin, "The Student Movement in the 1950s: A Reminiscence," *Radical America* (May-June 1968); Vickers, *Formation of the New Left*, pp. 66–68; SDS Collection, Box 3, Tamiment Institute.

61. Vickers, *Formation of the New Left*, pp. 68–69; Sale, *SDS*, pp. 24–25.

62. Vickers, *Formation of the New Left*, pp. 70–71; Sale, *SDS*, pp. 30–34. Sale, in what was either a careless formulation or a curious misreading of the politics of the period, suggested that Haber got into difficulties with LID because of fears that he would work too closely with other campus groups including YPSL and thus "embroil the LID in relations with Communist or quasi-Communist organizations."

63. Interview with Michael Harrington, 19 November 1982; Sale, *SDS*, pp. 35, 65; Thomas Hayden, "Who are the Student Boat-Rockers?" *Mademoiselle* (August 1961):334–335.

64. Interview with Steve Max, 14 May 1986; Sale, *SDS*, pp. 24–25, 35, 48, 89; Vickers, *Formation of the New Left*, p. 91.

65. Interview with Steve Max, 14 May 1986. The role of "red diaper babies" in the New Left has often been commented on, perhaps most perceptively by one of them, Dick Flacks: see, for example, his article entitled "Making History vs. Making Life: Dilemmas of an American Left," *Sociological Inquiry* 46 (1976):263–280. The most colorful comment on the topic

comes from Norman Podhoretz: "As one read about the student radical leaders in the press . . . one kept coming upon scions of what could be called the First Families of American Stalinism. . . . [The New Left] was in the end turning out to be a movement by the children of McCarthy's victims to avenge their parents on the flesh of the country which had produced him." Podhoretz, *Breaking Ranks: A Political Memoir* (New York: Harper & Row, 1979), p. 253.

66. Interview with Steve Max, 14 May 1986; Sale, *SDS*, p. 44.

67. Interview with Todd Gitlin, 29 December 1983.

68. Al Haber, "Memorandum on the Students for a Democratic Society," 20 May 1961, Reel 1, SDS Papers.

69. Thomas Hayden, "A Letter to the New (Young) Left," reprinted in Mitchell Cohen and Dennis Hale, *The New Student Left* (Boston: Beacon Press, 1966), p. 5; Sale, *SDS*, p. 33.

70. The Port Huron statement has never been reprinted in full, but has been excerpted in various collections, including Jacobs and Landau, *The New Radicals*, and Cohen and Hale, *The New Student Left*. See also Sale, *SDS*, pp. 42–59, 69–70.

71. On the Max-Hayden battle over the shape of the Port Huron statement see Sale, *SDS*, pp. 44–45; and the minutes of the meeting of SDS national executive committee held in Chapel Hill, 6–7 May 1962, Reel 1, SDS Papers.

72. *Dissent* 9 (Spring 1962):166. Harrington has criticized his own role at Port Huron on many occasions, most recently in the introduction to a reprint of his *Dissent* piece: "I carefully ignored the good advice I had given in my 1962 article. I became a tough faction fighter, treating sincere young radicals, who were at worst confused—and understandably so—as if they were the implacable foes of any criticism of Communism." Harrington, *Taking Sides: The Education of a Militant Mind* (New York: Holt, Rinehart & Winston, 1985), p. 59.

73. Interview with Steve Max, 14 May 1986; Sale, *SDS*, pp. 60–68. Documents from the LID-SDS confrontation can be found in Reel 1, SDS Papers.

74. Memorandum, 16–17 May 1961, Reel 1, SDS Papers.

75. Steve Max recalled of the aftermath of Port Huron: "From that point on the SDS leadership wouldn't trust liberals. Any time anybody came along with some ultra-left thing to say about liberals, their own experience confirmed that it was true. It was impossible to seriously argue the coalitionist viewpoint after that." Interview with Steve Max, 14 May 1986.

76. *Nation* 191 (2 July 1960):4.

77. *Nation* 200 (10 May 1965):492.

78. Interview with Todd Gitlin, 29 December 1983.

79. My interpretation of the Port Huron statement owes much to Steve Wasserman's article, "A Manifesto Lost in Time," *The Progressive* (December 1982):32–36.

80. Sale, *SDS*, pp. 154–159. Todd Gitlin emphasized the importance of the collapse of relations with the LID: "The LID insanity over Port Huron is a very important break point. For someone coming into the organization when I did [1963], it was never even an open question about whether one should feel some sort of pull towards that politics (even though I felt when I read Irving Howe's 'New Styles of Leftism,' that the things he said made sense)." Interview with Todd Gitlin, 29 December 1983.

81. "Peter, Paul and Mary," Warner Brothers recording, 1962; Bob Dylan, "The Times They Are A-changing," "Ballad for a Thin Man." Paul Cowan, *The Making of an Un-American* (New York: Viking, 1970), p. 8; David King Dunaway, *How Can I Keep from Singing: Pete Seeger* (New York: McGraw-Hill, 1981), pp. 210, 246.

82. Hayden was quoted in the *National Guardian*, 2 October 1965, interview with Todd Gitlin, 29 December 1983.

83. On Educational Research and Action Project (ERAP) see Sale, *SDS*, pp. 95–115, 131–150; Vickers, *Formation of the New Left*, pp. 81–82; Todd Gitlin and Nanci Hollander, *Uptown: Poor Whites in Chicago* (New York: Harper & Row, 1970); Gitlin, *The Whole World is Watching: Mass Media in the Making and Unmaking of the New Left* (Berkeley: University of California Press, 1980), pp. 167–168; Paul Potter, *A Name for Ourselves* (Boston: Little, Brown, 1971), pp.

136–153. Wini Breines offers a more positive evaluation of ERAP in *Community and Organization in the New Left, 1962–1968: The Great Refusal* (New York: Praeger, 1982), pp. 123–149.

84. Interview with Steve Max, 14 May 1986. Another SDS founder, Bob Ross, has written a very astute analysis of SDS internal dynamics in the mid-1960s. See Robert J. Ross, "Primary Groups in Social Movements: A Memoir and Interpretation," *Journal of Voluntary Action Research* 6 (1977):139–152. Some day, some clever editor will gather up such virtually inaccessible material as Ross's article, Dick Flack's "Making History vs. Making Life," Richard Rothstein's "Representative Democracy in SDS," Elinor Langer's "Notes for Next Time," Todd Gitlin's "Seizing History," and Carl Oglesby's "Notes on a Decade Ready for the Dustbin," for a documentary collection of the New Left's reflections on its own history.

85. Hayden, "Who are the Student Boat-Rockers?" p. 337.

86. Potter is quoted in Breines, *Community and Organization*, p. 70.

87. James Gilbert offered a perceptive obituary for the New Left: "Thinking back on the 1960s, I see this period as one of enormous energy and change, of a movement in civil rights that altered American history as much as anything ever has done. But I also see it as a profoundly anti-political decade, nothing in its premises or effects like the 1930s during the heyday of the old left. And, I am forced to wonder what might have happened—what might still happen—if the moral energy of the 1960s were ever joined to the political shrewdness of the 1930s." Sohnya Sayres et al., *The 60s Without Apology* (Minneapolis: University of Minnesota Press, 1984), p. 247.

INDEX